DEVELOPING SUSTAINABLE EDUCATION IN REGIONAL AUSTRALIA

Edited by Andrew Gunstone

© Copyright 2014
All rights reserved. Apart from any uses permitted by Australia's Copyright Act 1968, no part of this book may be reproduced by any process without prior written permission from the copyright owners. Inquiries should be directed to the publisher.

Monash University Publishing
Building 4, Monash University
Clayton, Victoria 3800, Australia
www.publishing.monash.edu

Monash University Publishing brings to the world publications which advance the best traditions of humane and enlightened thought.

Monash University Publishing titles pass through a rigorous process of independent peer review.

Series: Education

Design: Les Thomas

www.publishing.monash.edu/books/dsera-9781922235244.html

National Library of Australia Cataloguing-in-Publication entry:

Title:	Developing sustainable education in regional Australia / edited by Andrew Gunstone
ISBN:	9781922235244 (paperback)
Notes:	Includes bibliographical reference.
Subjects:	Education, Rural--Australia.
Dewey Number:	370.19346

Printed in Australia by Griffin Press an Accredited ISO AS/NZS 14001:2004 Environmental Management System printer.

The paper this book is printed on is certified by the Programme for the Endorsement of Forest Certification scheme. Griffin Press holds PEFC chain of custody SGS - PEFC/COC-0594. PEFC promotes environmentally responsible, socially beneficial and economically viable management of the world's forests.

Contents

List of Contributors v
Acknowledgements viii

1. Developing Sustainable Education in Regional Australia 1
   Bruce Waldrip, Andrew Gunstone and Margaret Plunkett

2. Educating for a Sustainable Future Through the Redevelopment of the Online Learning Experience for Off-Campus Students 8
   Judy Tennant, Andrew West, Margaret Plunkett, and Renata Howard

3. The Benefits of University Studies. 25
   The Perspectives of Pathway Students
   Stuart Levy

4. Development of a Postulated Model for Investigating Resilience and Retention of Teachers and Nurses 43
   A Review of Literature
   Jeffrey Dorman and Michael Dyson

5. Sustainable Education in a Small Regional Medical School 66
   Challenges and Opportunities
   Brian Chapman and William Hart

6. Engaging the Learner. 79
   A Framework for Sustainable Teaching
   Adam Bertram

7. Racial Behaviour Among Secondary School Students 99
   Khalim Zainal, Johari Talib, Fazilah Idris, Mansor Bin Mohd. Noor, Norshidah Mohamad Salleh

8. Investigating a Win-Win Situation 117
   Delivering Quality Swimming Experiences for Children in Local Primary Schools within the Gippsland Region, via Teacher Education
   Timothy Lynch

9. Education, Teaching Entrepreneurship and Indigenous Peoples . . 133
   Dennis Foley

10. "Going to School on Our Country". 161
    Expanding the Concept of Schooling in Semi-Sedentary Aboriginal and Sámi Communities in Australia and Sweden
    Zane Ma Rhea

11. The Koorie Footprints to Higher Education Program 189
    An Analysis of Program Strengths and Challenges
    Grania Sheehan, Tia Di Biase, and Kylie Clarke

List of Contributors

Adam Bertram is a lecturer in the Faculty of Education, Monash University. His research interests are pedagogical content knowledge (PCK), teacher research and teacher-educator research, particularly within the realm of science education. For his work on PCK, he has been invited to work with teachers and researchers nationally and internationally.

Brian Chapman is an Associate Professor and PBL Coordinator at Gippsland Medical School, and he teaches various branches of physiology in the MBBS curriculum. His teaching and research interests have included muscle energetics, thermodynamics and kinetics of membrane transport processes, educational multimedia for computer-based learning, macroeconomics, musicology, private piano tuition and medical education.

Kylie Clarke is the former Coordinator of the *Koorie Footprints to Higher Education* program, Monash University, Gippsland Campus, and former Program Coordinator Kitjarra wurrun-ngeen – Aboriginal Education Unit (Gordon Institute of TAFE).

Tia Di Baise is a former Research Assistant on the GAP Project and honours student, Psychology Department, Swinburne University of Technology.

Jeffrey Dorman is an Associate Professor in the Faculty of Education at Monash University, Gippsland. Jeff's research has focused predominantly on the determinants and outcomes of psychosocial environments in schools and classrooms. He is particularly interested in the use of structural equation modelling and multi-level analysis in learning environment research.

Michael Dyson is Head of School in the Faculty of Education at Monash University Gippsland. His research interests are focused on the re conceptualisation of pre-service teacher education, the educational use of ICT and alternative ways to conduct education in the 21st century.

Dennis Foley is of Aboriginal descent (Gai-mariagal/Wiradjuri), a Professor of Aboriginal Studies researching and publishing in the fields of Aboriginal history, cultural studies, management/entrepreneurship and education. He is a Fulbright and double Endeavour Fellow, having researched and lived in Hawaii, New Zealand and Ireland, researching Indigenous enterprise in Australia and the Pacifica together with the Irish Traveller.

Andrew Gunstone is an Associate Professor and Associate Head, Research at the David Unaipon College of Indigenous Education and Research, University of South Australia. His research interests include the historical and political relationships between Indigenous and non-Indigenous peoples. He is the Foundation Editor of the *Journal of Australian Indigenous Issues*.

William Hart is an Associate Professor and Director of Gippsland Medical School, and he teaches in areas related to his experiences over the past thirty years as a public health physician (Assistant Director of Public Health for Victoria), a part-time GP, and Chief Executive of a medical research consortium (Neurosciences Victoria Ltd. [NSV]).

Renata Howard is in the Gippsland School of Business and Economics at Monash University and researches the use of technology in teaching.

Fazilah Idris is an Associate Professor, has been lecturing since 1995 and teaches courses in English Proficiency, Leadership & Interpersonal Skills, Time Management and Ethnic Relations. Throughout her career, she has published books and numerous journal articles. Research interests includes personality, youth development and ethnic relations.

Stuart Levy is the Director of the Diploma of Tertiary Studies (DoTS) Pathway, Monash University. His research interests include International Relations, the First Year in Higher Education, student experiences of transition to tertiary study, and pathways to higher education that address social inclusion.

Timothy Lynch is a senior lecturer in the Faculty of Education at Monash University. He is an experienced classroom, Health and Physical Education (HPE) teacher and school leader. In 2006, he was the Teresa Carlson Award recipient (ACHPER Qld) in recognition of his health promotion within the community.

Zane Ma Rhea has worked nationally and internationally with Indigenous communities over the last 30 years. Her research examines the provision of education services to Indigenous people, focusing on systemic reform, teacher cross-cultural professional development, and the preservation and maintenance of Indigenous knowledge through the development of school-community-university partnerships.

Mansor Bin Mohd. Noor is a Professor and Principal Fellow at the Institute Of Ethnic Studies, Universiti Kebangsaan Malaysia. His area of specialisation is Ethnic Relations. He has done much research, writings and has published many books in ethnic relations. He has also been awarded many grants from the Malaysia Ministry of Higher Education.

Margaret Plunkett is a Senior Lecturer in the Faculty of Education at Monash University Gippsland. Her main research interests are in the areas of gifted education, rural education, alternative educational settings, and professional learning for teachers.

Norshidah Mohamad Salleh is a Senior Lecturer at Faculty of Education, University Kebangsaan Malaysia since 2000. Her area of specialisation is Special Education. She has conducted numerous research and writings in special education since 1993. She was also awarded four grants from the Malaysia Ministry of Higher Education since 2007 until the present.

Grania Sheehan is a former Senior Research Fellow, Gippsland Access and Participation (GAP) Project, Monash University Gippsland campus.

Johari Bin Talib is a Senior Lecturer at The Centre for General Studies, Universiti Kebangsaan Malaysia. His area of specialisation is Psychology. He was in the field of education for more than 35 years. He teaches Family Issues, Human Development and Writing Skills. His research interests includes social and education psychology.

Judy Tennant is in the Gippsland School of Business and Economics at Monash University and researches the use of technology in teaching, orientation and transition issues, the banking and finance industry in relation to monetary policy, and financial literacy.

Bruce Waldrip has a strong interest in how one can facilitate students' learning that focuses how they reason and justify their understanding. He has extensive experience in cultural aspects of learning.

Andrew West is in the Gippsland School of Business and Economics at Monash University and researches the relationship between business, accounting, and society, and the moral evaluations of these relationships, corporate governance, accounting and professional ethics, and sustainability reporting.

Khalim Bin Zainal is an Associate Professor at the Centre for General Studies, Universiti Kebangsaan Malaysia. He has been in the educational field for 30 years. He specialised in Educational Administration, Behaviour Management, Ethnic Relations and Leadership. He is also a Visiting Research Fellow at University of New South Wales, Sydney.

Acknowledgments

This edited book has resulted from the *Education for Regional Sustainability Conference* held at Monash University in November 2011. The conference was organised by the *Research in Educational Issues Network (REIN)*, a research group based at Monash University, Gippsland.

There are a number of people I would like to thank for their involvement in developing this edited collection.

The authors contributed their expertise to this book. My colleagues on the REIN executive, Harry Ballis, Brian Chapman, Jeff Dorman, and particularly Margaret Plunkett and Bruce Waldrip, assisted me in tasks such as organising referees. Bruce and Margaret also co-wrote with me the back cover details.

The Monash University Gippsland Research Office, in particular Philip Taylor, Tina D'Urbano and Paula Di Maria, provided funding and other support for the conference and edited book. Mark Manolopoulos copy-edited the book. Monash University Publishing, in particular Nathan Hollier, provided helpful advice.

Finally, I thank my wife Belinda and our children Jack, Liam and Ben for their love and support.

Andrew Gunstone
November 2013

Chapter 1

Developing Sustainable Education in Regional Australia

Bruce Waldrip, Andrew Gunstone and Margaret Plunkett

> We need a shared commitment to education that empowers people for change. Such education should be of a quality that provides the values, knowledge, skills and competencies for sustainable living and participation in society (Bonn Declaration, UNESCO 2009).

For the improvement of life in this world, there is a need to develop the understandings and capabilities required to make informed decisions. To achieve this, learning needs to be interdisciplinary and holistic such that it facilitates a reasoned problem solving approach, one that recognises the complexities and synergies between current and future issues impacting life on Earth. This need will require a rethink of our approach to learning and teaching.

Traditionally, educators, particularly university educators, have focused on the cognitive domain of learning but have largely ignored the affective domain that includes the ability to listen and respond, motivation for sustainability, and the ability to reflect and change behaviours (Shephard 2008). This approach could mean that a new focus is required within our education systems and approaches, so that affective outcomes such as values, attitudes and behaviours are explicitly covered, which could help students develop the ability to critically think and reason. Addressing these issues, including evidence-based learning, would place universities and schools in a position to instil some graduate attributes (Shephard 2008) and possibly stimulate a transformation that could ultimately facilitate change in approaches to learning.

In Australia, there is a tendency to view that everyone requires the same type of education. Reflecting on past evidence, it is noticeable that differences exist between the more populous metropolitan areas and the regional and rural areas. The current dominant approach is to develop common curricula (ACARA 2012) despite some educators stressing the need for diversity of approaches to cater for recognised differences. In particular, the need to address the lower academic achievement of regional and rural Australian students when contrasted with their metropolitan counterparts is now broadly recognised (ACER 2011; Bradley et al 2008; Lyons et al 2006). The recent PISA 2010 report indicated that Australian students' literacy performance had declined significantly between 2000 and 2009, with a widening gap between metropolitan and other students. The PISA results further revealed that the proportion of non-metropolitan students performing at high levels in reading and scientific literacy was much smaller than the corresponding metropolitan group, adding to this picture of systemic regional underachievement.

This pattern is highlighted in areas such as regional Victoria, where this negative pattern is impacted by higher school absentee rates, lower VCE performance results (VCAA 2010), a lower retention rate in senior high school (DEECD 2011) and less participation from lower socio-economic background students in further education (Parliamentary Library Paper 2009) when compared with metropolitan student data. Also, in Queensland, rural and remote students performed at a much lower level than their provincial and metropolitan counterparts (Masters 2009). Across many Australian states, lower SES students as well as rural and remote students (COAG 2011), are being disadvantaged by where they live. NAPLAN results for 2011 reveal that both regional and rural Victorian and Queensland students have lower literacy results at the middle school level. Despite intensive reading reforms at state and national levels, reading achievement has not improved (NAPLAN 2011; PISA 2009). Effective teaching of literacy skills is arguably the most critical aspect of educating students for education and life success. In addition to the recent PISA 2009 data, diverse sources within Australia show literacy difficulties to be frequent, with up to 30% of students at primary and high school experiencing significant weakness (Masters 2009; NAPLAN 2011), and almost 50% of Australian adults having literacy skills below the level needed to thrive in modern society (ABS 2008). This evidence suggests a real need to change what and how we teach and learn.

A persuasive body of research supports a focus on strong teacher-student relationships, effective teaching and learning strategies, and student goal-setting, as being critical in promoting student academic success (Hattie 2009). The most basic and probably the most challenging educational reform consists of a shift from viewing the teaching–learning process primarily as a transmission of knowledge to forms of teaching focused on active and collaborative knowledge construction, involving critical reflection and a recognition of complex inter-connected issues. This approach recognises the need to justify and verify one's understandings and to take into account other aspects of life including socio-cultural factors, life experiences and the development and recognition of cultural mores and values.

Furthermore, the increasing range of diverse needs of students provides a challenge that will need to be met through a range of approaches that address these needs mainly through creation of personalised learning environments. Coupled with greater mobility of the work force with increasing change of careers, questions arise as to how education can meet this demand. Questions could be raised about whether we are in fact producing distinct groups of students with different life expectations and hence a diverse range of educational expectations. For example, what are the expectations of school leavers compared to mature aged workers who might work in areas where there are little opportunities for education?

This expectation raises a series of questions to consider. Given the relatively lower levels of parental tertiary education, how can students from homes where neither parent has received post-school education, be encouraged to undertake higher education? With the current emphasis by governments to rank educational providers, how can the collective needs of some children, for example, Indigenous students be met? Is competition beneficial for attracting all types of learners? How does one re-distribute resources to those who are in most need? How do we reward the more effective academics and teachers who impact on learning? How do we measure this impact? How do we keep the most talented and motivated people in the teaching process? How does assessment become an on-going developmental process that invigorates and stimulates interest and understanding? This book attempts to address some of these issues.

This edited book is divided into three sections. The first section focusses on university education and contains three chapters from Tennant, West, Plunkett and Howard; Levy; and Dorman and Dyson. The second section looks at school education and contains four chapters from Chapman and Hart; Bertram; Zainal, Talib, Idris, Noor and Salleh; and Lynch. The third section explores Indigenous education and contains three chapters from Foley; Ma Rhea; and Sheehan, Di Biase and Clarke.

Tennant, West, Plunkett and Howard describe an ongoing business department project that investigates and implements research-led approaches to learning that improve the educational outcomes for off-campus students.

The project included the development of an online learning environment which "brings the university" to off-campus students and enhances their online learning experience. Interaction between students and teachers is considered a key component of a rich learning environment, and when combined with a well-designed website, enables a greater focus on meaningful interactions between staff and students. The adoption of the template encouraged academic staff to reflect on their teaching practices and it is hoped it will enable staff to devote more time to fostering dynamic interaction with students, an essential component of the overall learning experience.

Levy reports on the benefits of university studies as perceived by former students of the Diploma of Tertiary Studies (DoTS) pathway who were undertaking a variety of Monash degrees, or had graduated and were working in the Gippsland region. He describes how the student reflections reveal that, aside from the basic benefit of experiencing a pathway into university, DoTS students gain interdisciplinary learning opportunities, as well as the acquisition of generic graduate skills and attributes that provide them with a brighter view of their future. The experiences and voices of the DoTS students confirm that they take away from the engagement what all students are expected to leave with.

Dorman and Dyson explored the resilience and retention of pre-service and in-service teachers and nurses. The retention of new graduates in these professions is a significant issue. Retention can be related to the resilience of students, especially in courses that demand both academic and vocational development. Dorman and Dyson have attempted to delineate some of the key issues in resilience and retention of teachers and nurses. They postulated a model for resilience and retention of teachers and nurses. While much previous research has tended to focus on parts of models, the complex nature of resilience and retention requires approaches that capture the complexity of the constructs.

Chapman and Hart describe the experience of university academics responding to the challenges and exploiting the opportunities that attend the establishment of a new, small regional medical school. The educational challenges pertain to the recruitment and retention of suitably qualified academic and clinical staff to deliver a medical course to a graduate-entry cohort, given the limitations bearing on career progression and family support. The research challenges derive from limitations in infrastructure, the availability of honours and graduate research students, and on the collegiality that exists when teams of researchers are engaged in related pursuits. These studies reflect the opportunities for interdisciplinary collaboration that arise directly from some of the challenges faced within a small medical school. The relative smallness of the university's Gippsland Campus is a facilitating factor for such collaboration, allowing closer interaction between colleagues in separate schools within one small campus.

Bertram discusses engaging school learners and examines a research-based approach to teaching, which connects subject matter knowledge with pedagogical knowledge. Using Shulman's (1986) construct of Pedagogical Content Knowledge (PCK) and Loughran, Berry and Mulhall's (2006) development of Content Representations (CoRes), Bertram devised a small qualitative study with six teachers, to test the applicability of the theoretical construct of PCK in the classroom. Bertram believes that an explicit awareness of PCK offers educators a lens for engaging with their practice, which in turn offers possibilities for sharing of insights, pedagogies and content knowledge thereby promoting a sustainable professional body of knowledge for teaching. His findings confirmed this, illustrating that "the construct of PCK offered teachers an important and useful construct for shaping their pedagogical knowledge".

Zainal, Talib, Idris, Noor and Salleh deal with the pressing issue of racial tolerance within the school system, as a micro reflection of society as a whole. Although conducted in Malaysia, the study has synergies with regions within Australia, which are facing the issues associated with multiculturalism, often for the first time. When a range of nationalities exist, racial tolerance is particularly important, so an examination of attitudes towards race was felt to be valuable. The study involved 15 schools and 600 students of mixed backgrounds and gender across Negeri Sembian in Malaysia. While small gender/locality differences were found in responses, overall attitudes were positive. The authors believe the Malaysian national education system has given serious attention towards national unity, which has clearly helped create a tolerant relationship between the various ethnic groups, something that regional areas could learn from.

Lynch discusses a different approach to engaging university pre-service teachers in thinking about their teaching of swimming and water safety to primary school students. He examines how the implementation of the Educational Goals for Young Australians within Health and Physical Education in primary schools; "Swimming and water safety" lessons could be conducted more collaboratively. Through using swimming and water safety as the curriculum content, Lynch saw stronger partnerships being developed, which helped to support quality teaching particularly strengthening early childhood education. He argued that through initiating pathways with ASCTA and RLSSA the university pre-service teachers were able to promote a world-class curriculum and assessment, which they then implemented in local primary schools. This resulted in improved educational outcomes and strengthened accountability and transparency.

Foley examines the role of education programs, both through tertiary education and through workplace industry training, in regard to developing effective Indigenous businesspeople and entrepreneurs. Foley's argument is based on researching hundreds of Indigenous case studies throughout Australia, Hawaii and New Zealand. Foley contends that while these education programs are critical, the effectiveness of many of them, particularly formal programs is very limited. He analyses an entrepreneurship education system that has been adapted from its original setting in the United States, and modified to achieve very successful outcomes in working with Indigenous peoples in New Zealand and Ireland. Foley argues that the adaption of such a system in Australia could significantly assist in improving the lives of Indigenous people in Australia.

Ma Rhea examines "traditionally-orientated communities" and specifically two "communities of Aboriginal and Samí peoples who live on their traditional estates, in places that are far from the administrative, often metropolitan, centres that govern their lives within the nation-state". These two communities are in central Australia and in Northern Sweden. Ma Rhea examines and compares the history of government provided schooling in both communities. Ma Rhea argues that Indigenous peoples in these communities are advocating an education system that does not just provide "mainstream schooling" but also an education system that supports "these communities to create sustainable futures that enable them to grow and prosper in economically and socially viable, traditionally-oriented ways".

Sheehan, Di Biase and Clarke discuss the Koorie Footprints to Higher Education (KFtHE) program at Monash University, Gippsland. The aim of this program is to encourage local Indigenous secondary students to continue their education through to higher education. Sheehan, Di Biase and Clarke analyses the effectiveness of this program, reviewing program reports and interviewing relevant staff. They utilise an approach called the Design and Evaluation Matrix for University Outreach (DEMO) (developed by Gale, Seller et al 2010) to map the program characteristics of the KFtHE program. Sheehan, Di Biase and Clarke then develop a quantitative analysis of the effectiveness of the KFtHE program in enabling Indigenous people to successfully enter higher education.

References

ACER. 2011. 'PISA identifies challenges for Australian education'. http://www.acer.edu.au/media/pisa-identifieschallenges-for-australian-education (accessed December 10 2011).

Bradley, D., Noonan, P., Nugent, H. & Scales, B. 2008. Review of Australian Higher Education, Final Report. Canberra, ACT: Commonwealth of Australia.

DEECD. 2011. Summary Statistics Victorian Schools, February 2011. Melbourne: DEECD.

Department of the Parliamentary Library. 2009. Poverty rates by electoral divisions, 2006. Melbourne: Department of Parliamentary Services.

Lyons, T., Cooksey, R., Panizzon, D. & Pegg, J. 2006. Science ICT and mathematics education in rural and regional Australia. The SiMERR national survey. Canberra: Department of Education, Science and Training.

Masters, G. 2009. Improving literacy, numeracy and science learning in Qld primary schools. Melbourne: ACER.

McMillan, J. H. & Schumacher, S. 2006. Research in education: Evidence-based inquiry (6th ed.). Boston: Pearson.

National Assessment Program Literacy and Numeracy (NAPLAN). 2011. National Assessment Program – Literacy and Numeracy: Summary report. Australian Curriculum, Assessment and Reporting Authority (ACARA).

Shephard, K. 2008. 'Higher education for sustainability: seeking affective learning outcomes'. International Journal of Sustainability in Higher Education 9(1): 87–98.

UNESCO. 2009. 'Bonn Declaration, UNESCO World Conference on Education for Sustainable Development, Bonn, Germany, April 2009'. http://unesdoc.unesco.org/images/0018/001887/188799e.pdf (accessed February 9 2012).

Chapter 2

Educating for a Sustainable Future Through the Redevelopment of the Online Learning Experience for Off-Campus Students

Judy Tennant, Andrew West, Margaret Plunkett, and Renata Howard

Abstract

This chapter reports on an ongoing project conducted at the School of Business and Economics at Monash University's Gippsland campus. The aim of the project is to investigate and implement research-led approaches to learning that improve the educational outcomes of off-campus students. The project included the development of an online learning environment which "brings the university" to off-campus students and enhances their online learning experience. The project is informed by a constructivist approach to learning, the acknowledgement of different learning styles, the pedagogical requirements of the online learning environment, and the needs of students who study off-campus. It is part of an ongoing process to improve the quality of online learning and, due to its nature, continues to evolve.

To ensure the future sustainability of off-campus education, it is important that students experience a learning environment that is both appropriate and meaningful. Within the context of this project, there is considerable emphasis on providing ongoing professional development to staff to ensure that the level of student engagement continues to improve. This is based on the premise that a well-designed website on its own is insufficient to foster engagement and student learning. Interaction between students and teachers is a key component of a rich learning environment, which, together with a well-designed website, enables a greater focus on meaningful interactions between staff and students.

Introduction

Off-campus students are a major component of the overall student cohort enrolled at the Gippsland campus of Monash University. Re-developing online learning materials is part of a wider ongoing project to ensure the sustainability of off-campus education. Producing high quality online materials for off-campus students is an important element of the broader goals of improving the overall student learning experience, improving student learning outcomes, and increasing student retention.

This chapter describes the re-development of the online learning environment for off-campus students primarily through the design and implementation of a template through which learning material can be presented online. The chapter begins by reviewing the literature that informs the project and highlighting existing research relating to the off-campus learning experience. This research influenced the way in which the online learning template was constructed. This is followed by a description of the new online learning template and initial feedback from both staff and students. The support provided to academic staff is subsequently discussed, with the provision of (ongoing) technical support being recognised as integral to the project. The chapter concludes with a brief discussion of plans for a wider adoption of the online learning template.

Literature Review

Technological changes and developments do not occur in a conceptual or theoretical vacuum, and the development of a new online learning template for off-campus students at Monash University's Gippsland campus is no exception. This section presents the theoretical background that informed the development of the template.

Constructivism

During the early 20th Century, the models and lenses which had previously informed our thinking about education underwent enormous changes. A group of theorists, including Piaget (1896–1980), Vygotsky (1896–1934), Bruner (1915–present), and Dewey (1859–1952) all began working on a paradigm that was to become known as constructivism. Constructivism is essentially a philosophy about learning that proposes that meaning is constructed by the subject rather than existing externally and waiting to be discovered (Offord 2005). Consequently, learners build their own understanding of new ideas. It is, fundamentally, a theory about the limits of human knowledge, incorporating the belief that our own cognitive acts are behind the creation of knowledge. Moreover, our constructed understandings are influenced by our experiences, which are in turn influenced by our personal cognitive lens. According to Noddings (1993), constructivism may be characterised as both a cognitive position and a methodological perspective. As a cognitive position, constructivism holds that all knowledge is constructed, and the instruments of construction include cognitive structures that are either innate (Chomsky 1968, 1971) or are themselves products of developmental construction (Piaget 1972). As such, constructivism is fixed in the idea of an epistemological subject, questioning what it means to know and whether we can actually really know something.

Although the field of education has been heavily influenced by the constructivist paradigm, some theorists have been more influential than others, though this has certainly changed over time. Two of the major contributors were contemporaries, Jean Piaget and Lev Vysgotsky, who were developing their ideas in opposite parts of the world. Initially, Piaget's ideas played a major role in teacher education programs, particularly those relating to early childhood and primary education. Russian theorist Vysgotsky's work took longer to reach the West; even though *Thought and Language* was published in English in 1962, it was not until 1978, when *Mind in Society* was published, that his contribution was first noticed and the value of his work began to receive acknowledgement (Newman & Holzmann 1993).

Piaget is generally attributed as the formaliser of the theory of constructivism due to his articulation of the mechanisms by which knowledge is internalised by learners. He believed that learning occurred through the construction of one logical structure after another, with his theories about assimilation (base structure) and accommodation (continued revision of structure) helping to explain the active mechanism associated with the process of transformation or creation of knowledge that underpins constructivism. Vygotsky's (1978) contribution relates to the introduction of the social aspect of learning into constructivism. He also developed the concept of the Zone of Proximal Development (ZPD), whereby students solve problems beyond their actual developmental level (but within their level of potential development) under adult guidance or in collaboration with more capable peers.

Dewey's (1938) earlier work, which promoted an inquiry approach with an emphasis on education being grounded in real experience, fitted in with the underlying principles of constructivism. He argued that engagement in sustained inquiry (including studying, pondering, considering alternative possibilities, and arriving at a belief grounded in evidence) was what learning was all about. Bruner (1960) supported the views of his contemporaries and sought to initiate curriculum change based on the notion that learning is both an active and social process, in which students' current knowledge provides structure for the construction of new ideas or concepts.

How Can Constructivism Articulate into Practice?

The constructivist view of learning suggests a number of different curriculum and teaching practices. In the most general sense, it usually means encouraging students to use active techniques such as real-world problem-solving to create more knowledge, and then discussing and reflecting on how their understandings are changing. Added to this has been the emerging understanding about individual learning patterns and preferences that has arisen as a result of the recent focus in educational circles on learning styles (Hood 1995).

Learning Styles

The concept of individual approaches or ways of learning originated in the 1970s and became very popular within the field of education (Pashler *et al.* 2009), but was more heavily scrutinised in other fields for an apparent lack of theorisation (Pashler *et al.* 2009). However, much of the critique associated with learning styles has been related to the measurement process rather than to the underlying philosophy of the construct.

Although numerous definitions of learning styles exist, a popular interpretation is that they refer to "individual differences in approaches to tasks that can make a difference in the way in which and, potentially, in the efficacy with which, a person perceives, learns, or thinks" (Sternberg, Grigorenko & Zhang 2008: 486). For instance, at its most basic level, learning styles or preferences are said to occur in relation to how we:

- take in information or *content*;
- *process* information – i.e., make our own meanings and connections (some prefer to reflect, others need to be more active);
- provide *products* or forms of evidence of the meanings we have made (some like essays, others prefer poems or oral presentations); and,
- interact with the *learning environment* (some like quiet solo work, others like discussion, debate, and group work).

More than 30 years ago, Dunn and Dunn (1978) suggested to teachers that if students did not learn through the way that they were taught, then they must be taught in the way that they learn. Since then, a large body of literature has accumulated with some key researchers (Gardner 1999; Sternberg 1999) advocating that educators provide options and flexibility. Sternberg, Grigorenko and Zhang argue:

> The key principle is that for students maximally to benefit from instruction and assessment, at least some of each of instruction and assessment should match their styles of thinking. We do not advocate a perfect match all the time: Students need to learn, as does everyone, that the world does not always provide people with a perfect match to their preferred ways of doing things. Flexibility is as important for students as for teachers. But if we want students to show what they truly can do, match of instruction and assessment to styles is essential. (2008: 504)

While the underlying concept behind the idea of individual ways or preferences for learning holds appeal, learning style theory has been the subject of recent criticism. Pashler *et al.* (2009) reviewed the existing literature on learning styles and found that although numerous studies have purported to show the existence of different kinds of learners (such as "auditory learners" and "visual learners"), those studies have not used the type of randomised research designs that would make their findings credible. However, the report also found:

> ample evidence that children and adults will, if asked, express preferences about how they prefer information to be presented to them. There is also plentiful evidence arguing that people differ in the degree to which they have some fairly specific aptitudes for different kinds of thinking and for processing different types of information. (Pashler *et al.* 2009: 105)

Furthermore, their conclusion was not that educators should ignore expressed preferences for learning in particular ways, but rather that the methods used for assessing learning styles should be viewed cautiously, as they have not been rigorously tested: "We conclude therefore, that at present, there is no adequate evidence base to justify incorporating learning styles *assessments* into general educational practice" (Pashler *et al.* 2009: 105).

Nevertheless, as universities expand and enrol students from more diverse backgrounds, there is a need for recognition and accommodation of different learning styles in online environments. Federico (2000) argues that an understanding of learning styles is essential as it assists in the development of more appropriately tailored learning experiences. According to Mestre (2006: 30): "most current online situations best serve students who function well in a logical text-based, passive environment. But many students require more personalised attention in an interactive environment". Yet if universities want to accommodate different learning styles, there is a need to "move beyond text-based interactions and include visual or kinesthetic modalities, as well as intuition and thinking exercises" (Mestre 2006: 30). Furthermore, programming should be designed so that students are scaffolded in such a way that they have some control over their progress (Keeton, Sheckley & Griggs 2002).

This project sought to provide for a range of different learning preferences through the development of an online environment that maximises opportunities for flexibility and choice (retaining an element of individual control) within a scaffolded support structure. It is thus not dependent on the identification of individual learning styles of students, but rather incorporates the principles underpinning learning styles theory, and that complement a constructivist approach to learning.

Principles Underlying the Development of the Online Learning Environment

In preparation for the development of the online learning environment for off-campus Business degree students, a further review of the literature identified key principles that would inform the practical design of the learning template. Arguably the most important of these was the confirmation that off-campus learning can be a successful learning approach, and that the experience of off-campus students can be positive and compares well with that of on-campus students. If properly designed, online learning can be a positive engaging experience (Castle & McGuire 2010; Ward, Peters & Shelley 2010; Argaugh *et al.* 2009), and, according to Chen, Gonyea and Kuh (2008: 4): "[t]he engagement of distance learners compares favourably with that of campus based learners. Distance learners are generally as engaged and often more engaged than their campus based counterparts". Ogunleye (2010: 88) also found that "online course programmes contribute effectively to collaborative and cooperative learning".

Following the acknowledgement of different learning styles (as discussed above), it was apparent that learning material would need to be presented in different ways. The essential learning resource for many units, however, remains the prescribed textbook. As noted by Phillips and Phillips (2007: 21), there is a heavy reliance of accounting units (one of which is mandatory within the Business degree) on textbooks, especially at the first year.

Phillips and Phillips argue that: "the effectiveness of the most well-chosen textbook still depends on the reading behaviour of students" and identify a need to provide students with information regarding how to read and interact with the textbook. Furthermore, in developing materials for online learning, it is important to provide students with guidelines to maximise their interaction with the materials provided; Anderson (2008) notes the importance of providing "big picture" scaffolding to students. Accordingly, additional materials that would complement the textbook, accommodate different learning styles and would also be available online, could include visual material (such as diagrams, mindmaps, and video presentations), audio recordings, as well as extra written (printable) material that provides guidance to the textbook.

Using a range of media such as audio and video provides a different perspective to the learning materials than just text. The use of software such as Camstudio and Debut allows the lecturer to demonstrate practical exercises via a combination of screen capture and audio. This is particularly applicable to more quantitative units such as accounting, finance, and statistics. Sugar, Brown and Luterbach (2010: 2–3) found that the use of screen casting "can have positive effects on student learning and can be pedagogically equivalent to their face-to-face instruction counterparts". Other video software that combines still images with audio allows lecturers to provide short presentations of key concepts that are tailored specifically for off-campus students (rather than recording lengthy on-campus lectures and making these available online). Hartsell and Yuen (2006: 31) observed that online video-based instruction "brings courses alive by allowing online learners to use their visual and auditory senses to learn complex concepts and difficult procedures", a view shared by Wouters, Paas and van Merrienboer (2008).

Learning objectives are the central platform for evaluating the effectiveness of teaching and learning (Stokes, Rosetti & King 2010; Baker *et al.* 2008; Phillips & Phillips 2007). They should reflect the cumulative nature of learning and cognitive development, and emphasis should ideally be placed on clearly expressed learning objectives for both the unit as a whole and for individual weeks. Baker, Almerico and Thornton (2008: 27) note that the American Association of Collegiate Schools of Business (AACSB) requires that "accredited business schools require course objectives to be written in compliance with Bloom's taxonomy cognitive domain". The importance of learning objectives should accordingly be clear in any online learning environment.

The importance of learner-teacher and learner-learner interaction via discussion boards is heavily stressed in much of the literature. Anderson (2008), for example, developed a "conceptual model of online learning", within which a key principle is the establishment of a discourse between and amongst students and teachers, and between students and the teaching resources. Brindley, Walti and Blaschke (2009: 2) claim that: "access to education should not mean merely access to content … rather it should mean access to a rich learning environment that provides opportunity for interaction and connectedness". According to Michinov *et al.* (2011: 245): "learning in an online environment is most successful when students feel they participate". Intuitively, students are more likely to continue with a unit when they feel part of the unit. Encouraging students to participate in online discussions is one way of developing and fostering a sense of belonging, especially if participation is stimulated early in the semester. Many other authors express similar opinions as to the importance of incorporating participation and engagement into online learning environments (see, e.g., Ma & Yuen 2011; Arbaugh 2010; Hrastinski 2009; Garsky & Blau 2009; Young 2006).

Construction of a Revised Template

Over recent decades, several learning management systems (such as WebCT, Blackboard, and Moodle) have been developed, allowing academics to provide learning material related to units and courses online. One of the advertised advantages of these systems is that they allow educators a great deal of flexibility in terms of how they present their material and what tools they use. The systems typically provide various tools, such as discussion forums and quizzes, but do not prescribe how or whether they should be used or how learning material should be presented. This flexibility allows these products to be adopted in a wide range of educational settings, with each user customising it to their own needs.

The disadvantage of such "bare-bones" learning management systems is that there is no assurance that the principles for developing online learning environments (discussed above) will be followed by individual educators. There is nothing within the learning management system to encourage the presentation of learning objectives for each topic, the use of audio and video resources, or visual overviews. In order to optimise the online learning environment, there is accordingly a need for greater formalisation, sacrificing some flexibility in order to address the principles discussed above.

This project involved the development of a formal template for online learning material that could be used across a range of units and disciplines and which would specifically encourage the presentation of learning objectives for each topic, the use of audio and video resources, and a visual overview of the unit. Flexibility in terms of what specific learning materials are made available and other online tools (such as discussion boards and quizzes) would remain.

The development of the new template for off-campus students is a further development of a number of previous projects. An existing Bachelor of Business and Commerce template was developed for the Faculty of Business and Economics as part of a research-based pilot project during the move to WebCt by Tennant et al. (2004). This was then further developed by staff from the Gippsland School of Business and Economics to the current format. This template provided a structure for organising files and folders in WebCT and Blackboard, as well as a set of links to student-support services. As part of the research undertaken in developing this earlier template, two test sites were developed and a usability study conducted with students to determine which style was preferred by students (see Tennant & Webber 2008). One finding was that students preferred to have all learning material relevant to a particular week or topic grouped together. This preference has been carried through to the new template.

Although the new template was uploaded and used within Blackboard (2011) and Moodle (2012), it was designed using Microsoft Expression Web. For each unit, the template includes:

1. A standardised "topic map" webpage. This provides a visual overview of the unit, diagrammatically showing how the topics relate to each other, with an audio or video clip introducing the unit as a whole. Each of the topics on the diagram is clickable and links to its own separate page. An example topic map is provided in the Appendix.

2. Standardised topic pages for each topic. Each of these pages has prominent areas for Learning Objectives, Audio/Video resources, Commentary and Activities, and Other Resources. An example topic page is provided in the Appendix.

Developing this as an Expression Web template allowed for consistency in formatting across all units. Several areas of the template were then mapped as "editable regions" within which individual academics could add text or links to documents or other files. This allows each academic to customise the topic map to suit their unit, to input their own learning objectives, and add their own commentary, activities, audio/video and other resources as they desire. All of the development and updating of learning material is performed outside of the learning system, and is uploaded into

Blackboard/Moodle on completion (typically at the beginning of each semester).

The template was considered to have a number of advantages for both students and academics. For students, the "topic map" provides a visual overview of the unit that complements the written presentation of topics found in most textbooks. This enables students to easily identify connections between different topics or sections of the unit, to see which topics are closely related and which topics develop knowledge already covered in other topics. These relationships are not often made explicit, nor are they easily identifiable in traditional learning resources (the learning modules in Blackboard and the presentation of topics in Moodle are both entirely linear).

The standardisation of topic pages themselves allows students to easily navigate learning material in a range of units and across disciplines. Learning objectives for each topic would, for example, be in exactly the same place in every unit. The inclusion of sections on "audio/video" and "other resources" also allows students to quickly and easily see what resources are available for each topic.

For academics, the template encourages consideration of some of the key principles underlying online learning environments discussed above. The inclusion of a visual topic map forces a consideration of the relationships between topics in the unit that may previously have gone unnoticed or unacknowledged. The mandatory section on Learning Objectives requires academics to formulate learning objectives for each individual topic, and the sections on "Audio/Video" and "Other Resources" suggests some consideration of what resources may be available and useful for each topic. Although it is possible that academics could leave these sections blank, they cannot be deleted and it would be obvious that material had been omitted.

Developing and updating the learning material offline and external to Blackboard also has several benefits: facilitating peer review of online learning material, as all academics have access to the material for each unit and do not have to be granted access by the unit leader, and providing an additional backup in the event of a staff member leaving or falling ill.

Outcomes and Feedback

The template was implemented in a number of postgraduate and undergraduate units in 2011 and 2012. In general, although some learning was necessary for academics to use the template, their experiences were positive. In some cases it has encouraged the development of audio/video materials and it has allowed academics to focus on more active involvement on the discussion forums during the semester. Many of the Accounting and

Finance topics in the trial units now incorporate video walk-throughs of end-of-chapter problems in Excel using Camstudio/Debut screen recording software. Other units have made increasing use of other software, such as Soundslides, to incorporate audio into short PowerPoint-style presentations. The choice of the actual format for video/audio is not prescribed but is chosen by each academic to reflect the needs of individual units. Some academics also noted that once the learning material had been prepared within the template, setting up the unit's site in a subsequent semester was less onerous.

Feedback on this project was obtained in a number of different ways. For four postgraduate Accounting and Finance units, academics coordinating equivalent on-campus units offered at another campus within the University, were given access to the Blackboard sites and asked to provide feedback. All feedback received was positive, one academic commenting that:

> I have had a look at the AFG9071 site and it is excellent. I can understand why students have reacted positively to it – you can see a lot of work has gone into it and it is very informative. The links to the support services are important, but I am particularly impressed by the video tutorials (most of which are on Youtube). These are excellent.

Students enrolled in five units were asked to complete a short online survey at the end of their semesters. A total of 22 questionnaires were completed, and a summary of the main findings are presented below:

> When asked if the information provided on the Blackboard site assisted their learning in the semester, 20 answered "Yes", 2 answered "Neutral". None answered "No".

> When asked if, in future, they would prefer the Blackboard format adopted in semester 1, 2011 over what they had experienced in other units and previous semesters, 16 answered "Yes", 5 answered "Neutral", 1 answered "No".

> When asked the extent to which they found the unit easier or more difficult to navigate, compared to other units and previous semesters, 13 answered either "Much easier" or "Easier" to navigate, 9 answered "Neutral". None considered the new format to be more difficult to navigate.

Some of the comments regarding their impressions and experiences of the site include: "Very well organised. Very easy to navigate. Clear learning pathways"; "I thought that the interaction that the new processes created was very valuable to my learning"; "Basically, it is well organised and I can find what I want"; "The website was great and easy to navigate. All unit content should be delivered like this." Formal university teaching evaluations for two of the units also included comments related to the redesigned Blackboard site. When asked what the best aspects of the units were, responses included: "Everything. The content is very interesting and with all the resources provided online helps [me] understand the unit very well. I felt like I was at the university" and "The online resources for this unit were fantastic." A number of other comments referred to the use of audio or video resources on the sites, and how they assisted their learning. For example, one student wrote that: "The soundslides certainly cement the learning process. I think I learn better from an audio perspective than from a reading perspective".

As discussed above, unlike "bare-bones" learning management systems, the template specifically highlights the use of such resources.

Supporting the Implementation of the New Template

From the beginning of this project, the importance of technical support was clear, particularly given the increased pressure being placed on academics to achieve research outcomes. Persuading some academics to adopt new ways of constructing and operating within an online learning environment can be difficult, and the provision of ongoing support and training was considered essential. With this in mind, the project team comprised both academic and technical-support personnel. This allowed all team members to be familiar with the intricacies of the design of the template and future training needs of academic staff as the template became more widely adopted.

Following an initial trial of the new template in several postgraduate units and the positive feedback received from students, it was decided to roll out the template across all off-campus Business units offered at the Gippsland campus from Semester One 2012. To support the implementation of the template, a number of things had to occur. Firstly, all staff needed to have access to a common network drive where all unit materials are stored. Staff were then allocated a one hour one-on-one orientation session. An Academic Support Officer met each staff member at their workstation. The Expression Web software was installed on the staff member's computer and access to the network drive was checked. To further assist staff in getting started, a topic folder and a blank topic template page had already been created for each week of the semester ready for staff to edit. Staff were then shown where their unit folder was located on the network drive, and using these blank pages, the Expression Web software was demonstrated. Written instructions on creating and editing topic pages were given to staff during the initial orientation session.

Some staff members required no extra assistance beyond the initial set-up and orientation session; however, many staff did require extra help once they were ready to format the first week's material into the template. Generally this was a second half-hour appointment where the Academic Support Officer sat with the academic staff member as they worked through editing a topic page. The Academic Support Officer also provided ongoing support as required. This generally entailed minor troubleshooting and answering any questions academic staff had about editing the template.

Once the topic pages were ready to be uploaded to the Learning Management System (Blackboard), the Academic Support Officer assisted staff with uploading the template files where required. Written instructions were also provided to staff. It is anticipated that as academic staff become proficient in working with Expression Web, less assistance will be required, though occasional support will still be necessary.

Conclusion

The online learning template described above, created as part of a redevelopment of the online learning environment for off-campus students, was adopted in a small number of units in 2011 and is being introduced into all off-campus Business units offered by the Gippsland campus in 2012. The motivation and design of the template has its roots in a constructivist approach to learning and the acknowledgement of differing learning styles. The template was designed to encourage academics to engage with their students in a variety of ways, using both traditional text-based material as well as video and audio tools, while maintaining some consistency across units. This encourages staff to maximise opportunities for flexibility and choice within a scaffolded support structure, thereby providing for a range of different learning preferences. Specific attention was also paid to the importance of learning objectives both for units as a whole and for individual topics.

While it is recognised that the provision of well-structured content alone is insufficient to provide a stimulating learning environment, it is an important part of the process, and the initial, positive, feedback from students and staff has been very encouraging. Adoption of the template has encouraged academic staff to reflect on their teaching practices and the nature of materials provided, and it is hoped that it will also enable staff to devote more time to fostering dynamic interaction with students, an essential component of the overall learning experience. This construction of the template is only the beginning of a wider project aimed at fostering an improved learning experience and student outcomes. Going forward, further staff training will be conducted to encourage staff to enrich the learning environment by creating ongoing interaction between academics and students, and between students themselves. Further research will be conducted in relation to how well the redeveloped learning environment is meeting these aims.

Chapter 2: Appendix 1

Html Template Screenshots

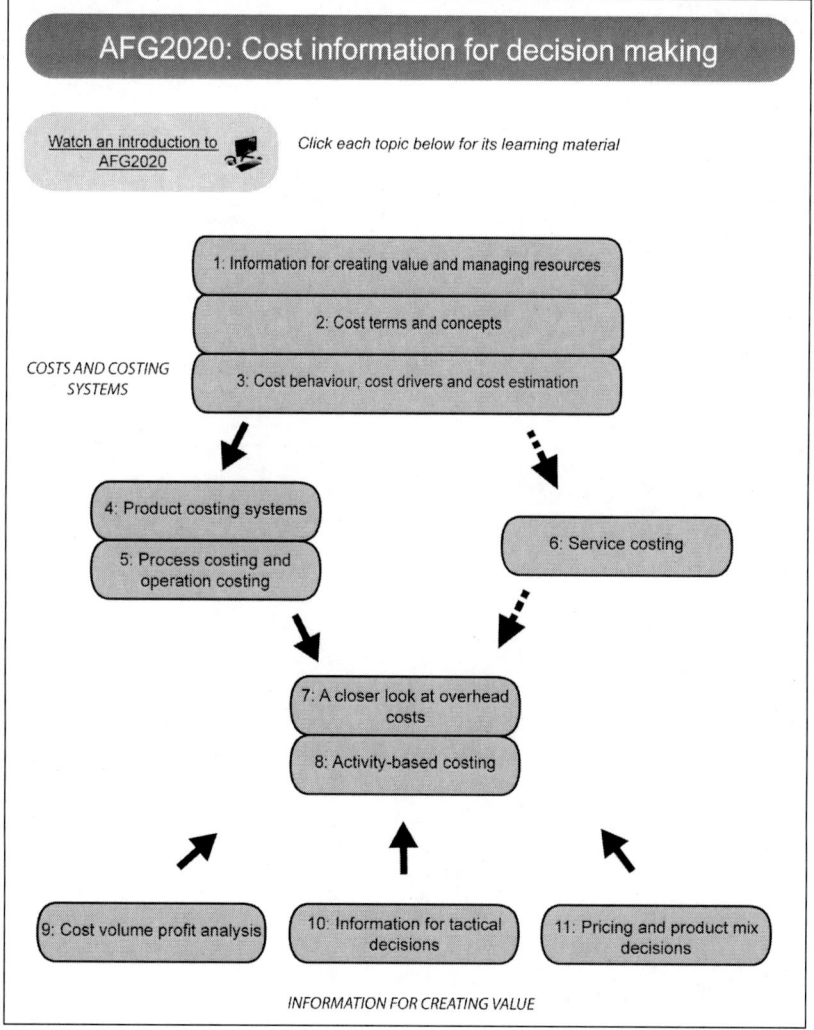

Sample topic map

Topic 8: Activity-based costing

Learning Objectives

At the end of this topic you will be able to:

1. Discuss the limitations of conventional costing systems;
2. Describe ABM (activity-based management) and ABC (activity-based costing) models, and apply ABC to the cost of products and services;
3. Explain the differences between product costs prepared using ABC and conventional systems;
4. Discuss the circumstances in which ABC should be implemented, and the barriers to implementation;
5. Identify and discuss other relevants aspects of ABC systems.

Audio/Video

Listen to an introduction to this topic

Watch a video walk-through of Problem 8:50:

Part One

Part Two

Commentary and Activities

Activity-based costing (ABC) is one of the most significant developments in management accounting in recent decades (dating to the 1980s) and has had a substantial impact not only on how products are costed, but in how other aspects of the business (such as customers and suppliers) are managed. This topic follows on directly from the last, as it deals primarily with how manufacturing overheads can be accurately allocated to products, overcoming some of the problems of the other methods you have come across.

Read through chapter 8 and the topic notes. Pay attention to how ABC represents a 'contemporary' management accounting technique, that has the potential to alleviate problems associated with more 'conventional' techniques ABC does, of course, have its owns problems, however! It is also worth reading Kaplan & Norton's (1988) article in which they introduce ABC, it will give you a good understanding of the issues involved.

There is a strong practical element to this, so work through the exercises at the end of the chapter and make sure that you are able to perform the learning objectives above.

Other Resources

Download and read Kaplan & Norton's article introducing ABC from 1988

Work through a prior exam question on this topic

Download a mindmap of chapter 8

Publisher's powerpoints for chapter 8

Sample topic page

References

Anderson, T. 2008. 'Towards a Theory of Online Learning'. In Anderson, T. (ed.). *The Theory and Practice of Online Learning*. Second ed. Edmonton: Athabasca University.

Arbaugh, J. B. 2010. 'Sage, Guide, Both or Even More? An Examination of Instructor Activity in Online MBA Courses'. *Computers and Education* 55(3): 1234–1244.

Argaugh, J. B., Godfrey, M. R., Johnson, M., Pollack, B. L., Niendorf, B., & Wresch, W. 2009. 'Research in Online and Blended Learning in the Business Disciplines: Key Findings and Possible Future Directions'. *Internet and Higher Education* 12: 71–87.

Baker, R., Almerico, G. M., & Thornton, B. 2008. 'Evaluating the Effectiveness of a Course-Objective Writing Development Teacher Training Program'. *Contemporary Issues in Educational Research* 1(4): 27–34.

Brindley, J. E., Walti, C., & Blaschke, L. M. 2009. 'Creating Effective Collaborative Learning Groups in an Online Environment'. *The International Review of Research in Open and Distance Learning* 10(3): http://www.irrodl.org/index.php/irrodl/article/viewArticle/675/1271 (accessed 6 January 2011).

Bruner, J. 1960. *The Process of Education*. Cambridge: Harvard University Press.

Castle, S. R., & McGuire, C. J. 2010. 'An Analysis of Student Self-Assessment of Online, Blended and Face-to-Face Learning Environments: Implications for Sustainable Education Delivery'. *International Education Studies* 3(3): 36–40.

Chen, P., Gonyea R., & Kuh, G. 2008. 'Learning at a Distance: Engaged or Not?'. *Innovate: Journal of Online Education* 4(3). http://www.innovateonline.info/pdf/vol4_issue3/Learning_at_a_Distance-__Engaged_or_Not_.pdf (accessed 7 July 2011).

Chomsky, N. 1968. *Language and Mind*. New York: Harcourt Brace Jovanovich.

Dewey, J. 1938. *Education and Experience*. New York: Simon & Schuster.

Dunn, R., & Dunn, K. 1978. *Teaching Students Through Their Individual Learning Styles*. Reston: Reston Publishing Company, Inc.

Hood, K. 1995. 'Exploring Learning Styles and Instruction'. http://jwilson.coe.uga.edu/EMT705/EMT705.Hood.html (accessed 4 October 2011).

Federico P (2000) Learning Styles and Student Attitudes Toward Various Aspects of Network-Based Instruction' *Computers in Human Behavior* 16: 359–379.

Gardner, H. 1999. *The Disciplined Mind: What All Students Should Understand*. New York: Simon & Schuster.

Gorsky, P., & Blau, I. 2009. 'Online Teaching Effectiveness: A Tale of Two Instructors'. *The International Review of Research in Open and Distance Learning* 10(3): http://www.irrodl.org/index.php/irrodl/article/view/712/1270 (accessed 11 January 2011).

Hartsell, T., & Yuen, S. 2006. 'Video Streaming in Online Learning'. *AACE Journal* 14(1): 31–43.

Hrastinski, S. 2009. 'A Theory of Online Learning as Online Participation'. *Computers and Education* 52(1): 78–82.

Keeton, M. T., Sheckley, B. G., & Griggs, J. K. 2002. *Efficiency and Effectiveness in Higher Education*. Dubuque: Kendall/Hunt Publishing Company.

Ma, W., & Yuen, A. 2011. 'Understanding Online Knowledge Sharing: An Interpersonal Relationship Perspective'. *Computers and Education* 56(1): 210–219.

Mestre, L. (2006). 'Accommodating Diverse Learning Styles in an Online Environment'. *Reference and User Services Quarterly* 46(2), 27–32.

Michinov, N., Brunot, S., Le Bohec, O., Juhel, J., & Delaveil, M. 2011. 'Procrastination, Participation and Performance in Online Learning Environments'. *Computers and Education* 56(1): 243–252.

Newman, F., & Holzman, L. 1993. *Lev Vygotsky: Revolutionary Scientist*. London: Routledge.
Noddings, N. 1993. *Educating for Intelligent Belief or Unbelief*. New York: Teachers College Press.
Offord, L. 2005. 'The Mozart of Psychology: Lev Semenovich Vygotsky'. http://vygotsky.afraid.org/ (accessed 14 February 2012).
Ogunleye, A. O. 2010. 'Evaluating an Online Learning Programme from Students' Perspectives'. *Journal of College Teaching and Learning* January: 79–89.
Pashler, H., McDaniel, M., Rohrer, D., & Bjork, R. 2009. 'Learning Styles: Concepts and Evidence'. *Psychological Science in the Public Interest* 9: 105–119.
Phillips, B. J., & Phillips, F. 2007. 'Sink or Skim: Textbook Reading Behaviours of Introductory Accounting Students'. *Issues in Accounting Education* 22(1): 21–24.
Piaget, J. 1972. 'Intellectual Evolution from Adolescence to Adulthood'. *Human Development* 15(1):1–12.
Sternberg, R. J. 1999. 'The theory of successful intelligence.' *Review of General Psychology* 3: 292–316.
Sternberg, R. J., Grigorenko, E. L., & Zhang, L. 2008. 'Styles of Learning and Thinking Matter in Instruction and Assessment'. *Perspectives on Psychological Science* 3: 486–506.
Stokes, L., Rosetti, J. L., & King, M. 2010. 'Form Over Substance: Learning Objectives in the Business Sore'. *Contemporary Issues in Education Research* 3(11): 11–20.
Sugar, W., Brown, A., & Luterbach, K. 2010. 'Examining the Anatomy of a Screencast: Uncovering Common Elements and Instructional Strategies'. *International Review of Research in Open and Distance Learning* 11(3): 1–20.
Tennant, J., & Webber, W. 2008. 'Helping Academics Meet Quality Standards in Online Teaching'. Edmondson, B. 9ed.). *Collected Wisdom: Off Campus Learning and Teaching Symposium, Papers and Posters*. Churchill: Off Campus Learning Centre, Monash University.
Tennant, J., Birch, L., Lismann, S., & Plones, W. 2004. 'Piloting a New Online Learning Management System'. Presented at the AARE Conference, 2004. http://www.aare.edu.au/04pap/ten04490.pdf (accessed 5 January 2012).
Vygotsky, L. S. 1962. *Thought and Language*. Cambridge: MIT Press and Wiley.
Vygotsky, L. S. 1978. *Mind in Society: The Development of Higher Psychological Processes*. Cambridge: Harvard University Press.
Ward, M. E., Peters, E., & Shelley, K. 2010. 'Student and Faculty Perceptions of the Quality of Online Learning Experiences'. *International Review of Research in Open and Distance Learning* 11(3): 57–77.
Wouters, P., Paas, F., & van Merrienboer, J .J. G. 2008. 'How to Optimize Learning from Animated Models: A Review of Guidelines Based on Cognitive Load'. *Review of Educational Research* 78(3): 645–675.
Young, S. 2006. 'Student Views of Effective Online Teaching in Higher Education'. *American Journal of Distance Education* 20(2): 65–77.

Chapter 3

The Benefits of University Studies

The Perspectives of Pathway Students

Stuart Levy

Abstract

The reflections of former students of the Diploma of Tertiary Studies (DoTS) pathway reveal that among the benefits of university study were opportunities for interdisciplinary learning and the acquisition of generic graduate skills and attributes that provide them with a brighter view of their future. Their voices, contextualised against existing transition literature and research, provide insights into how under-represented student cohorts value their experiences of university. Through a supported immersion pathway students from under-represented and/or poorly prepared backgrounds with limited opportunities to experience university are assisted to develop the attitudes and learning skills considered necessary for successful engagement with higher education. Graduates acknowledge that their attitudes towards education were changed and the transformative nature of higher education provided them with greater confidence, life skills and broader horizons. In addition to a career qualification, graduates also expressed a high regard for learning that well equips them to participate in their communities as lifelong learners.

Introduction

This chapter reports on the benefits of university studies as perceived by former students of the Diploma of Tertiary Studies (DoTS) pathway who were undertaking a variety of Monash degrees, or had graduated and work in the Gippsland region. During 2009 and 2010, 40 students responded to letters inviting them to participate in semi-structured interviews exploring their experiences of university study. Thirty-nine interviews were subsequently transcribed, approved by participants, de-identified, assigned pseudonyms, and their reflections thematically collated. The results of this project are reported more fully in *Student Voices in Transition: The Experiences of Pathways Students* (Levy & Earl 2012). The student reflections reveal that, aside from the basic benefit of experiencing a pathway into university, DoTS students gain interdisciplinary learning opportunities, as well as the acquisition of generic graduate skills and attributes that provide them with a brighter view of their future. Their voices, when contextualised against existing transition literature and research, provide insights into how the personal value of experiencing university can be understood.

The purpose of pathways such as the DoTS is to prepare students for successful university study. One measure of success is the extent to which they equip students with the skills and results to be able to articulate into degrees. For pathways students, who are often from under-represented and/or poorly prepared student groups who cannot meet conventional entry requirements, an important goal is also the cultivation of attitudes and learning skills necessary to experience success at university (Wilson 2009). For over a decade, the DoTS pathway has been equipping students for university studies by exploring the benefits of acquiring generic skills and an appreciation of graduate attributes.

A quantitative assessment of the DoTS at Monash University's Gippsland, Berwick, and Peninsula campuses between 2005 and 2008 identified levels of student success satisfactory to warrant its steady expansion (Hourigan *et al.* 2009). As an immersion pathway, the DoTS students undertake two core units alongside six disciplinary-specific first-year units. Graduates then have the opportunity to enter the second year of a degree with full credit and commence Monash degrees as second year students. The DoTS provides higher education opportunities to individuals from under-represented student groups who demonstrate an ability to satisfy institutional performance benchmarks within the pathway program.

Between 2005 and 2009, 64% of the DoTS students progressed into Monash degrees, with this figure rising to between 68% to 70% for the period 2007 to 2009 (Powell & Hourigan 2010). As second year students in the period 2005 to 2008, student progress rates (the proportion of load passed by a student) ranged between 79.6% and 86.9%. Retention rates (the extent to which students complete or continue their studies) ranged between 83.1% and 92.3%, and average weighted marks ranged between 57% and 60.7% (Hourigan *et al.* 2009). These levels of success are comparable with the performance of conventional entry students on each of the respective campuses. At a quantitative level, these students have been equipped via the DoTS to study alongside their peers on an equal footing. As determined by Evans' (2000: 4) literature review of university transition, reliable indicators of students' potential for success were "previous post-secondary qualifications". As a consequence, the DoTS pathway provides a useful mechanism to assist Monash University to address government social inclusion targets (Bradley 2008).

In interviews, the students attributed their subsequent academic success to the DoTS pathway. A common interview theme was the extent to which they identified the explicit teaching of study skills within the core units as an important part of their transition into university. For example, Jenna identified the explicit focus upon the transition experiences of students as a "first step" that eased the anxiety and difficulty in adapting to the university learning environment:

> I think it's just a first step in to uni ... I don't know what I would have done not having done it. Going into first year, like "oh my god this is uni, I'm only getting passes and the learning is very full on and stressful." I think it's a process for learning at university and there are units to help you with that ... It's definitely the individual DoTS units that help with learning what's required of a university student.

A second recurring interview theme was a perception that DoTS students had benefitted from an induction into the university style of learning and scholarship, and had been placed in a position of advantage with respect to their peers. Rachel identified as integral to her transition additional staff support in the acquisition of skills necessary for success at university:

> The DoTS tutor taught us everything we needed to know to be successful at university, and we basically all have, we're all doing better than most of the other students who didn't do DoTS ... there is a big difference between us DoTS students and the people that didn't do DoTS from how much we actually succeed, how much knowledge we actually pick up compared to them. With the referencing – we're really good at it now and they are not. There are people [I know] that are doing well that didn't do DoTS, but not the majority of them.

Many other students also attributed staff interest in a student-centred approach to learning as fundamental in developing their capacities to become "good" students. Rachel's view was representative of many past student reflections and suggests the DoTS students believed they acquired skills and insights into the practices of university learning that set them apart from their peers who directly entered first year.

What is confirmed by combining the quantitative analysis of student performance with their qualitative interview reflections is the importance of preparing students for success. It has been widely acknowledged that first year is when students acquire the skills, outlooks, values and patterns of behaviour necessary to be successful at university (McInnis *et al.* 1995: 121; see also Pike & Kuh 2005; Krause 2005; Brinkworth *et al.* 2009; Leese 2010). For DoTS students, their pathway year was effectively their first year at university. Therefore, it is important to embed strategies to facilitate students' understanding of "what is expected of them", "how to navigate the university system", and how to develop a "sense of cultural competence" (Wilson 2009: 4–7).

Wilson (2009: 11) asserts "the dual aims of any first year course are helping students 'learn the curriculum' and assisting them to 'learn to be successful students'". This is, arguably, most necessary when students are among those considered least academically prepared, and is often recognised by institutions that recruit younger students or those "from traditionally less well-represented social backgrounds" (Smith 2003: 91). Even if universities continue to conceive teaching students how to learn as being outside of their core business (Smith 2003: 93; Bamforth 2010: 51), it is clearly appreciated by the students as a core function of a university education. It is also a demonstrably effective approach when applied within the DoTS pathway program.

The Benefits of Imparting Generic Skills

A university education is presumed to prepare students to contribute to national development goals and become the professionals necessary for 21st-Century workplaces (Bamforth 2010). The generic skills that underpin graduate attributes are intended to equip students with the dispositions necessary to "continue learning throughout their lives, not only in formal contexts ... but at home, at work, and in the community" (Candy *et al.* 1994: 32; see also Bamforth 2010: 58; Brookfield 1987). More recently, such attributes have been institutionally promoted as a means of addressing the "educational needs of an ever more diverse group of learners" (Pitman & Broomhall 2009: 440). Yet discipline-specific knowledge and skills continue to dominate first year curricula, and generic skills are not explicitly taught to new students because they are expected to "either arrive at university with a strong set of generic skills appropriately contextualised for application, or ... student's fill any gaps in this area during study" (Bamforth 2010: 50). Effective pathways programs should not have such expectations of their students nor excuse themselves from the responsibility to directly address these learning needs. Neither should universities, if they seek to address government social inclusion agendas that further add to the diversity of their student bodies (Bradley 2008).

Initially, the learning interests of the overwhelming majority of students entering the pathway are dominated by vocational ambitions. While these provide students with robust motivation (Lehmann 2009) and an enviable clarity of purpose for pursuing higher education (Wilson 2009), it has been recognised that acquiring generic skills contributes "significantly to student confidence ... and commitment" (Bamforth 2010: 51). As a consequence, one of the objectives of the DoTS core units has been to explicitly cultivate among students a broader appreciation of the nature and benefits of a university education. As proposed by Winchester-Seeto and Bosanquet (2009: 511), it is "vital that the learning and teaching of graduate capabilities occurs at the program and especially at the unit level if there is to be any degree of success in embedding the capabilities in everyday student learning experiences". The effectiveness of this strategy is evident in the student interviews when participants were invited to reflect upon their perceived benefits of a university education.

Many students expressed a belief that university provides an opportunity to broaden individual horizons of opportunity and possibility, and the skills they acquired changed their attitudes toward, and ideas about, learning. Simon came to recognise that learning is not simply an institutional activity:

> Something I learnt back then [DoTS] was that learning is more than just going to university, life experiences are also learning. And being able to draw on things I've learnt is enjoyable.

In response to being asked "what makes a good student?", Jean-Paul suggested:

> You'd say good marks, wouldn't you? But I just think someone that takes in what they are learning, not just does the assignment and forgets about it ... I'm remembering things and thinking more about things outside uni in general because of it, whereas in high school, you'll do all this work just to get this mark.

Of interest here is the move beyond institutionally-measured performance to considering the application of knowledge beyond the classroom. The benefits of a university education were considered by past students to represent more than the sum of its parts.

Embedding generic skills "offers an opportunity for students at the foundation level to identify and begin to build the academic skills necessary for success" (Bamforth 2010: 51). This has been the approach of the DoTS core units over the past decade, explicitly and critically introducing students to the concepts of lifelong learning, critical thinking, and independent learning. As the majority of students self-identify as first-in-family, or first-in-generation to attend university, it is important to clearly explain the purpose and benefits of a university education. Without ready access to role-models who are able to explain what is required to be successful at university, or the long-term benefits of a bachelor degree, pathway students do not necessarily have the social support required to sustain their commitment (Urquhart & Pooley 2007). Neither do they initially approach their studies with expectations of acquiring anything other than vocationally-specific skills and knowledge. By contextualising and demystifying the nature of university learning within the core DoTS units, students are better equipped to appreciate and understand the expectations placed upon them as learners (Levy & Murray 2003; Ballantyne *et al.* 2009). Those who have been successful are then able to identify relevant skills and attitudes for tertiary study and attribute their acquisition as a fundamental benefit of the pathway.

Lifelong learning is presumed to equip graduates with desirable learning attitudes that provide them with an insight into the value of ongoing education. It has been recognised as:

> crucial to preparing workers to compete in the global economy. But it is important for other reasons as well. By improving people's ability to function as members of their communities, education and training increase social cohesion, reduce crime, and improve income distribution. (World Bank 2003: xvii)

Higher-education institutions share these views and consider the provision of lifelong learning opportunities as part of their "social and community responsibilities, as well as a key business strategy in an increasingly competitive market" (Pittman & Broomhall 2009: 455). While most often discussed as an underpinning strategy for providing education to increasing numbers of people, it is interesting to see how lifelong learning finds expression among the pathways students. Negina identified lifelong learning as one of the principal benefits of undertaking a pathway into university:

> From my studies last year, it's lifelong learning. Like you learn through your life, if you're educated and you've got the knowledge, then the world is your oyster. So once you're educated, you can do anything you want to. You're not relying on anyone.

Many past students also suggested that the opportunity to successfully experience a pathway program resulted in changed attitudes toward education. For example, Lisa exhibited a genuine enthusiasm for learning and planned to return to study a graduate program:

> I'm actually interested in learning now, I never used to be. But I've got these plans, when I become a nurse I'll come back and I'll do more. I want to do emergency nursing already, I've decided. I'll come back and do more classes for emergency nursing, get my diploma.

Evident among many of the former students were awakened ambitions to pursue study beyond undergraduate qualifications – an embodiment of the concept of lifelong learning. Many former pathways students have pursued vocationally-specific graduate programs and several have undertaken Masters and Doctoral degrees.

Critical thinking is introduced to students, initially as an important study skill, and then as a fundamental attitude of university graduates. Encouraging students to recognise the importance of thinking outside a box has proven successful, as witnessed by Helen's consideration of the post-secondary differences between herself and her friends:

> For me it [university] was to get my job. But I think I've become a better thinker and I look at things a lot different ... I think uni really taught me to look outside the box and not be so straight and narrow, which is what I grew up with and I guess it's just a better way of thinking and giving people more opportunities ... The thinking, like critical thinking, [a] willingness to look at things in another way and another perspective ... I think that's a big one. I just look at some of my friends and I think our whole thinking about things changed.

This approach often proves challenging for students who enter university with pragmatic, vocational ambitions and who do not easily recognise how their views of the wider world have been shaped. Daniel remarked:

> I was brought up in a very narrow existence ... Just the idea that people could think differently to that was foreign to me at first. It was confronting for a little while. The thing that hit me the most was the realisation that I really didn't know as much as I thought I did. Coming to uni just broadened the scope of possibilities for me ... It's discomforting when you recognise how little you know, but it's beneficial just because broader horizons, broader opportunities ... It was good to have one place where you could learn [generic skills] without being limited by being in a particular discipline.

In writing about disciplinary differences, Ballard and Clanchy (1988: 14) observe that "[s]tudents take some time to realize that the world comes to them, not pure, not undifferentiated, but already parcelled out, distinctively signposted and labelled". The same may be said of students' attitudes towards knowledge more generally. Introducing students to viewpoints perhaps foreign to their own, and cultivating a critical capacity for evaluation, becomes a principal function of the DoTS. In efforts to achieve this objective, the multi-disciplinary nature of the pathway appears to have a distinct advantage for some students. Melinda noted:

> In comparison to nursing tutes there were a lot of different viewpoints and opinions and I really liked getting exposure to those different, sometimes not the same as mine, opinions ... With DoTS it was good because there were lots of different people doing different things, but with nursing everyone feels the same way about the profession ... You get stuck, if you're in a faculty or a field, you get stuck all the time with very similar views. [DoTS] sort of makes you wake up a little bit that there are different ways that things can happen and they still function, they still work even if it's not done your way.

Within tutorials, the students were often openly cynical or dismissive of the idea of critical thinking, sometimes accepting it grudgingly as little more than another university oddity, much like academic referencing. In retrospect, however, many of them recognised the acquisition of critical thinking skills and attitudes as an integral part of their university education. Although students may take some time to recognise and accept critical thinking as a lived activity rather than simply a study skill (Brookfield 1987; Allen 1997), getting them there is clearly a crucial role of pathways.

All students new to university are introduced to their responsibility to become an independent learner in order to effectively transition into a learning environment that does not provide the same level of guidance and support typically offered in secondary school. It is widely acknowledged that becoming a self-regulating learner is a skill students need to acquire in order to be successful in adult learning environments (Wilson 2009; see also Marshall & Rowland 2006; Burns 2006). Successful DoTS students identified this as another important attribute acquired at university, which they then applied to their working lives. Simon paired independent learning with critical thinking as important graduate skills and believed they provided a foundation for future success:

> I think everyone should learn the skills that a university offers – independent learning, critical thinking. I think being able to critically think and analyse a situation, to learn how to listen as opposed to just hear, to understand, to challenge what's being said so then you can get a different idea on that and start making your own ideas. I think those two skills, it doesn't matter what form of life, being able to do that, I think, is beneficial to an individual, to everyone.

Graduate Attributes, Personal Growth, and Life Skills

Interviews revealed that in addition to acquiring an appreciation of generic skills, former DoTS students who undertook degrees also acquired the graduate attributes Monash University seeks to instil in all students. By the time they entered their degrees, or graduated from them, the vocational focus of many students had been augmented with a deeper and broader appreciation of the nature of a university education. "Monash University prepares its graduates to be responsible and effective global citizens who engage in an internationalised world, exhibit cross-cultural competence and demonstrate ethical values"; they are expected to be "critical and creative scholars who produce innovative solutions to problems, apply research skills to a range of challenges and communicate perceptively and effectively" (Monash University 2011). Pitman and Broomhall (2009: 451) suggest graduate attributes prepare bachelors-degree students for post-graduate-level studies. At a pathway level, embedding the foundations of these could be more modestly argued to be an appropriate preparation for students seeking entry into bachelors' degrees.

Many former students ultimately appreciated that the acquisition of disciplinary knowledge, along with critical analysis and information literacy skills, are all part of being a critical and creative scholar. Developing a commitment to learning is a significant achievement for many of the students and represented a significant change in the attitudes they brought into the pathway. Jenna acknowledged that her decision to attend university carried with it a responsibility for her own learning:

> I don't think I'm the best, I think my average is a distinction, that's what I aim for. But I know there are other students who put in more time and effort and get high distinctions for it. I think I do alright. I don't think I put in anywhere near as much time and effort [at high school] as I do now. I think it was, I choose to be here, this is my decision whereas in high school it was very much I have to be here, I have to learn this, whereas now it is my decision and it's up to me to do it.

Monash university graduates are prepared to become responsible and effective global citizens (Monash University 2011). One way in which this is evident among the former DoTS students is in their interest in events and issues beyond the personal. While some of this could be attributed to their developing maturity, it could equally be attributed to the outcomes of their studies. For example, Anna attributed her personal changes to university study because it had been her principal source of influence after secondary school:

> I think it teaches you really how to be a better person. I really do think that [university teaches you] to appreciate everything, and I'm sure, because I haven't really been exposed to anything after high school, but it's taught me to be a better person.

Similarly, Chloe felt the graduate attributes she acquired equipped her to positively engage with the world:

> It just opens you up to so much more and you actually, I find that I pay attention to so many more things, like I never even took notice of what the news said, or what things said and now I can actually question stuff and pay attention to things that are going on in the world ... It's good knowing what's going on.

Critical analysis, information literacy, and multi- and inter-disciplinarity are recognised as components of becoming a critical and creative scholar (Monash University 2011). Serena believed "seeing the bigger picture", being "aware of other things" gaining "in-depth knowledge in other areas" are fundamental to being more analytical:

> I think it gives you more of a – you see the bigger picture. You're sort of more aware of other things. You have more of an in-depth knowledge into other areas and you look at things in a different light. You analyse things more. You feel more confident. Because you've done this, you can do something else … I think it just gives you more hope in life, more hope that you can do bigger and greater things.

Significantly, Serena believed these benefits provide a foundation for "more hope in life".

A university education is supposed to be transformative, the skills and attitudes acquired are supposed to change the value and identities of graduates, and this is evident in the reflections of many pathways students. Denise observed:

> If you're open minded enough to what you're exposed to and are willing to take some of it on board … then it does change who you are. But those changes aren't just in your knowledge, it's who you are personally as well. I found that I became, for the most part, a stronger person, more open minded and I could say what I wanted to say. Whereas before university I wasn't necessarily like that. So it can be transformative.

Such evaluations confirm the findings of Wood and Lithauer (2005:1012) that students attributed personal growth and "developed self-knowledge, an improved sense of self-worth, self-management and communication skills and that their attitudes in general became more positive" to the experience of studying at university. These perceived outcomes correlate very closely with the reflections of Jenna:

> I think I've grown as a person as well as in my studies. I think I'm a lot more independent and self-sufficient, more confident in what I can do as well. I criticise everything now, I can't watch telly without being critical. I watch something and I think; that's just stupid. I know that there's more than one side. In all my assignments I try to find the other side of whatever I'm arguing, even if it's just one person and everyone else says it's this, and then I try to understand why they say it is.

Among pathways students who could not access degree programs via conventional entry mechanisms, these are significant personal developments because of the positive correlation between self-efficacy and academic achievement (Wood & Lithauer 2005: 1014; see also Bandura 1997; Levy & Campbell 2007).

In reflecting upon the benefits of a pathway into university, Copernicus believed the learning curve extended as far as to questioning his own beliefs and certainties along with those of others. A process that made him a "better person", "open to new things" and "critically analytical":

> Big learning curve in terms of figuring out where you want to go. Even to the point of looking at yourself and figuring out who you are ... I'm realising it more so now when I look back and think about it and think "wow", it really opens your eyes to things, and makes you think about who you are and question your current beliefs ... It makes you a better person, I think, because I no longer go around thinking that what I know is right and I don't necessarily believe in what everyone else says either. You know, I'm always open to new things and critically analysing everything now. Including you.

Views such as these suggest success at university permits students to look at themselves in a "new and different way" and positively contributes to their sense of self-efficacy. For these students, a central benefit of experiencing university was the acquisition of an enriched range of life skills that extended beyond the purely academic (Wood & Lithauer 2005: 1003).

For some students, life skills and graduate attributes are inseparable and demonstrate the extent to which they have engaged with the learning opportunities provided by university and become lifelong learners. For Max, critical analysis and communication skills are useful life skills. They are part of an experience he would never trade, justifying his decision not to leave "school" and providing him with a positive view of the future:

> The whole critical thinking, like I think some DoTS students will probably have an advantage over others because the knowledge is quite broad and it can be applied to almost any facet of life. So it was really quite handy. It's life skills, not just tertiary skills. It's life skills as well and I found it quite helpful. It's just really valuable. The experience I've had, like I say, I wouldn't trade it and I'm so glad I didn't leave school now. I'm looking forward to what's in the future as well, like it's only just another stepping stone, but yes helpful. I think that's all. But even just the people skills you learn being here are quite valuable at work, like just the communication skills and that independence is valuable.

Likewise, Daniel believed one of the benefits of university education was a broadening of his mental horizons, and this was a phrase that recurred throughout his interview. His exposure to a "variety of perspectives" and being taught "how to deal with them" represented a "preparation for life":

> Broadening your mental horizons, that's the easiest way to describe it. Coming to uni, coming to a forum where you have so many different perspectives in a small space, in a relatively open forum in the sense that you have the opportunity to listen to those perspectives. That's a benefit all of its own, because that prepares you better than the rote knowledge that you get for dealing with people in the work place. Because out there you'll come across a massive variety of perspectives, in here they teach you how to deal with them. To a point, it's a preparation for life, to be able to deal with people's perspectives ... to interact with them you need to be able to think, you need to be able to see it from their point [of view], to recognise that they're different.

Being able to see things from other people's perspectives and to recognise their differences are expressions of the "compassion and empathy" and "cross-cultural sensitivity" expected from responsible and effective global citizens (Monash University 2011).

Conclusion

Among those students who successfully utilised the DoTS to enter and complete degrees, it is very evident that their university experiences changed their attitudes towards education. When invited to reflect upon their experiences, even many years after the fact, it is apparent the pathway remained a significant memory for the majority of students interviewed. Previous research (Pike & Kuh 2005: 278) suggests first-generation university students, which many of these students were, experience university differently. They are "less engaged overall and less likely to successfully integrate diverse college experiences; they perceived the college environment as less supportive and reported making less progress in their learning and intellectual development" (Pike & Kuh 2005: 289). While this may be true of some students, it does not appear to be the experience of the successful DoTS students who were interviewed. Their reflections appear to more closely align with the findings of Pascarella, Pierson, Wolniak and Terenzini (2004: 274) who found "the positive impact of the specific academic/classroom involvement ... was significantly stronger for first-generation than other students". This led them to conclude that higher education experiences provided a "bigger bang-for-the-buck for first generation students ... because these experiences act in a compensatory manner and this contributes comparatively greater incremental increases" (Pascarella et al. 2004: 279–80). This is, of course, the rationale of pathways. The generic skills and attitudes imparted to students are intended to provide the foundations upon which to successfully engage with the enterprise of university learning.

Obviously, there are differences in terms of how best to provide these foundations for students. Smith (2003: 92) believes the best way to impart study skills is within specific disciplines, and if "taught outside a specific discipline, the students feel that they lack focus; they quickly lose interest and vote with their feet". In contrast, the research of Brinkworth, McCann, Matthews and Nordstrom (2009: 157) "[h]ighlight a call for non-specialised transition programs to meet the needs of first year students and facilitate the transition from secondary to tertiary education". The differences between these positions may be accounted for by a focus upon simply skills in the case of Smith and a broader interpretation of the transition needs of new students held by Brinkworth and colleagues. The testimonies of the DoTS students suggests their transition into higher education was a much more complex undertaking than simply skills acquisition, and the opportunity to learn in a multi-disciplinary, immersion context provided them with a greater appreciation of the applications and benefits of the skills and attitudes they acquired.

The complexity of transitioning into university is well captured by the reflections of Sorcha who expressed a quite nuanced appreciation of how students have to come to terms with higher-education disciplines:

> DoTS gave me that foundation ... I never would have studied if I didn't get DoTS. There's a lot of advantages for doing DoTS. Having the taste, having the feel for what I want to study, I think the overwhelming thing is that you think you want to be something, even at my age, but the commitment and the lingo – are you going to fit the discourse? The ideology? And you've got to analyse all of that and say, "well am I part of that? Or is it totally something different to what I want to do?" The 12 months sort of not only gave you what kind of student you can be ... but helps you to tune in to whether you're on the right path.

Importantly, Sorcha acknowledged success ultimately relies upon students demonstrating appropriate levels of commitment and dedication.

As expected, former pathways students who volunteered to be interviewed were overwhelmingly grateful for the opportunity to undertake university study. The extent to which they attributed their subsequent university success to the pathway, however, was genuinely surprising. The transformative nature of first year for successful students is often overlooked by staffs unless they are reminded by students. Tara, when asked how she would now describe her first year experience, had little hesitation in describing it as life changing:

> I guess I have to say life changing, so to speak, because it's a bit of a combination of everything. You have really good times and you have times when you're really stressed and really tired, but at the same time I guess the whole year of uni and with DoTS it changes the way you think. And it changes everything, you don't take things at face value anymore, you question things, and that sort of thing.

Anna attributed the pathway with providing the means by which to undertake university and for, perhaps, making her a better person:

> If there wasn't a program like DoTS I probably wouldn't be here at all … I think DoTS maybe made me a better person. And I'm not just saying that because you're here. I say it to people that I speak to, that I'm friends with. I do thank my lucky stars that there is a program like DoTS at Monash that people who only got an [entry] score of 57 can come and do, and still be able to do what they want. But you have to want to do it.

She also acknowledged it provided her with the opportunity to study what she was interested in. As observed by Ballantyne, Madden and Todd (2009: 311; see also Lehmann 2009), vocational ambitions drive these students to be successful and "may contribute to their enjoyment of study, identification of the traditional role of a student and, most significantly, sense of purpose and motivation to succeed". Anna confirmed that a pathway provides those students "who want to do it" with the necessary vehicle for success.

Sir John Monash famously declared "[a]dopt as your fundamental creed that you will equip yourself for life, not solely for your own benefit but for the benefit of the whole community" (Serle 1982: 481). The extent to which DoTS students have adapted to the university learning environment and absorbed important aspects of its culture is evident from Meg's reflections on what she gained from her experiences:

> It gives you those skills, those tools to make it through life … If you've been through a lot of things and you get a lot of tools to deal with

that from uni, you can then help other people to better their lives. I think without uni I wouldn't be half as determined or willing or strong. I'm not that smart, but I wouldn't be as analytical as I am now and critical. I'm critical of everything now. I never used to really, like I only questioned things that were personal to *me* and important to *me*, but now I watch the news and I'm like, "well how do they know that?" I think that it really helps you have a whole new outlook on life and everybody should be able to have that opportunity.

Pathways provide important opportunities to broaden university participation rates among previously under-represented student groups. The experiences and voices of the DoTS students confirm that they take away from the engagement what all students are expected to leave with. They graduate with generic skills and attributes, a career qualification, and a high regard for learning that well equips them to participate in their communities as lifelong learners.

References

Allen, M. 1997. *Smart Thinking: Skills for Critical Understanding and Writing*. Oxford: Oxford University Press.

Ballantyne, J., Madden, T., & Todd, N. 2009. 'Gauging the Attitudes of Non-Traditional Students at a New Campus: An Australian Case Study'. *Journal of Higher Education Policy and Management* 31(14): 301–313.

Ballard, B., & Clanchy, J. 1988. 'Literacy in the University: An Anthropological Approach'. In Taylor, G., Ballard, B., Beasley, V., Bock, H., Clanchy, J., & Nightingale, P. (ed.). *Literacy by Degrees*. Milton Keynes: Open University Press.

Bamforth, C. J. 2010. 'Improving Undergraduates' Performance via an Embedded Generic Skills Program'. In Devlin, M., Nagy, J., & Lichtenberg, A. (ed.). *Research and Development in Higher Education: Reshaping Higher Education: Proceedings of the 33rd Higher Education Research and Development Society of Australasia Annual International Conference*, 6–9 July, Melbourne.

Bandura, A. 1997. *Self-Efficacy: The Exercise of Control*. New York: WH Freeman & Company.

Bradley, D., Noonan, P., Nugent, H., & Scales, B. 2008. *Review of Australian Higher Education, Final Report*. http://www.deewr.gov.au/HigherEducation/Review/Documents/PDF/Higher%20Education%20Review_one%20document_02.pdf (accessed 20 May 2011).

Brookfield, S. 1987. *Developing Critical Thinkers: Challenging Adults to Exploring Alternative Ways of Thinking and Acting*. Milton Keynes: Open University Press.

Burns, P. 2006. *Success in College: from Cs in High School to As in College*. Lanham: Rowman & Littlefield Education.

Candy, P., Crebert, G., & O'Leary, J. 1994. *Developing Lifelong Learners through Undergraduate Education*. Canberra: Australian Government Publishing Service.

Evans, M. 2000. 'Planning for the Transition to Tertiary Study: A Literature Review'.

Journal of Institutional Research 9(1): http://www.aair.org.au/articles/volume-9-no-1/9-1-planning-for-the-transition-to-tertiary-study-a-literature-review (accessed 26 May 2011).

Hourigan, C. 2009. *Bachelor Pass Admission Pathways and Academic Performance at Monash South Africa*. University Planning and Statistics, Office of the Pro Vice-Chancellor Planning and Quality, 24 August, Monash University.

Krause, K. 2005. 'The Changing Face of the First Year: Challenges for Policy and Practice in Research-Led Universities'. Keynote Paper, First Year Experience Workshop, 31 October, University of Queensland.

Leese, M. 2010. 'Bridging the Gap: Supporting Student Transitions into Higher Education'. *Journal of Further and Higher Education* 34(2): 239–251.

Lehmann, W. 2009. 'University as Vocational Education: Working Class Students' Expectations for University'. *British Journal of Sociology of Education* 30(2): 137–149.

Levy, S., & Campbell, H. 2007. 'Promoting Motivation and Engagement Among Academically at Risk Students'. *Widening Participation and Lifelong Learning* 9(3): 18–25.

Levy, S., & Earl, C. 2012. *Student Voices in Transition: The Experiences of Pathways Students*. South Africa: Van Schaik Publishers.

Levy, S., & Murray, J. 2003. 'Demystifying Tertiary Success: Strategies for Broadening Participation and Initiating Lifelong Learning'. *Journal of Higher Education Policy and Management* 5(2): 42–45.

Marshall, L., & Rowland, F. 2006. *A Guide to Learning Independently*. Fourth ed. Frenchs Forest: Pearson Education Australia.

McInnis, C., James, R., & McNaught, C. 1995. *First Year on Campus: Diversity in the Initial Experience of Australian Undergraduates*. Canberra: Australian Government Publishing Service.

Monash University. 2011. *Monash Graduate Attributes Policy*. http://www.policy.monash.edu/policybank/academic/education/management/monash-graduate-attributes-policy.html (accessed 2 May 2011).

Pascarella, E. T., Pierson, C. T., Wolniak, G. C., & Terenzini, P. T. 2004. 'First Generation College Students: Additional Evidence on College Experience and Outcomes'. *The Journal of Higher Education* 75(3): 249–285.

Pike, G. R., & Kuh, G. D. 2005. 'First- and Second-Generation College Students: A Comparison of Their Engagement and Intellectual Development'. *The Journal of Higher Education* 76(3): 276–300.

Pitman, T., & Broomhall, S. 2009. 'Australian Universities, Generic Skills and Lifelong Learning'. *International Journal of Lifelong Education* 28(4): 439–458.

Powell, N., & Hourigan, C. 2010. *Diploma of Tertiary Studies DoTS Qualification Review*. University Planning and Statistics, Office of the Pro Vice-Chancellor Planning and Quality, Monash University.

Serle, G. 1982. *John Monash: A Biography*. Carlton: Melbourne University Press in association with Monash University.

Smith, K. 2003. 'School to University: Sunlit Steps, or Stumbling in the Dark?' *Arts and Humanities in Higher Education* 2(1): 90–98.

Urqhart, B., & Pooley, J. 2007. 'The Transition Experience of Australian Students to University: The Importance of Social Support'. *The Australian Community Psychologist* 19(2): 78–91.

Wilson, K. 2009. 'Success in First Year: The Impact of Institutional, Programmatic and Personal Interventions on an Effective and Sustainable First-Year Student Experience'. Paper presented at the 12th Pacific Rim First Year in Higher

Education 2009 Conference: Preparing for Tomorrow Today: The First Year Experience as foundation. http://www.fyhe.com.au/past_papers/papers09/content/html/keynote.html (accessed on 6 September 2010).

Winchester-Seeto, T., & Bosanquet, A. 2009. 'Will Students Notice the Difference? Embedding Graduate Capabilities in the Curriculum'. The Student Experience. Proceedings of the 32nd HERDSA Annual Conference, 6–9 July, Darwin.

Wood, L. A., & Lithauer, P. 2005. 'The "Added" Value of a Foundation Programme'. *South African Journal of Higher Education* 19(5): 1002–1019.

World Bank. 2003. *Lifelong Learning in the Global Knowledge Economy: Challenges for Developing Countries*. Washington: World Bank.

Chapter 4

Development of a Postulated Model for Investigating Resilience and Retention of Teachers and Nurses

A Review of Literature

Jeffrey Dorman and Michael Dyson

Abstract

This chapter reviews national and international literature on the resilience and retention of pre-service and in-service teachers and nurses. The importance of increasing participation rates in Australian tertiary education has been identified as a key area of action by Australian governments and reports like *The Bradley Report* (Bradley *et al.* 2008). This is especially so for locations like the Latrobe Valley, Victoria, which has a history of poor participation. While getting students into tertiary institutions is an important issue, it is also important to keep the students in the institutions once they arrive. The retention of new graduates in these professions is also a significant issue. As such, the retention of students is a key issue. Retention can be related to the resilience of students, especially in courses that demand both academic and vocational development. While it is easy to focus on individual student attributes as predictors of resilience and retention, the learning environments provided in universities at both the class and institutional levels warrant closer examination. This chapter studies resilience and retention and its antecedents with a particular focus on pre-service and beginning teachers and nurses. A model that encapsulates current theoretical perspectives on these issues is postulated as a way forward for empirical investigations.

Introduction

For many tertiary students who graduate as teachers or nurses, the reality is that they will not be practising in five years' time. Indeed, the attrition rate in teaching is such that as many as 50% of beginning teachers will leave the profession within the first five years (Ingersoll 2007; Ingersoll & Smith 2003; Watlington *et al.* 2010). Furthermore, teacher retention statistics mask the reality that some practising teachers are physically present but not contributing professionally (Beltmann, Mansfield & Price 2011).

Shortages of nursing staff are also evident and are linked to occupational stress, workloads and insufficient resourcing (Evans *et al.* 2006; Evans & Huxley 2009; Jackson, Firtko & Edenborough 2007). In short, just like teachers, nurses are undervalued. In one of the few studies into undergraduate retention, Gaynor *et al.* (2006) noted that the attrition rates for first year undergraduate nursing students ranged from 25–27%.

The concept of retention has appeared in social science literature over the past two decades. It has been linked to stress and burnout. Significant research has been conducted in these fields (Dorman 2003; Tait 2008). By contrast, the issue of resilience is a relatively new concept without a substantive research history. Its relevance and importance to nurses and teachers is undeniable. The purpose of this chapter is to introduce and discuss the concepts of resilience and retention of teachers and nurses. An elaborate causal path model for future research is proposed and its components will be discussed.

Resilience

The concept of resilience in young children, adolescents and adults has developed into a significant field of research and associated theoretical discussion on coping with risks (Wagnild 2009). This research contrasts with researching deficit issues that focus on illness and psychopathology (Windle, Bennet & Noyes 2011). That is, the direction of resilience research has shifted from the negative outcomes and damage caused by risk factors to researching the positive attributes of how to cope with risk factors (Sun & Stewart 2007). Internationally, these concepts have been related to resilience in Antonovsky's *salutogenic model* (Antonovsky 1996) and Bronfenbrenner's *ecological model* (1979). These conceptualisations contextualise human development and provide a place for the environment in research on resilience. As such, resilience is not simply a personal attribute but a dynamic that involves environmental situations or risk factors and what personal and environmental protective factors exist (Beltman *et al.* 2011).

The complexity of defining the construct of resilience has been widely recognised and it has created considerable challenges when developing an operational definition of resilience (Masten 2007). While no one definition of resilience exists, there is general agreement in the literature that it involves the ability of individuals to cope with adversity, stress and achieve goals in the face of obstacles. Give this lack of clarity about a definition, researchers need to be particularly careful not to confound the predictors of resilience with the construct itself.

Assessing Resilience

Connor and Davidson (2003) suggest that resilience is about thriving in the face of adversity. Natural disasters (e.g., floods, cyclones, and bushfires) often bring out the resilience in people. Indeed, the ability to "bounce back" is fundamental to the concept of resilience. In developing a six-item *Basic Resilience Scale*, Smith *et al.* (2008) refer to the basic meaning of the word resile: to bounce or spring back.

Two established instruments used to assess resilience are the *Resilience Scale* (Wagnild & Young 1993) and the *Connor-Davidson Resilience Scale* (CD-RISC) (Connor & Davidson 2003). Both of these scales have twenty-five items and tap several underlying constructs. For example, the Resilience Scale assesses perseverance, equanimity, meaningfulness, self-reliance and existential aloneness. The psychometric properties of these instruments have been studied with shortened versions of these instruments available. While Campbell-Sills and Stein (2007) developed a ten-item version of the CD-RISC, Vaishnavi, Connor and Davidson (2007) validated a scale consisting of only two of the original twenty-five CD-RISC items. Overall, this conceptual and empirical work attests to the contemporary nature of much national and international resilience research.

Resilience in Teaching

Teachers require a diverse range of skills and knowledge to enable them to be effective teachers within the classroom. However, teaching goes beyond having a deep understanding of a subject area and the ability to teach it to others. Teachers must have strong self-efficacy, sound classroom management skills, highly developed organisational skills, and an ability to interact with people from a diverse range of backgrounds and motivations. They constantly face new challenges from students and the wider school community, in addition to working in a profession that is constantly evolving and demanding more from its employees. How do teachers adapt successfully to these challenges? Why do some cope better than others? Research shows there is a significant link between a teacher's resilience level and their ability to adapt to such challenges.

Pre-Service Teachers' Resilience

In order for resilience to exist, there needs to be some stressor or risk factor that requires an individual to act in response to the risk; "resilience is a mode of interacting with events in the environment that is activated and nurtured in times of stress" (Tait 2008: 58). Pre-service teacher resilience risk factors may relate to individual traits, such as poor self-efficacy, a lack of confidence, poor organisational skills, poor social skills and difficulty identifying oneself as a teacher (Hong 2010); contextual risk factors may relate to the course structure, timetabling, family commitments, financial strain and work commitments (Beltman *et al.* 2011; Le Cornu 2009).

The mix of academic studies together with compulsory vocational experience in teacher education courses adds an additional layer of complexity to these risk factors. It can be difficult to successfully integrate these two areas and adjust accordingly to the ebbs and flows that occur during and after each teaching-round practicum. Pre-service teachers are faced with a host of practical challenges, including classroom management, pastoral care, and administrative duties (Buchanan 2011). As many issues are contextually based, it is impossible for tertiary education courses to address all of the specific, practical realities that pre-service teachers encounter. Given the diverse range of risk factors present during a pre-service teacher education course, it is imperative that pre-service teachers have sufficient generic, adaptable skills and resources to be able to face risks and adapt positively to them. As Bobek (2002: 202) states: "pre-service teachers must recognise and develop the resources that will sustain their resilience as they enter the initial career stages of the profession".

What protective factors may apply to resilience in a pre-service teaching course? Students would benefit from having a clear understanding of the realities of their course, including an awareness that practicum is a compulsory, demanding, stressful component of their course. It is also important that an individual have some notion of what it means to be a contemporary teacher. Developing an identity as a teacher is an evolving process, and part of that process involves internalising teacher attributes. Without a strong sense of teacher identity, pre-service teachers are exposing themselves to risk factors that may impact on their ability to continue (Hong

2010). Other protective factors may include supportive family, familiarity with the campus, staff and peer academic and social support.

Beginning Teachers' Resilience

According to Windle (2011), resilience is considered a process of adapting to significant trauma or stress by utilising resources that an individual possesses and being able to bounce back from the trauma. In relation to teaching, potential stressors or risk factors may include classroom management issues, aggressive behaviour from students, time management and workload pressures, teaching outside area of expertise, school location, environmental change (personal and professional), parental interference, a lack of administrative, collegial and leadership support, and working in a disadvantaged environment with insufficient resources (Bobek 2002).

The way in which teachers react to these risk factors is important. Risk factors that relate to working conditions have been linked to high attrition rates for beginning teachers (Ingersoll & Smith 2003) who may not have the experience or protective resources to manage the situation effectively, and may therefore decide to leave. If, on the other hand, these stressors are considered from a resilience perspective and the individual has protective factors to utilise, they are more likely to experience a successful outcome and be motivated to continue in the profession. Bobek (2002: 202) sees teacher resilience as "a critical element in classroom success and retention". A resilient teacher will not only have personal success, but will also have a positive influence on students (Gu & Day 2007).

The protective factors that may be effective in combating these stressors include a teacher's ability to de-personalise the event, and self-reflect (Howard & Johnson 2004) on how the situation was handled and consider alternative solutions for future events. Indeed, "learning from past experience increases available resources and thus improves one's resilience for dealing with future circumstances" (Bobek 2002: 202). However, it is important to note that an individual's resilience to a stressor may be context-specific; they may react differently in the future, depending on the type of stressor and how regularly it occurs (Beltman *et al.* 2011; Gu & Day 2007; Herrman *et al.* 2007). It follows that resilient individuals will be enabled to develop and increase their pool of protective resources as they are exposed to different stressors over time (Bobek 2002).

Sound collegial relationships within the school community can enhance teacher resilience. It is often useful to de-brief and reflect on issues with colleagues who understand the nature of teacher work. More experienced colleagues may be able to offer strategies to cope with the demands of the job in a more effective way. Whereas beginning teachers view their profession from a micro perspective – they are focussed on daily logistics of classroom management, administrative duties and teaching – more experienced teachers are able to put issues into a more realistic and long-term perspective. The mentor can provide useful insights about teaching as a profession, in addition to more specific information on the school environment.

Protective factors that can be taught and enhanced will not only enable individuals to cope with the demands of the teaching profession, but will also enable them to adapt successfully and remain encouraged and committed to dynamic and ever-changing educational settings (Bobek 2002; Gu and Day 2007; Howard and Johnson 2004). It is, however, the responsibility of higher education providers, schools, governments and communities to ensure that learning opportunities and the necessary physical resources are made available to teachers to learn and foster resilience (Howard & Johnson 2004).

There are significant benefits for resilient teachers. From an individual perspective, teachers will feel a great sense of self-efficacy, they will be effective teachers with strong social support networks and they will remain committed to the teaching profession for the long term. Resilient teachers will also have a positive impact on burnout and stress levels (Gu and Day 2007; Howard and Johnson 2004). It is argued that some attrition is needed within a profession to enable change and innovation (Ingersoll & Smith 2003). However, it is imperative that quality retention (Day & Gu 2009) is sought; every effort should be made to retain resilient teachers within the profession.

Resilience in Nursing

As a service-orientated occupation like teaching, nursing is also a stressful profession (Gillespie *et al*. 2007; McVicar 2003). McAllister and McKinnon (2009) note that nursing involves constant helping and caring which require a high degree of self-giving. The work environment is stressful and, collectively, nurses have high levels of unhappiness, reduced self-efficacy, and a high attrition rate (Clinton & Hazelton 2000; Leighton 2005). Despite these attributes, the study of resilience has been largely overlooked by higher education nursing courses (see Hodges, Keeley & Grier 2005; Jackson *et al*. 2007). Importantly, Hodges, Keeley and Grier (2005) linked resilience with career retention: resilient nurses do not leave the profession when temporarily overwhelmed.

A study by Gillespie *et al.* (2007) focused on the experience of operating-room nurses, and defined resilience in terms of personal competence, strength in adversity, acceptance, control and belief in mystical powers. They proposed a five-dimensional model for predictors of this resilience: hope, self-efficacy, coping, workplace culture, and age. According to Jackson *et al.* (2007), resilience is an essential quality of successful nurses. They identified five strategies to develop resilience: building positive professional relationships; maintaining positivity; developing emotional insights to understand one's own risk and protective factors; using life balance and spirituality; and becoming more reflective to elucidate meaning from events.

Retention

As discussed earlier, teaching and nursing are being reviewed due to the high attrition rates experienced in pre-service courses and the beginning years of each profession. It has been suggested that some level of attrition is healthy to ensure a dynamic, innovative, qualified and competent workforce (Ingersoll & Smith 2003; Plunkett & Dyson 2011). Nevertheless, it is imperative that action be taken by governments and employers to improve staffing retention levels.

This section has a focus on the reasons for high attrition rates within teaching and nursing, and explores initiatives introduced by education and health care providers to determine if these measures have any long-term, positive impact on both pre-service and in-service retention levels. Initiatives that enhance and develop resilience may result in improved retention rates (Bobek 2002; Cameron & Brownie 2010; Tait 2008). In exploring the concept of retention, research invariably studies the reasons why individuals leave a course or a profession. Few studies have approched the issue from the perspective of ascertaining why teachers and nurses stay in their profession.

In examining the high attrition rates in the beginning years of an individual's career, some researchers consider the notion that there may be gaps between theoretical components of higher education courses, and the realities of the workplace. Even though course practica offer insights into a profession, there are still gaps between what is taught at university and the actual working environment that graduates encounter (Australian Education Union 2006; Australian Primary Principals' Association 2006; Buchanan 2011; Gaynor *et al.* 2006). The apparent lack of integration between theory and practice can be demonstrated in the field of teaching, where the theory may not prepare students adequately to carry out pastoral, managerial and administrative responsibilities of a teacher (Buchanan 2011), even though these duties are integral to the profession of teaching. However, as indicated by Dyson:

> It would also seem that when practice is valued over theory an increasing emphasis is placed on training as distinct from an emphasis placed on education. This suggests that when the concept of education is prioritised, rather than training, and on the synergy rather than the separation of theory and practice, we have the potential to build the professional status of a profession of education as distinct from preparing skilled and competent service providers. (2009: 59)

The separation of theory and practice may be caused partially by a lack of collaboration between higher education providers and practicum providers (i.e., schools and hospitals). However, it is also significant to investigate if the transitional needs of graduating students are being satisfactorily identified and addressed at the workplace by schools and hospitals (Buchanan 2011; McAllister & McKinnon 2009). Indeed, collective ownership can result in neither the higher education providers nor the practicum providers taking responsibility on important induction issues.

Retention of Teachers

Individuals are motivated into a career in teaching for several reasons. For many people, the idea of engaging with and educating a younger generation is often appealing. Also, the international mobility of the profession is an attractive aspect of teaching, especially for young people. Other aspirants, unsure of what employment they seek, enrol in education while they determine what profession they wish to enter. For other individuals, they enter the teaching profession after an established career in another field with the aim of educating others in their area of expertise. Lastly, there are extrinsic reasons, including long holidays, pay and status (Kyriacou & Coulthard 2000) that may entice an individual to enrol in a teaching course.

For some individuals, their reasons for enrolling in a teaching course are misguided and uninformed: what they are wanting out of a career and what teaching can offer are mismatched (Kyriacou and Coulthard 2000). Teaching practica offer the first insight into the realities of teaching, and it is during this time that student teachers begin to understand the workload and challenges of teaching.

One of the greatest concerns of teacher attrition is the substantial costs associated with significant and sustained teacher turnover rates. In America, the estimated cost of replacing public school teachers that leave the profession is $2.2 billion per year (Watlington *et al.* 2010). In addition to these financial costs, educational costs to students and the larger school community must also be considered. When a teacher leaves the profession, expertise, experience and local knowledge are lost. Wong (2004) argues that the ultimate aim of a school is student success and this is primarily determined by the quality of the teacher. If teaching quality is not sustained due to constant staff turnover, student performance can be affected. Of concern is that high turnover rates are associated with a greater percentage of beginning teachers. It is estimated that up to 50% of teachers leave the profession within the first three to five years (Rinke 2008). Australian research undertaken by the Australian Primary Principals' Association (APPA 2007) supports these figures. From a survey pool of 1351 respondents, 24% indicated that they will leave the profession within five years. A survey of 1200 beginning teachers by the Australian Education Union (2006) showed that 45% of beginning teachers were not planning to be teaching in 10 years' time.

The situation is worse for rural Australia, where, according to the APPA: "86% of survey respondents chose to only seek teaching appointments in urban centres. Around 55% did not consider rural schools and approximately 80% did not consider remote schools as employment prospects" (2007: 30).

A potential pressure on beginning teachers is the working conditions of the school where a teacher is employed. The availability (or lack of) initial and continuous support provided by a school, colleagues, the leadership team and administration can impact greatly on the level of job satisfaction experienced by a beginning teacher. Beginning teachers invariably spend many hours developing lesson plans, getting to know students, and developing strategies for successful classroom management. Without the support of the school environment, the beginning teacher may feel isolated and become quickly disillusioned with the profession (Buchanan 2011; Tait 2008).

In Australia, the introduction of contract-based employment has had a significant impact on teacher morale and teacher willingness to continue in the profession. Without security, teachers can feel vulnerable and insecure about the position they hold, and may not connect as effectively with the school community (Plunkett & Dyson 2011). Additionally, schools are a state responsibility, and mobility across Australian states is somewhat restricted, as each state has different registration requirements and different curricula.

These impediments are intensified in rural settings, where, due to the small size of the local school community and limited staffing numbers, teachers are required to take on more diverse teaching and administrative responsibilities. A significant time period is required to become familiar with the local environment and develop social links with the wider school community. In addition, an individual must consider the relocation requirements (e.g., accommodation, schooling for dependents, childcare). Although local recruitment would remove some of this pressure, the number of vacancies advertised for rural teaching positions highlights the existence of staff shortages (Australian Primary Principals' Association 2006).

Retention of Nurses

In Australia and internationally, lower than desired retention rates within the nursing profession are a leading cause of labour force shortages. High attrition rates are not only prevalent with registered nurses. Research shows that attrition levels are also high at a pre-service level. It is important that governments and health providers address this issue to enable the increasingly demanding health needs of individuals and society to be met in a safe and appropriate manner (Johnstone 2007), and also to reduce the high financial cost of nursing attrition.

The nursing profession is quite diverse and staff employment is widespread across a range of health care fields. The nursing profession is the largest within the health care profession, and makes up a large percentage of Australia's total labour force (Gaynor *et al.* 2007). In 2009, there were 260,121 registered nurses in Australia who were employed (or looking for employment) in nursing (Australian Institute of Health and Welfare 2011). Given the large number of nurses required in the global community, it is a serious concern that there are labour shortages within the profession internationally (Gaynor *et al.* 2006; Leurer, Donnelly & Domm 2007). Locally, labour shortages are also prevalent within the nursing profession. The Australian Health Workforce Advisory Committee 2004, cited in Eley, Eley and Rogers-Clark (2010), anticipated that from 2010, the yearly demand was expected to be 10,000 new nurse graduates with a shortfall of 4000.

One of the reasons behind the shortages may be attributed to the ageing population of the profession (Australian Government Department of Health and Ageing 2008; Cowin & Hengstberger-Sims 2006). This can be demonstrated in Australia: "In 1999, the 40–44 years age group included the greatest number of nurses of all the age groups; by 2009, it was the 50–54 years age group that included the most nurses" (Australian Institute of Health and Welfare 2011: 3). Imminent retirements and their impact on the health care sector are cause for concern, given the ageing nurse workforce.

However, it is not the primary cause for the significant shortfall of labour supply.

Attrition rates are of concern to governments and health care providers, yet rather than looking into ways to increase retention "solutions have tended to be restricted to measures that increase supply" (McAllister & McKinnon 2009: 372). An increase in labour supply may meet industry demands in the short-term, but it is unsustainable. It is not a simply a matter of new nurses replacing retiring nurses. Indeed, some new nurses replace nurses who leave after only one year of service. Exiting nurses take with them a wealth of knowledge and experience that takes time to rebuild. This may also have a detrimental impact on the quality of care provided to patients (Leurer *et al.* 2007). Governments must consider the cost of staff turnover. In the USA, it has been estimated that the "the costs of nurse turnover range from $22,000 to $64,000 per nurse" (Jones & Gates, cited in Wisotzkey 2011: 15). This cost could be reduced with an increase in retention rates. Therefore, it is important to investigate the reasons behind nursing attrition so that a long-term strategy can be developed to encourage current nurses to remain in the profession.

According to Booth (2011), one of the primary reasons for reduced retention rates relates to the "overwhelming and lost" feeling many beginning nurses experience when they commence their employment after graduation. There is a significant transition between clinical placements as a pre-service nurse and working independently with a presumed level of competency (Booth 2011; Cowin 2002). It seems likely that health care providers do not provide the crucial learning environment needed by beginning nurses, with experienced health professionals lacking in their ability and willingness to guide and nurture new staff. In response to this reality in Australia, Transition to Practice (TTP) programs, or Graduate Nurse Programs (GNP) (Procter *et al.* 2011) have been introduced to provide transitional arrangements and a continuous learning environment for newly registered nurses. Booth (2011) describes initiatives aimed at enhancing beginning nurse experiences and transition into the profession, including the use of visual supports, such as a video that presents different daily scenarios and rationale for the nurse's actions. This visual support is aimed at providing the beginning nurse with insight into the daily activities of the profession. Another fundamental factor affecting nursing retention is job satisfaction. Key indicators of job satisfaction are the autonomy to influence outcomes, and clearly defined task delegation (Cowin 2002; Wisotzkey 2011). If nurses feel they have an element of ownership over their work, they will feel more in control and value the responsibility given to them.

One initiative has been the introduction of nursing mentors to provide support and insight into different areas within nursing care. A mentor is seen as someone who can bridge the gap between the beginning nurse and the employer, by providing sound advice and experience to the beginning nurse, while being willing to listen and offer support to the new employee.

Dyson's (2009) model of *reflective mentoring* would be a useful mentoring procedure to be taught to beginnning nurses and their mentors. The process of reflective mentoring (Dyson 2002) was first developed as a model for the internship program which formed the final year of the Bachelor of Education program at Monash University. It was founded on the ALACT (Korthagan 1999) model of teacher reflection, with two additional components: the inclusion of the role of the mentor teachers and a framework to facilitate reflection, which was the National Competency Framework for Beginning Teachers (NPQTL 1996). This model of "reflective mentoring" was successful and found to be – as expressed by the interns and mentor teachers – a useful alternative to traditional models of supervision. However, when the linear ALACT (Korthagan 1999) process was used just as a cyclical process, that is, visiting concerns or issues, the possibilities for real change or transformation appeared to be limited. It seems to be essential that movement also take place above the current plane of consciousness so that a real transformation is possible in both the pre-service teachers (PSTs) and their mentors.

In response to this limitation, a revised model (Dyson 2009) deals not only with the stand-alone single events but an ongoing transformative process involving both the mentor teacher and the PST. In essence, the model involves support and guidance, a relationship built on trust, frequent conversations, the creation of a non-judgmental environment, and returning to issues and problems for further discussion. The development of the revised process of reflective mentoring came about through embracing Bauman's (2001) concept of tertiary learning and Arendt's (1990) concepts of thinking and judging, actors and spectators. As Coulter (2002: 22) suggests, PSTs need to be "thinking and judging actors and spectators", and as Bauman (2001) asserts, tertiary learners need to be capable of breaking regularity, preventing habitualisation and rearranging the fragmentary experiences into patterns. The new version also incorporates the upward movement to an open worldview (Heylighton 2000), and both the cyclic and the transformative natures of the process illustrate how the PST and the mentor teacher engage in regular and meaningful conversations about daily events and experiences.

This model embraces the potential for a gradual movement towards transformative independence and the recognition of interdependence (i.e., the development of a worldview). It has the potential to assist in both the pre-service and in-service preparation and ongoing development of those in the professions of teaching and nursing.

A Postulated Model for Resilience and Retention of Teachers and Nurses

In developing a model for resilience and retention of teachers and nurses, the above literature was reviewed and other potential predictor variables investigated. This model is shown in Figure 1. It attempts to encapsulate the antecedents and mediating variables that hypothetically influence resilience and retention. In this model, the key predictor variables are social and emotional competence and the learning environments at the university and the workplace (i.e., school or hospital). Other variables that mediate the effects of these predictors on resilience and retention include aspirations, motivation, self-efficacy, engagement, and well-being. It is noteworthy that resilience is a mediating variable that has a direct effect on career intentions. Each of these variables is briefly discussed below.

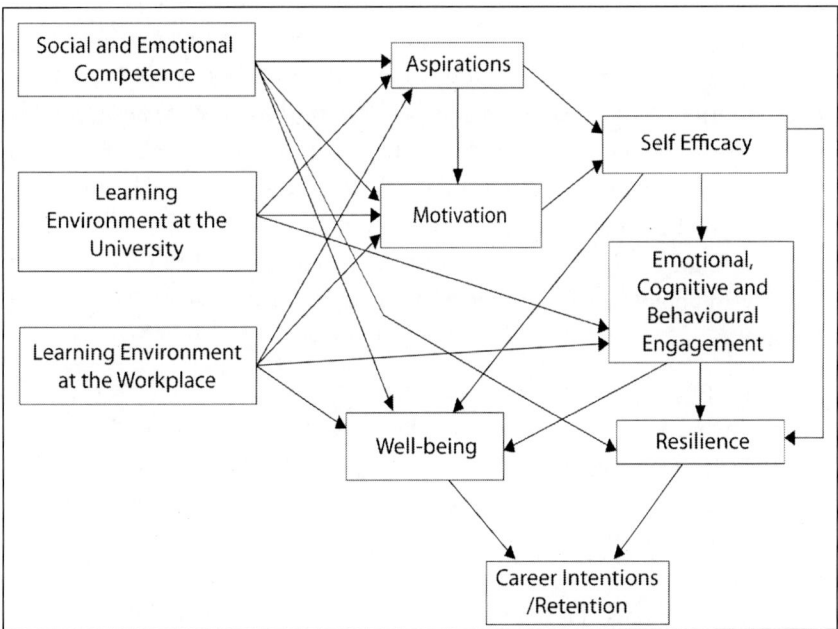

Figure 1. Postulated research model

Social and emotional competence

Social and emotional competence (SEC) refers to a set of life skills that all individuals need to function effectively (see Jennings & Greenberg 2009). Much attention has been paid to the development of such skills in children and adolescents. For example, Durlak *et al.* (2011) presented findings from a meta-analysis of 213 school-based, universal social and emotional learning (SEL) programs involving 270,034 kindergarten-through-to-high-school students. Compared to controls, SEL participants demonstrated significantly improved social and emotional skills, attitudes, behaviour, and academic performance.

While the importance of SEC of young people is well-acknowledged, relatively little research has been conducted on the SEC skills of adults. SEC is especially important for adults who work in demanding human environments like schools and hospitals. Teachers and nurses need to be able to cope with conflict, make sound choices and deal with difficult situations in positive ways. Furthermore, they need to perform such tasks on a regular basis. By contrast, socially and emotionally incompetent teachers are prime targets for burnout, with emotional exhaustion leading to depersonalisation and a lack of personal accomplishment (see Maslach & Leiter 1999).

Social and emotional competence can be considered an outcome of social and emotional learning (SEL). According to Jennings and Greenberg's (2009) extensive review, SEL has five components: self-management (managing emotions and behaviours to achieve one's goals); self-awareness (recognising one's emotions and values as well as one's strengths and weaknesses); social awareness (showing understanding and empathy for others); relationship skills (forming positive relationships, working in teams, dealing effectively with conflict); and responsible decision making (making ethical, constructive choices about personal and social behaviour). The importance of socially and emotionally competent teachers is summed up by Jennings and Greenberg:

> Socially and emotionally competent teachers set the tone of the classroom by developing supportive and encouraging relationships with their students, designing lessons that build on student strengths and abilities, establishing and implementing behavioral guidelines in ways that promote intrinsic motivation, coaching students through conflict situations, encouraging cooperation among students, and acting as a role model for respectful and appropriate communication and exhibitions of prosocial behavior. (2009: 492)

Learning Environments at the University and the Workplace

Learning environment research focuses on the psychosocial dimensions of the environment: the atmosphere or climate that pervades a particular setting. The strong tradition of environment research has been to conceptualise environments in terms of Murray's (1938) *beta press* – the perceptions of the milieu inhabitants – with instruments assessing particular dimensions of the environment (e.g. Personalisation). Moos' (1987) conceptualisation of human environments as having relationship, personal growth, and system maintenance and change dimensions has guided research in this field since the late 1960s. Moos also developed a suite of social-climate scales including the *Work Environment Scale* and the *Ward Atmosphere Scale*. Research on the psychosocial dimensions of environments has made substantial progress during the past 40 years (see Dorman 2002; Fraser 2012). Edited books by Khine and Fisher (2003) and Fisher and Khine (2006) have reported research on the assessment, determinants and outcomes of learning environments.

Studying associations between environment and student outcomes has been the most prolific area of learning environment research. Early career teachers and nurses are exposed to both university and workplace environments. In the present model, it is hypothesised that these environments influence the career intention/retention of early career teachers and nurses; that is, the environment is a determinant or antecedent to the career intentions of teachers and nurses.

Potential Mediating Variables
Well-Being

Well-being has developed into a very significant area of interest for school staff, researchers and administrators in Victoria and beyond. Much of this interest has focused on student well-being rather teacher well-being. Similarly, patient well-being rather than nurse well-being is the focus of hospitals. One major issue concerning well-being is its disparate conceptualisation. Fraillon's (2004) review of well-being literature suggests five substantive dimensions to the construct: physical, economic, psychological, cognitive and social. Fraillon went on to define well-being in terms of intrapersonal and interpersonal dimensions. Seifert (2005) noted that well-being is a dynamic concept that includes subjective, social and psychological dimensions, as well as health-related behaviours. The well-known and well-documented *Ryff Scales of Psychological Well-Being* assess autonomy, environmental mastery, personal growth, positive relations with others, purpose in life, and self-acceptance (Seifert). It is plausible to hypothesis that the well-being of teachers and nurses is related to career intentions/retention.

Emotional, Cognitive, and Behavioural Engagement

Over the past 10 years, research has identified academic engagement to be a key contributor to school and university success (Fredricks, Blumenfeld & Parks 2004). There is a strong correlation between student engagement and achievement (Jimerson, Campos & Greif 2003), and research findings have also documented a steady decline in student engagement with schooling. Students' interest, enthusiasm, and intrinsic motivation for learning wane, with noteworthy losses during the transitions from primary to middle school and middle to high school (Wigfield et al. 2006). By contrast, students who are engaged show sustained behavioural, emotional and cognitive involvement in learning. As such, it is useful to conceptualise engagement as having emotional, cognitive and behavioural components. According to Skinner and Belmont, they "select tasks at the border of their competencies, initiate action when given the opportunity, and exert intense effort and concentration in the implementation of learning tasks" (1993: 572). Highly engaged students challenge themselves to excel. Indeed, the issue of student engagement is central to students optimising their learning and development.

Two broad explanatory frameworks have been proposed to generally account for a lack of engagement by students. A first framework suggests that inappropriate curricula content (Luke et al. 2003; Pendergast et al. 2005) influences engagement, while a broader framework explains student engagement in terms of sociocultural and psychological factors (Martin & Marsh 2006). However, two important areas of confusion remain. The first focuses on the distinction between indicators (features inside the engagement construct) and facilitators (causal factors) of engagement (Sinclair et al. 2003).

One of the most important characteristics of student engagement is that it is malleable. According to Finn and Rock (1987), engagement results from an interaction between the individual and the context, and it is responsive to changes in these variables. For this reason, dimensions of the psychosocial environment at university and the workplace have been considered important predictors of engagement. Within this viewpoint, the importance of relationships, and, in particular, teacher-student relationships to engagement, is noted (see Atweh et al. 2007). This position is supported by empirical studies. Furrer and Skinner (2003) found that relatedness to parents, teachers and peers each uniquely contributed to students' engagement, especially emotional engagement.

Motivation

Student motivation to perform academic tasks remains a key issue in schools today with a significant and persistent proportion of students not completing high school. Much of the research on academic motivation has employed the conceptual foundations of self-determination theory (Deci & Ryan 2008). With this theory, autonomy is a basic psychological need of all humans, with self-rule and the capacity to take ownership of one's actions essential components of the motivated student. As noted by Guay, Ratelle and Chanal (2008), self-determination theory rejects control, rewards and competition. Importantly, self-determination theory proposes a multidimensional construct in which a person might be intrinsically motivated, extrinsically motivated or even amotivated to perform certain behaviours. Vallerand's substantial research agenda has contributed enormously to research on academic motivation. In the late 1980s and early 1990s, Vallerand *et al.* (1993) proposed a seven-dimension academic motivation construct with three intrinsic motivation dimensions (viz., knowledge, accomplishment, and stimulation), three extrinsic motivation dimensions (viz., identified, introjected, and external) and one amotivation dimension. Other self-determination theorists have proposed a hierarchy in which intrinsic motivation is at the highest end of a continuum, followed by three extrinsic motivation dimensions (in order: identified regulation, introjected regulation and external regulation) (see Ryan & Connell 1989). According to Ratelle *et al.* (2004), positive outcomes in schools (e.g., persistence, concentration) are linked with self-determined motivation and negative outcomes are associated with nonself-determined forms of motivation (see also Vallerand, Fortier & Guay 1997).

Aspirations

A third potential mediating variable is student aspirations. This area has a significant research history in educational sociology where research on reducing the effects of social disadvantage on student outcomes has been conducted. Marjoribanks (2002) presented a mediation-moderation model of family and school capital influences on students' outcomes. In that model, aspirations were conceptualised as influencing student characteristics which, in turn, influence outcomes.

Self-Efficacy

The broad psychological concept of self-efficacy has been the subject of much theorising and research over the past two decades (see e.g., Bandura 1997;

Schunk 1995). Within this field, one particularly strong area of interest is that of academic efficacy, which refers to personal judgments of one's capabilities to organise and execute courses of action to attain designated types of educational performances (Zimmerman 1995). Consistent with self-efficacy theory, academic efficacy involves judgments on capabilities to perform tasks in specific academic domains. Accordingly, within a classroom-learning environment, measures of academic efficacy must assess students' perceptions of their competence to undertake specific activities. It is therefore not surprising to find that much academic efficacy research has focused on specific areas of the formal school curriculum. For example, Pajares (1996) investigated academic efficacy at mathematics-related tasks. Similarly, Schunk and Rice (1993) studied self-efficacy among students receiving remedial educational services. Zeldin and Pajares (2000) explored the self-efficacy beliefs of women in mathematical, scientific and technological careers. This model hypothesises that self-efficacy is influenced by the social and emotional competence of the individual teacher or nurse and that, in turn, self-efficacy influences resilience and, hence, career retention.

Conclusion

The attrition rates of teacher and nurses in Australia are very high, with substantial associated costs to employers and indeed the individual teachers and nurses who leave the profession prematurely. This chapter has attempted to delineate some of the key issues in resilience and retention of teachers and nurses. The postulated model for resilience and retention of teachers and nurses has been developed from literature in these and allied fields of research. The next step in this research agenda is to test empirically this complex model. While much previous research has tended to focus on parts of models, the complex nature of resilience and retention requires approaches that capture the complexity of the constructs. Programs to analyse the fit of hypothesised multilevel structural equation models to collected data are readily available and should be employed in studying the predictors of resilience and retention of teachers and nurses.

References

Antonovsky, A. 1996. 'The Salutogenic Model as a Theory to Guide Health Promotion'. *Health Promotion International* 11: 11–18.
Arendt, H. 1990. 'Thinking and Moral Considerations: A Lecture'. *Social Research* 57(1): 417–446.
Atweh, B., Bland, D., Carrington, S., & Cavanagh, R. F. 2007. 'School Disengagement: Its Constructions, Investigation and Management'. Paper presented at the annual conference of the Australian Association for Research in Education, Fremantle, Western Australia.
Australian Education Union (AEU). 2006. *Beginning Teachers List Workload, Behaviour, Management, Pay and Class Size as Top Concerns.* Melbourne: AEU.
Australian Government Department of Health and Ageing. 2008. *Report on the Audit of Health Workforce in Rural and Regional Australia, April 2008.* Canberra: Commonwealth of Australia.
Australian Institute of Health and Welfare (AIHW). 2011. *Nursing and Midwifery Labour Force 2009.* Bulletin no. 90. Cat. no. AUS 139. Canberra: AIHW.
Australian Primary Principals' Association (APPA). 2007. *Reports on the Experiences of Beginning Teachers.* Canberra: APPA.
Bandura, A. 1997. *Self-Efficacy: The Exercise of Control.* New York: Freeman.
Bauman, Z. 2001. 'Education: Under, For and In Spite of Post Modernity'. In Bauman, Z. (ed.). *The Individualised Society.* Oxford: Blackwell Publishers.
Beltman, S., Mansfield, C., & Price, A. 2011. 'Thriving Not Just Surviving: A Review of Research on Teacher Resilience'. *Educational Research Review* doi: 10.1016/j.edurev.2011.09.001, accessed 23 October 2012.
Bobek, B. L. 2002. 'Teacher Resiliency: A Key to Career Longevity'. *Clearing House* 75(4): 202–205.
Booth, B. 2011. 'Alarming Rise of New Graduate Nurse Attrition'. *Journal of Practical Nursing* 61(1): 3.
Bradley, D., Noonan, P., Nugent, H., & Scales, B. 2008. *Review of Australian Higher Education: Final Report.* Canberra: Department of Education, Employment and Workplace Relations.
Bronfenbrenner, U. 1979. *The Ecology of Human Development: Experiments by Nature and Design.* Cambridge: Harvard University Press.
Buchanan, J. 2011. 'Teacher Dis/appointments? Transitions Into and Out of Teaching'. *Curriculum Perspectives* 31(1): 12–23.
Campbell-Sills, L., & Stein, M. B. 2007. 'Psychometric Analysis and Refinement of the Connor-Davidson Resilience Scale (CD-RISC): Validation of a 10-Item Measure of Resilience'. *Journal of Traumatic Stress* 20(6): 1019–1028.
Cameron, F., & Brownie, S. 2010. 'Enhancing Resilience in Registered Aged Care Nurses'. *Australasian Journal on Ageing* 29(2): 66–71.
Clinton, M., & Hazelton, M. 2000. 'Scoping Practice Issues in the Australian Mental Health Nursing Workforce'. *Australian and New Zealand Journal of Mental Health Nursing* 9(3): 100–109.
Connor, K., & Davidson, J. 2003. 'Development of a New Resilience Scale: The Connor-Davidson Resilience Scale (CD-RISC)'. *Depression and Anxiety* 18(2): 76–82.
Coulter, D., & Wiens, J. 2002. 'Educational Judgement: Linking the Actor and the Spectator'. *Educational Researcher* 31(4): 15–25.
Cowin, L. 2002. 'The Effects of Nurses' Job Satisfaction on Retention: An Australian Perspective'. *Journal of Nursing Administration* 32(5): 283–291.

Cowin, L. S., & Hengstberger-Sims, C. 2006. 'New Graduate Nurse Self-Concept and Retention: A Longitudinal Survey'. *International Journal of Nursing Studies* 43(1): 59–70.

Day, C., & Gu, Q. 2009. 'Veteran Teachers: Commitment, Resilience and Quality Retention'. *Teachers and Teaching: Theory and Practice* 15(4): 441–457.

Deci, E. L., & Ryan, R. M. 2008. 'Self-Determination Theory: A Macrotheory of Human Motivation, Development, and Health'. *Canadian Psychology* 49(3): 182–185.

Dorman, J. 2002. 'Classroom Environment Research: Progress and Possibilities'. *Queensland Journal of Educational Research* 18(2): 112–140.

Dorman, J. P. 2003. 'Relationship Between School and Classroom Environment and Teacher Burnout: A LISREL Analysis'. *Social Psychology of Education* 6: 106–127.

Durlak, J. A., Weissberg, R. P., Dymnicki, A. B., Taylor, R. D., & Schellinger, K. B. 2011. 'The Impact of Enhancing Students' Social and Emotional Learning: A Meta-Analysis of School-Based Universal Interventions'. *Child Development* 82(1): 405–432.

Dyson, M. 2002. 'Integrating Computer Mediated Communication Into a Final Pre-Service Teacher Education Internship: A Model and a Pilot Study as a Supervision Adjunct'. Paper presented at the Australian Computers in Education Conference, Hobart, Tasmania.

Dyson, M. 2009. *A Journey to Transformism in Australian Teacher Education: Reconceptualising Teacher Education in the 21st Century*. Saarbrucken: VDM.

Eley, R., Eley, D., & Rogers-Clark, C. 2010. 'Reasons for Entering and Leaving Nursing: An Australian Regional Study'. *Australian Journal of Advanced Nursing* 28(1): 6–13.

Evans, S., & Huxley, P. 2009. 'Factors associated with the recruitment and retention of social workers in Wales: employer and employee perspectives'. *Health & Social Care in the Community*, 17(3): 254–266.

Evans, S., Huxley, P., Gately, C., Webber, M., Mears, A., Pajak, S., & Katona, C. 2006. 'Mental Health, Burnout and Job Satisfaction Among Mental Health Social Workers in England and Wales'. *British Journal of Psychiatry* 188: 75–80.

Finn, J. D., & Rock, D. A. 1997. 'Academic Success Among Students at Risk for School Failure'. *Journal of Applied Psychology* 82: 221–234.

Fisher, D. L., & Khine, M. S. (ed.). 2006. *Contemporary Approaches to Research on Learning Environments*. Singapore: World Scientific.

Fraillon, J. 2004. 'Measuring Student Well-Being in the Context of Australian Schooling: Discussion Paper. Carlton South: MCEETYA.

Fraser, B. J. 2012. 'Classroom Learning Environments: Retrospect, Context and Prospect'. In Fraser, B. J., Tobin, K. G., & Mc Robbie, C. J. (ed.). *Second International Handbook of Science Education*, vol. 2. Dordercht: Springer.

Fredricks, J. A., Blumenfeld, P. C., & Paris, A. H. 2004. 'School Engagement: Potential of the Concept, State of the Evidence'. *Review of Educational Research* 74: 59–109.

Furrer, C., & Skinner, C. J. 2003. 'Sense of Relatedness as a Factor in Children's Academic Engagement and Performance'. *Journal of Educational Psychology* 95: 148–162.

Gaynor, L., Gallasch, T., Yorkston, E., Stewart, S., Bogossian, F., Fairweather, C., & Turner, C. 2007. 'The Future Nursing Workforce in Australia: Baseline Data for a Prospective Study of the Profile, Attrition Rates and Graduate Outcomes in a Contemporary Cohort of Undergraduates'. *Australian Journal of Advanced Nursing* 25(2): 11–20.

Gaynor, L., Gallasch, T., Yorkston, E., Stewart, S., & Turner, C. 2006. 'Where Do All the Undergraduate and New Graduate Nurses Go and Why? A Search for Empirical Research Evidence'. *Australian Journal of Advanced Nursing* 24(2): 26–32.

Gillespie, B. M., Chaboyer, W., Wallis, M., & Grimbeek, P. 2007. 'Resilience in the Operating Room: Developing and Testing of a Resilience Model'. *Journal of Advanced Nursing* 59(4): 427–438.

Gu, Q., & Day, C. 2007. 'Teachers Resilience: A Necessary Condition for Effectiveness'. *Teaching and Teacher Education: An International Journal of Research and Studies* 23(8): 1302–1316.

Guay, F., Ratelle, C. F., & Chanal, J. 2008. 'Optimal Learning in Optimal Contexts: The Role of Self-Determination in Education'. *Canadian Psychology* 49(3): 233–240.

Herrman, H., Stewart, D., Diaz-Granados, N., Berger, E., Jackson, B., & Yuen, T. 2011. 'What is Resilience?' *Canadian Journal of Psychiatry* 56(5): 258.

Heylighen, F. 2000. 'What is a World View'. *Principia Cybernetica Web*. http://pespmc1.vub.ac.be/worldview (accessed 17 June 2010).

Hodges, H. F., Keeley, A. C., & Grier, E. C. 2005. 'Professional Resilience, Practice Longevity, and Parse's Theory for Baccalaureate Education'. *The Journal of Nursing Education* 44(12): 548.

Hong, J. Y. 2010. 'Pre-Service and Beginning Teachers' Professional Identity and Its Relation to Dropping Out of the Profession'. *Teaching and Teacher Education: An International Journal of Research and Studies* 26(8): 1530–1543.

Howard, S., & Johnson, B. 2004. 'Resilient Teachers: Resisting Stress and Burnout'. *Social Psychology of Education* 7(4): 399–420.

Ingersoll, R. M. 2007. 'A Comparative Study of Teacher Preparation and Qualifications in Six Nations'. CPRE Policy Briefs, RB-47. Washington: Institute of Education Sciences.

Ingersoll, R. M., & Smith, T. M. 2003. 'The Wrong Solution to the Teacher Shortage'. *Educational Leadership* 60(8): 30–33.

Jackson, D., Firtko, A., & Edenborough, M. 2007. 'Personal Resilience as a Strategy for Surviving and Thriving in the Face of Workplace Adversity: A Literature Review'. *Journal of Advanced Nursing* 60(1): 1–9.

Jennings, P. A., & Greenberg, M. T. 2009. 'The Prosocial Classroom: Teacher Social and Emotional Competence in Relation to Student and Classroom Outcomes'. *Review of Educational Research* 79(1): 491.

Jimerson, S. R., Campos, E., & Grief, J. L. 2003. 'Toward an Understanding of Definitions and Measures of School Engagement and Related Terms'. *California School Psychologist* 8: 7–27.

Johnstone, M. 2007. 'Nurse Recruitment and Retention: Imperatives of Imagining the Future and Taking a Proactive Stance'. *Contemporary Nurse: A Journal for the Australian Nursing Profession* 24(2): iii-v.

Khine, M. S., & Fisher, D. L. (ed.). 2003. *Technology-Rich Learning Environments: A Future Perspective*. Singapore: World Scientific.

Korthagen, F. A., & Kessels, J. P. 1999. 'Linking Theory and Practice: Changing the Pedagogy of Teacher Education'. *Educational Researcher* 28(4): 4–17.

Kyriacou, C., & Coulthard, M. 2000. 'Undergraduates' Views of Teaching as a Career Choice'. *Journal of Education for Teaching* 26(2): 117–126.

Le Cornu, R. 2009. 'Building Resilience in Pre-Service Teachers'. *Teaching and Teacher Education: An International Journal of Research and Studies* 25(5): 717–723.

Leighton, K. 2005. 'Transcultural Nursing: The Relationship Between Individualist Ideology and Individualized Mental Health Care'. *Journal of Psychiatric and Mental Health Nursing* 12(1): 85–94.

Leurer, M., Donnelly, G., & Domm, E. 2007. 'Nurse Retention Strategies: Advice from Experienced Registered Nurses'. *Journal of Health Organization and Management* 21(3): 307.

Luke, A., Elkins, J., Weir, K., Land, R., Carrington, V., Dole, S., Pendergast, D., Kapitzke, C., van Kraayenoord, C., Moni, K., Mcintosh, A., Mayer, D., Bahr, M., Hunter, L., Chadboume, R., Bean, T., Alvermann, D., & Steven, L. 2003. *Beyond the Middle: A Report about Literacy and Numeracy Development of Target Group Students in the*

Middle Years of Schooling. Canberra: Commonwealth Department of Education, Science and Training.

Marjoribanks, K. 2002. *Family and School Capital: Towards a Context Theory of Students' School Outcomes*. Dortrecht: Kluwer.

Martin, A., & Marsh, H. 2006. 'Academic Resilience and Its Psychological and Educational Correlates: A Construct Validity Approach'. *Psychology in the Schools* 43(3): 267–281.

Maslach, C., & Leiter, M. P. 1999. 'Teacher Burnout: A Research Agenda'. In Vandenburghe, R., & Huberman, A. M. (ed.). *Understanding and Preventing Teacher Stress: A Sourcebook of International Research and Practice*. Cambridge: Cambridge University Press.

Masten, A. 2007. 'Resilience in Developing Systems: Progress and Promise as the Fourth Wave Rises'. *Development and Psychopathology* 19(03): 921–930.

McAllister, M., & McKinnon, J. 2009. 'The Importance of Teaching and Learning Resilience in the Health Disciplines: A Critical Review of the Literature'. *Nurse Education Today* 29(4): 371–379.

McVicar, A. 2003. 'Workplace Stress in Nursing: A Literature Review'. *Journal of Advanced Nursing* 44(6): 633–642.

Moos, R. H. 1987. *The Social Climate Scales: A User's Guide*. Palo Alto: Consulting Psychologists Press.

Murray, H. A. 1938. *Explorations in Personality*. New York: Oxford University Press.

National Project on the Quality of Teaching and Learning (NPQTL). 1992. *The Development of National Competency Standards for Teaching*. Canberra: Commonwealth of Australia.

Pajares, F. 1996. 'Self-Efficacy Beliefs and Mathematical Problem Solving of Gifted Students'. *Contemporary Educational Psychology* 21: 325–344.

Pendergast, D., Flanagan, R., Land, R., Bahr, M., Mitchell, J., Weir, K., Noblett, G., Cain, M., Misich, T., Carrington, V., & Smith, J. 2005. *Developing Lifelong Learners in the Middle Years of Schooling*. Carlton South: MCEETYA.

Plunkett, M., & Dyson, M. 2011. 'Becoming a Teacher and Staying One: Examining the Complex Ecologies Associated with Educating and Retaining New Teachers in Rural Australia?' *Australian Journal of Teacher Education* 36(1): 32–47.

Procter, N., Beutel, J., Deuter, K., Curren, D., de Crespigny, C., & Simon, M. 2011. 'The Developing Role of Transition to Practice Programs for Newly Graduated Mental Health Nurses'. *International Journal of Nursing Practice* 17(3): 254–261.

Ratelle, C., Guay, F., Larose, S., & Senécal, C. 2004. 'Family Correlates of Trajectories of Academic Motivation During a School Transition: A Semiparametric Group-Based Approach'. *Journal of Educational Psychology* 96(4): 743–754.Rinke, C. 2008. 'Understanding Teachers' Careers: Linking Professional Life to Professional Path'. *Educational Research Review* 3(1): 1–13.

Ryan, R. M., & Connell, J. P. 1989. 'Perceived Locus of Causality and Internalization: Examining Reasons for Acting in Two Domains'. *Journal of Personality and Social Psychology* 57(5): 749–761.

Schunk, D. H. 1995. 'Self-Efficacy and Education and Instruction'. In Maddux, J. E. (ed.). *Self-Efficacy, Adaptation, and Adjustment: Theory, Research, and Application*. New York: Plenum.

Schunk, D. H., & Rice, J. M. 1993. 'Strategy Fading and Progress Feedback: Effects on Self-Efficacy and Comprehension Among Students Receiving Remedial Reading Services'. *Journal of Special Education* 27: 257–276.

Seifert, T. A. 2009. *The Ryff Scales of Psychological Well-being*. http://www.liberalarts.wabash.edu/ryff-scales/, accessed 15 July 2012.

Sinclair, M. F., Christenson, S. L., Lehr, C. A., & Anderson, A. R. 2003. 'Facilitating Student Engagement: Lessons Learned from Check & Connect Longitudinal Studies'. *The California School Psychologist* 8: 29–42.
Skinner, E. A., & Belmont, N. J. 1993. 'Motivation in the Classroom: Reciprocal Effect of Teacher Behavior and Student Engagement Across the School Year'. *Journal of Educational Psychology* 85: 571–581.
Smith, B., Dalen, J., Wiggins, K., Tooley, E., Christopher, P., & Bernard, J. 2008. 'The Brief Resilience Scale: Assessing the Ability to Bounce Back'. *International Journal of Behavioral Medicine* 15(3): 194–200.
Sun, J., & Stewart, D. E. 2010. 'Promoting Student Resilience and Well-Being: Asia-Pacific Resilient Children and Communities Project'. In Lovat, T., Toomey, R., & Clement, N. (ed.). *International Research Handbook on Values Education and Student Wellbeing*. Dordrecht: Springer.
Tait, M. 2008. 'Resilience as a Contributor to Novice Teacher Success, Commitment, and Retention'. *Teacher Education Quarterly* 35(4): 57.
Vallerand, R., Fortier, M., & Guay, F. 1997. 'Self-Determination and Persistence in a Real-Life Setting: Toward a Motivational Model of High School Dropout'. *Journal of Personality and Social psychology* 72: 1161–1176.
Vallerand, R. J., Pelletier, L. G., Blais, M. R., Briere, N. M., Senecal, C., & Vallieres, E. F. 1993. 'On the Assessment of Intrinsic, Extrinsic, and Amotivation in Education: Evidence on the Concurrent and Construct Validity of the Academic Motivation Scale'. *Educational and Psychological Measurement* 53(1): 159–172.
Vaishnavi, S., Connor, K., & Davidson, J. 2007. 'An Abbreviated Version of the Connor-Davidson Resilience Scale (CD-RISC), the CD-RISC2: Psychometric Properties and Applications in Psychopharmacological Trials'. *Psychiatry Research* 152(2–3): 293–297.
Wagnild, G. 2009. 'A Review of the Resilience Scale'. *Journal of Nursing Measurement* 17(2): 105–113.
Wagnild, G. M., & Young, H. M. 1993. 'Development and Psychometric Evaluation of the Resilience Scale'. *Journal of Nursing Measurement* 1(2): 165–178.
Watlington, E., Shockley, R., Guglielmino, P., & Felsher, R. 2010. 'The High Cost of Leaving: An Analysis of the Cost of Teacher Turnover'. *Journal of Education Finance* 36(1): 22–37.
Wigfield, A., Eccles, J. S., Schiefele, U., Roeser, R., & Davis-Kean, P. 2006. 'Development of Achievement Motivation'. In Eisenberg, N. (ed.). *Handbook of Child Psychology, Vol. 3: Social, Emotional, and Personality Development*. Sixth ed. New Jersey: John Wiley & Sons.
Windle, G. 2011. 'What is Resilience? A Review and Concept Analysis'. *Reviews in Clinical Gerontology* 21(2): 152–169.
Windle, G., Bennett, K., & Noyes, J. 2011. 'A Methodological Review of Resilience Measurement Scales'. *Health and Quality of Life Outcomes* 9(1): 8.
Wisotzkey, S. 2011. 'Will They Stay Or Will They Go? Insight Into Nursing Turnover'. *Nursing Management* 42(2): 15–17.
Wong, H. K. 2004. 'Induction Programs that Keep New Teachers Teaching and Improving'. *NASSP Bulletin* 88(638): 41–58.
Zeldin, A. L., & Pajares, F. 2000. 'Against the Odds: Self-Efficacy Beliefs of Women in Mathematical, Scientific and Technological Careers'. *American Educational Research Journal* 37: 215–246.
Zimmerman, B. J. 1995. 'Self-Efficacy and Educational Development'. In Bandura, A. (ed.). *Self-Efficacy in Changing Societies*. Cambridge: Cambridge University Press.

Chapter 5

Sustainable Education in a Small Regional Medical School

Challenges and Opportunities

Brian Chapman and William Hart

Abstract

This chapter describes the experience of university academics responding to the challenges and exploiting the opportunities that attend the establishment of a new, small regional medical school. The challenges and the opportunities arise in relation to both education and research. The educational challenges pertain to the recruitment and retention of suitably qualified academic and clinical staff to deliver a medical course to a graduate-entry cohort, given the limitations bearing on career progression and family support. The research challenges derive from limitations in infrastructure, the availability of honours and graduate research students, and on the collegiality that exists when teams of researchers are engaged in related pursuits. The educational opportunities have come from being free of any limitations of tradition or inertia that often prevail at older, larger institutions. This freedom has resulted in four significant educational innovations that have been exported back to the parent faculty. A similar freedom in the research field has facilitated an independent critique of traditional methods of standard-setting in medical examinations, as well as identification of widespread error in the pedagogy of thermodynamics and bioenergetics in undergraduate textbooks. This latter project involved interdisciplinary collaboration that was itself facilitated by the smallness of the campus in which the medical school is located.

Introduction

A new regional medical school, such as Monash University's Gippsland Medical School (GMS) with its small cohort of students, presents special challenges and opportunities. The challenges lie in finding sufficient numbers of qualified staff to deliver lectures, facilitate small-group teaching and conduct written examinations and Objective Structured Clinical Examinations (OSCEs). The opportunities lie in developing and testing novel approaches to enrolment and curriculum delivery, and in questioning methods of teaching and assessment. These opportunities may then translate into innovation across the broader Faculty, or even beyond one University.

This chapter reviews the rationale for establishing a new rural medical school, outlines the challenges and opportunities encountered, and highlights how these opportunities have resulted in GMS-led developments in five areas of medical education and research.

About Gippsland Medical School

Gippsland Medical School was created in 2006 under the leadership of Professor Chris Browne to provide a graduate-entry four-year program for students to progress to the degrees of Bachelor of Medicine and Bachelor of Surgery (MBBS) within the Faculty of Medicine, Nursing and Health Sciences (FMNHS) at Monash University's Gippsland Campus based in Churchill, Victoria. The first intake of students commenced in 2008 with a cohort size of 57, of whom 45 became the school's first graduates on 1 December 2011. The intake quota was increased incrementally each year towards its current limit of 100 students, resulting in initial enrolments of 73, 79, 90 and 87 in the years 2009 to 2012, respectively.

Thus, GMS is a relatively new, small, rural medical school.

Why a Rural Medical School?

Rural Australians have poorer health status and less access to health services than do urban Australians. This is demonstrated by lower life expectancy, higher morbidity rates and lower levels of service provision (Australian Institute of Health and Welfare 2008). There is a "doctor shortage" in rural Australia. As shown in Table 1, there are 332 doctors per 100,000 population in major cities, whereas in outer regional areas there are only 157 doctors per 100,000 population (Australian Institute of Health and Welfare 2009).

Region	Greater Melbourne	Gippsland
Area (km2)	8806	42,000
Population	4,600,000	250,000
Population density (/km2)	522	5.9
Doctor availability per 100,000 people	332	157

Table 1. Population comparisons between greater Melbourne and Gippsland

Recruiting students with a rural background and training students in a rural location may predict the number of doctors who choose to return to rural practice (Henry *et al.* 2009; Rabinowitz & Paynter 2002). Thus, in 2007, Monash University established a four-year, graduate-entry version of its medical training degree (MBBS) on its regional Gippsland campus. The aspirations and early implementation of this Gippsland Medical School (GMS) are described by Hart and Browne (2010). The intention is that, through their experiences in Gippsland, many new doctors will choose to remain in or return to rural areas to provide services to otherwise underserved populations.

To this end, several advantages of offering training in a rural setting are evident:

- exposure to real rural health issues;
- acculturation to rural life;
- rural contextualisation of medical problems;
- community-based training; and,
- continuity of patient care.

In the first five graduate-entry student cohorts at GMS, rural and regional Victorian students have come from Geelong, Shepparton, Tawonga, Woodend and Gippsland, while the Gippslanders have come from Birchip, Churchill, Hazelwood, Moe, Sale, Tanjil South, Toongabbie, Traralgon, Warragul, Wodonga, Wonthaggi and Yarram (see Table 2). This is an encouraging recruitment pattern in view of the generally lower educational attainment of rural school students, particularly in Gippsland, relative to the general population (see Dow *et al.* 2011: 31).

In the first four years of course delivery at GMS, we have identified a number of challenges and opportunities. Some of these will be generic and applicable to any small rural medical school, while others may be more related to the particular needs, assets and human resources of GMS.

GMS first-year cohort					
Year	Enrolment	Rural	Gippsland	International	*Other
2008	57	8	8	5	36
2009	73	9	7	6	51
2010	79	13	10	9	47
2011	90	27	8	21	34
2012	87	24	6	9	48

Table 2: Distribution of origin of first-year cohorts at GMS
* Other students are from Melbourne (mostly) and other Australian cities.

Challenges in Education

Facing the imperative of delivering a medical education program, the primary challenge is to find sufficient academic and clinical staff to deliver lectures, facilitate small-group teaching, and conduct written examinations and OSCEs. This challenge has been met at GMS by appointing a small number of core academic staff – mostly on full-time appointments, with others being on fractional appointments – heavily supplemented by visiting lecturers mostly drawn from the ranks of academics who already teach the same material into the first two years of the undergraduate MBBS program delivered at Monash's Clayton Campus. While this involves considerable travel time and expense, we have been fortunate that visiting lecturers enjoy the experience of teaching a small graduate-entry cohort, resulting in very high retention rates for our visiting staff from the Clayton Campus.

Challenges associated with the attraction and retention of a sustainable core of permanent academic staff derive from issues such as career progression, spousal employment/support, and children's education. While the last two of these issues impact on all kinds of staff, the issue of academic career progression is particularly significant in a small, rural medical school with a graduate-entry program. There are limited opportunities for administration and extremely rare opportunities for supervision of honours and higher degree students (see below).

Challenges in Research

The challenges here pertain to the lack of infrastructure, the lack of research students and issues of collegiality.

Lack of Infrastructure

The lack of "wet laboratory" space at GMS (i.e., laboratories equipped to supply gas and running water and to facilitate the disposal of solid, liquid and volatile waste) is probably the greatest single factor militating against GMS academics' being able to develop a biomedical research career trajectory comparable to those possible at the Clayton Campus.

Lack of Research Students

The academic program at GMS is limited entirely to graduate-entry MBBS students. Thus, there is no cohort of science students available for recruitment into honours and higher degree programs. (There are some limited opportunities for teaching into some of the programs offered to undergraduates by the School of Applied Science and Engineering [SASE] at the Gippsland campus, but this does not compare with the student recruitment possibilities that obtain in relation to the large biomedical science undergraduate cohorts found at the Clayton Campus.) Moreover, the graduate-entry MBBS cohort have already self-selected themselves out of the likelihood of pursuing a research career in medical science – to a large extent they simply want to become doctors.

Collegiality

The diverse nature of the small cohort of academic staff at GMS, coupled with the above-mentioned lack of research students, means that there are no identifiable groups or teams of people sharing common academic interests. Nonetheless, the small staff cohort does facilitate some degree of interdisciplinary collegiality.

Moreover, several members of GMS staff are very research-active in the fields of public health and health services research, medical education and simulation methodology. These endeavours are not discussed further in this chapter. The School's research grant income in 2012 exceeds $1 million.

Opportunities in Education

Introduction of Multiple Mini-Interviews (MMIs) for Student Selection

Following Eva *et al.* (2004), we implemented the Multiple Mini-Interview (MMI) method of student selection in 2008 (see Table 3). The MMIs are run in circuits, each circuit comprising a group of ten interview stations, each station being manned by a single examiner/interviewer. Candidates rotate through the ten stations, commencing at each station with two minutes of reading time outside the interview room, during which time the candidate reads a document in which a scenario or problem is laid out for discussion at the respective interview which then runs for eight minutes. Each examiner thus has a two-minute "window" in which to complete the examiner's report on each respective interview. A recent review by Prideaux *et al.* (2011) suggests that the MMI has relatively good predictive validity and reliability. Our own preliminary data (Hart, McGrail, Nestel & Bullock, submitted) show that the MMI is a feasible and practical alternative to tradition interviews. We have found a significant correlation between scores on admission on the MMI and subsequent performance in the clinical skills tests, the Objective Structured Clinical Examination (OSCE). Structured course evaluation interviews with our final year students have also provided strong support to the view that the MMI selects medical students who possess the so-called "non-cognitive" attributes essential for good medical practice – attributes such as communication skills, empathy and ethical reasoning.

	Long interview before a panel of 3	Multiple mini-interviews on 1
No. panelists per station	3	1
No. panelists per circuit	3	10
No. stations in parallel per circuit	1	10
No. circuits in parallel	8	3
No. panelists in parallel	24	30
Duration per station	35 minutes interview + 10 minutes review	8 minutes (5 questions) + 2 minutes review
Duration per student	35 minutes	100 minutes
Students per hour: per circuit	1.33	6
Students per hour: all circuits	10.67	18
Panelists per student	3	10
Panelist hours per student	2.25	1.67

Table 3: Comparison of Long Interview and MMI methods

As a result of feedback on the utility of the MMI as implemented at GMS, the Central medical school at Monash (Clayton) has introduced the MMI to replace the traditional selection interview from 2011. Table 3 shows the main features distinguishing the "long" interviews used previously at Clayton from the MMIs used from the outset at GMS. In this table, the word "circuit" refers to the whole collection of stations experienced by a single student: thus, a long-interview "circuit" comprises one station while a MMI "circuit" comprises 10 stations.

Novel Timetabling of Problem-Based Learning Delivery

In the first year of the graduate-entry MBBS curriculum, problem-based learning (PBL) involves two small-group meetings per case conducted weekly. The first meeting is a 1-hour Briefing Session in which the case Narrative is read aloud and discussed one paragraph at a time. During this discussion, unfamiliar terms are identified for clarification and learning objectives are identified for research. When the entire Narrative has thus been analysed, there is a general discussion aimed at distributing the learning objectives into seven Research Tasks of roughly equal weight, each task being assigned to a particular Researcher. Each Researcher is required to post the resulting Research Report in the respective PBL group's discussion forum by an agreed deadline, allowing the Tutor and all group members to read all seven Reports prior to the second meeting. There is also a requirement for Tutors to provide feedback to the Researcher and respective Discussant (see below), indicating any areas requiring expansion or correction, thereby allowing any amended version (if required) to be posted to the discussion forum prior to the second meeting.

The second meeting is a 2-hour Workshop in which all seven Research Reports are discussed in turn and the new knowledge is consolidated among the group, with any outstanding issues being identified for further study. The meeting closes with a final summary by the Chair, relating the new knowledge back to the Narrative.

From 2002 until 2009, the PBL Briefing Sessions at the Central Medical School in Clayton were scheduled on Mondays, with the Workshops being scheduled on Fridays. Although a number of the PBL Tutors lobbied hard from 2006 onwards to have the two meetings scheduled on the same day (commencing with the previous week's Workshop followed by the current week's Briefing Session), the necessary changes to the timetable were constantly invoked by the course managers as placing the whole idea of change into the "too hard basket". On the other hand, when PBL was being planned at GMS, one of the Clayton Tutors who had been recruited to help set up the program found immediate fertile ground in which to plant the idea of same-day scheduling for the two weekly meetings. This resulted in the adoption of this idea from the outset, with obvious advantages for timetabling, the recruitment and retention of PBL Tutors, and the spreading of the research and reading workloads over a full week rather than over the four-day interval between Monday and Friday. This success became known at the Central Medical School and was implemented there in 2010, following significant changes in course management personnel.

Introduction of the Discussant Role in PBL

A problem commonly encountered in PBL Workshops is that too much time is spent with research reports being presented as didactic lectures, especially where the report is presented as a slide show. This is largely a waste of time. If the students have read the research report, they do not need it presented to them. If the students have not read the research report, then little is to be gained by having the report read to them in a way that does not encourage their active engagement. Formal student and tutor focus groups during 2008 and 2009 suggested that first-year PBL groups were relying too heavily on "mini lectures" delivered by researchers, at the cost of adequate discussion and problem analysis. We required a method of stimulating informed discussion so that students could benefit from sharing information and enhancing their problem-solving skills.

In 2010 we attempted to address this problem at GMS by introducing a "Discussant" role into the PBL process. The aim here was to break the sense of ownership between the researcher and the research report by requiring a person other than the researcher, i.e., the discussant, to lead an informed discussion of the research report rather than simply present the report. We introduced the discussant role in a controlled experiment as part of our evaluation protocol for internal quality control. PBL groups were randomly assigned to either Discussant status or Control status for the first nine weeks of first semester and then swapped over to the alternate status for the remaining eight weeks.

After nine weeks, all students were invited to complete a 10-item survey as to their experiences with PBLs. Comparison of the survey results between the Discussant and Control groups revealed enhancement of all ten items surveyed, with significant enhancement of each of the following six items:

- enjoyment of PBL tutorials;
- facilitation of sharing of knowledge;
- sense of added value from PBL tutorials to other lectures and tutorials;
- encouragement of group interaction and discussion;
- looking forward to weekly PBL tutorials; and,
- a sense of experiencing informed discussion rather than mini-lectures.

The PBL Tutors also provided supportive feedback on how the Discussant status improved the quality of the PBL process. We therefore decided to implement the Discussant mode of PBL delivery for all groups in future, commencing second semester of 2010. Our findings were communicated to a Faculty education seminar in September 2010 attended by MBBS course management personnel from Clayton who decided to adopt the Discussant mode for their undergraduate MBBS cohort commencing first semester 2011. This proved successful, and so both the central undergraduate cohort and the GMS graduate-entry cohort are continuing to use Discussant mode PBL delivery in 2012.

With the advent of Moodle as the method of eLearning delivery for the MBBS at GMS in 2012, we have added another refinement to the PBL process by requiring all research reports to be posted as Word™ documents in Moodle Discussion Forums. PBL Tutors are required to read the reports and, using Track Changes and Comments, provide minimalist feedback in a timely manner by private email to the researcher and discussant for each task. The Tutors are not required to provide corrections, just to indicate where there might be a problem or where a topic might need more detailed explanation. There is then an opportunity for researchers to post amended versions of their reports, if necessary, before the PBL Workshop takes place. At the time of writing, these new methods seem to have worked well during the first six weeks of first semester in 2012.

Creation of an Interactive Multimedia Application for Teaching "Heart Sounds"

Medical students are usually introduced to basic cardiac physiology through detailed consideration of the Wiggers diagram containing plots of aortic pressure, left ventricular pressure, left atrial pressure, left ventricular volume, the electrocardiogram and the first two heart sounds *versus* time. Although existing multimedia animations of this diagram afford valuable dynamic insight into the events of the cardiac cycle, a group of GMS academics identified a need to create a more effective self-directed learning experience for studying heart sounds. We devised a multimedia tutorial using ToolBook™ v9.5 that presents the sounds so that the locus of control is with the student and allows the sounds to be appreciated and studied in a way that is more directly complemented with highly specific, clinically relevant tutorial assistance.

The resulting module provides the student with the following features:

- a self-directed presentation of heart sounds and their relation to the major events of the cardiac cycle in normal and diseased states;
- a combination of the visual-learning power of the graphical representation of sounds with a self-summarising interactive tutorial style involving the use of 3-layered hypertext;
- the heart sounds are presented at a pace that is totally under student control as either (a) endless repetition or (b) single occurrence of either (i) a complete, or (ii) a partial, cardiac cycle; and,

- the visual representation of heart sounds as a means of (a) enabling students to select which portions of the cycle they wish to study, and (b) focusing specific tutorial information about the nature and origin of each sound.

This work was produced through rapid consultation between specialists all located within the same small department and modified equally rapidly as the software was trialled in various formal Clinical Skills sessions presented to the GMS first-year cohort in 2010. This work was communicated at an ANZAME Conference in 2010 (Chapman *et al.* 2010).

Opportunities in Research

Medical Education Research

Standard-setting in MBBS examinations is universally regarded as being of great importance by medical educators. Of all the various methods that have been tried over the years, that attributed to William Angoff (1971) is the most widely used (Mills & Melican 1988), and is purported to produce a criterion-referenced standard (Amin *et al.* 2006) that seeks to establish competence (Norcini 2003). This method is used at the Clayton Campus and also at GMS. To implement the method correctly, a panel of academic experts is convened to examine each assessment item on an examination paper and estimate the proportion of "borderline" students that would be expected to answer the question correctly. The proportions thus derived are then summed over the entire paper to determine the pass mark. This method is inherently problematic for implementation in a small rural medical school because of the small number of experts available to reach a consensus decision on each assessment item. Moreover, the method itself is open to question in terms of its purported claim to provide a criterion-based absolute standard. Critical reflection on the historical literature reveals widespread concerns about this issue, concerns that the more recent medical education literature seems increasingly prone to ignore.

In view of these problems perceived at GMS, an enquiry into the general issues regarding the Angoff method has been initiated. This work is currently in progress at GMS and is to be published elsewhere embracing the following issues and findings:

- a critical analysis of the claim that the Angoff method is criterion-referenced rather than norm-referenced;

- the finding that actual correlations between examiners' borderline estimates and actual low-performing students' results are often extremely weak and sometimes negative;
- a finding that a shift from didactic lecture-based teaching to active task-based learning can greatly alter the performance statistics of individual assessment items, significantly reducing their apparent difficulty while also significantly reducing their discriminating power;
- a re-appraisal of Angoff's original description of his method, suggesting that it has been almost universally applied in a norm-referenced manner, whilst purporting to be a criterion-referenced absolute standard; and,
- a suggested way forward as to how Angoff's original suggestion might be given a more prescriptive implementation strategy to enable a more truly criterion-referenced test to be devised.

Theoretical Biomedical Research: Review and Critique

One of us has developed a transdisciplinary collaboration with a biochemist and a mathematician from the School of Applied Science and Engineering (SASE) at our Gippsland Campus. The focus of the collaboration arose from finding pedagogical errors in a multimedia resource supporting teaching in the areas of thermodynamics and bioenergetics. On inspection of standard biochemistry textbooks, we discovered that these errors were widespread and had been so for over forty years. The errors were found to be clustered into three categories:

- confusion about entropy and reversibility;
- confounding of coupled reactions with sequential reactions in misguided attempts to show how exergonic reactions might drive endergonic reactions; and
- confusion about the proximity to equilibrium of living processes.

A fresh approach has been developed, based on the Second Law imperative that free energy be dissipated (identical to the requirement that entropy be created), leading to the identification and formulation of a Probability Isotherm, being the probabilistic and ultimately kinetic equivalent of the more well-known Van't Hoff Isotherm (Chapman *et al.* 2011). A historical survey was also completed, documenting the course of survival of these errors as biochemical knowledge increased and pedagogical fashions changed, altering the size and shape of pedagogy in thermodynamics and bioenergetics (Larkins *et al.* 2011).

We have also begun to identify "spillover" of these misconceptions into biochemical research, leading to misinterpretation of experimental data in the research literature. This work remains in progress.

These studies reflect the opportunities for interdisciplinary collaboration that arise directly from some of the challenges faced within a small medical school. The relative smallness of the university's Gippsland Campus is a facilitating factor for such collaboration, allowing closer interaction between colleagues in separate schools within one small campus.

Conclusion

A new, small, regional medical school provides novel opportunities for innovation in teaching and learning and in research. The new School possesses several advantages, such as fewer "traditional" ways of doing things, and a smaller, tight-knit faculty. Examples of innovation from the Monash Gippsland Medical School include:

- use of multiple mini-interviews (MMIs) for student selection;
- timetabling of problem-based learning (PBL) delivery;
- introduction of the Discussant role to the PBL process; and,
- development of an interactive multimedia application for teaching "Heart Sounds".

All of these innovations, trialled in Gippsland, are now being implemented in the main (Central) medical school at Monash's Clayton Campus, which is much older and much larger. The smallness of both GMS and its campus location has also facilitated productive interdisciplinary collaboration.

References

Amin, Z., Chong, Y. S., & Khoo, H. E. 2006. *Practical Guide to Medical Student Assessment*. London: World Scientific Publishing Co.

Angoff, W. H. 1971. 'Scales, Norms, and Equivalent Scores'. In Thorndike, R. L. (ed.). *Educational Measurement*. Second ed. Washington: American Council on Education.

Australian Institute of Health and Welfare (AIHW). 2008. *Indicators of Health Status and Determinants of Health*. Rural Health Series no. 9 Cat no PHE 103 Canberra: AIHW.

Australian Institute of Health and Welfare (AIHW). 2008. *Rural, Regional and Remote Health*. Cat. no. PHE 97. Canberra: AIHW.

Australian Institute of Health and Welfare. 2009. *Medical Labour Force 2007*. National Health Labour Force Series no. 44, Cat. no. HWL 45. Canberra: AIHW.

Chapman, B., Larkins, J. M., & Mosse, J. A. 2011. 'The Probability Isotherm: An Intuitive Non-Equilibrium Thermodynamic Framework for Biochemical Kinetis'. *Proceedings of the Australian Conference on Science & Mathematics Education 2011*, The University of Melbourne, 28–30 September 2011: 169–174.

Chapman, B., Villanueva, E., Somers, G., & Nestel, D. 2010. 'Putting the Student in Control: An Interactive Multimedia Application for Teaching Heart Sounds'. ANZAME 10 Conference, July, Townsville.

Dow, K. L., Allan, M., & Mitchell, J. .2011. *Gippsland Tertiary Education Plan: Report of the Expert Panel*. Melbourne: State Government, Victoria.

Eva, K. W., Rosenfeld, J., Reiter, H. I., & Norman, G. R. 2004. 'An Admissions OSCE: The Multiple Mini-Interview'. *Medical Education* 38: 314–326.

Hart, W., & Browne, C. 2010. 'Reducing Health Inequalities by Training More Rural and Indigenous Doctors: The Role of the Medical School'. *2010 World Universities Congress Proceedings* 1, 20–24 October 2010: 831–838.

Henry, J. A., Edwards, B. J., & Crotty, B. 2009. 'Why Do Medical Graduates Choose Rural Careers?' *Rural and Remote Health* 9(1): Article No. 1083. http://www.rrh.org.au/articles/subviewnew.asp?ArticleID=1083. (accessed 19 December 2012).

Larkins, J. M., Mosse, J. A., & Chapman, B. 2011. 'Is the Evolution of Biochemistry Texts Decreasing Fitness? A Case Study of Pedagogical Error in Bioenergetcs'. *Proceedings of the Australian Conference on Science & Mathematics Education 2011*, The University of Melbourne, September 28–30t, 2011: 187–192.

Mills, C. N., & Melican, G. J. 1988. 'Estimating and Adjusting Cutoff Scores: Features of Selected Methods'. *Applied Measurement in Education* 1: 261–275.

Norcini, J. J. 2003. 'Setting Standards on Educational Tests'. *Medical Education* 37: 464–469.

Prideaux D., Roberts, C., Eva, K., Centeno, A., McCrorie, P., McManus, C., Patterson, F., Powis, D., Tekian, A., & Wilkinson, D. 2011. 'Assessment for Selection for the Health Care Professions and Specialty Training: Consensus Statement and Recommendations from the Ottawa 2010 Conference'. *Med Teach*. 33(3): 215–223.

Rabinowitz, H., & Paynter, N. 2002. 'The Rural Vs Urban Practice Decision'. *JAMA* 287(1): 113.

Chapter 6

Engaging the Learner

A Framework for Sustainable Teaching

Adam Bertram

Abstract

Engagement of learners is often viewed by all stakeholders as vital in educational processes. If students are not "engaged" then are learning opportunities diminished? Engagement is, however, widely multi-faceted and not all forms support authentic learning. For instance, it could be encouraged at the superficial level (the "wow" factor) where deep processing of content is absent, or on the opposite end of the learning spectrum, through deep engagement where students are meaningfully participating in their own learning. This chapter explores how teachers might authentically engage their students, at all levels from early childhood through to postgraduate levels, to encourage this deep learning. This chapter reports on a study that used an educational framework, a Content Representation (CoRe), with practicing primary and secondary science classroom teachers (n = 6). Findings from the study revealed that the CoRe focussed these teachers to explore and connect their content knowledge with appropriate teaching strategies that would enhance deep student learning. The teachers claimed that the CoRe enhanced their professional knowledge in ways that would authentically engage students in learning and meaning-making.

Introduction

Student "engagement" at all levels of education is a hot topic in the current political and educational agendas of our government. But what is "engagement"? Is it merely a grab-bag of tricks that entertains? How can we be sure that our teaching is authentic and meaningful for our students? This chapter presents research on an educational framework which has been tested with practicing primary and secondary science classroom teachers (n = 6). The teachers claimed that Content Representations (CoRes), after using them in their practice, were a powerful and useful tool in helping them to understand their own professional knowledge of teaching and learning – connecting their subject-matter knowledge with their teaching knowledge in ways that enhanced meaningful student learning. Implications from the study suggest that this framework may also be of use to all teachers across the learning spectrum, from early childhood to adult education, including lecturers and tutors at the undergraduate and postgraduate levels. This chapter presents useful possibilities for all educators and helps to strengthen student engagement and learning across the varied domains of educational fields in ways which promote a sustainable professional body of knowledge for teaching.

Pedagogical Content Knowledge (PCK)

It is known that the scholarship of teaching involves a lot more than a basic understanding of "how to teach" or simple instruction. There is much more to teaching than this rudimentary ideology. Decades of research into teaching has found that the knowledge possessed or required by teachers is in fact vastly complex (Loughran, Berry & Mulhall 2006). As a result, many researchers have focused their studies on questioning the forms of knowledge that teachers require, possess and develop (see also Borko & Putnam 1996; Calderhead 1996; Shulman 1986). One component which has stimulated much interest in academia is that of pedagogical content knowledge (PCK). PCK is an amalgam of teachers' content and pedagogic knowledge which presents itself in its own right as the unique specialist knowledge that teachers have in transforming their knowledge of the content into knowledge of the content "for" teaching (Park & Oliver 2008). In other words, PCK represents the specialised knowledge of a teacher for teaching specific content to particular students which helps students learn and strengthens their engagement in their learning.

PCK was born out of concern that essential questions were not being asked about teaching during teacher knowledge research of the 1970s and early 1980s (Shulman 1986). When analysing the skills and competencies teachers required, Shulman felt there was a "missing paradigm" (1986: 7) absent amongst the research. The author recognised that it was not only important for teachers to possess knowledge of content and knowledge of pedagogy but that there existed a specific domain of knowledge which blended these two together in powerful "ways of representing and formulating the subject that makes it comprehensible for others" (1986: 9). Shulman proposed that this form of knowledge (which he called PCK) was a distinct category from both knowledge of pedagogy and content, and claimed that PCK:

> is of special interest because it identifies the distinctive bodies of knowledge for teaching. It represents the blending of content and pedagogy into an understanding of how particular topics, problems, or issues are organised, represented, and adapted to diverse interests and abilities of learners, and presented for instruction. Pedagogical content knowledge is the category most likely to distinguish the understanding of the content specialist from that of the pedagogue. (1987: 8)

Suddenly, Shulman had opened a new direction in the quest to understand the knowledge required by teachers. Not only did PCK offer a new way of valuing teachers' work but, as Seixas (2001) wrote, it reclaimed:

> the sustained consideration of 'content' within the purview of pedagogical research, a place that had been largely eclipsed by generic process-product research of the 1980s. This was the first, and arguably the most important to date, of research programs arching across subject areas and disciplines, which also took the distinctiveness of subjects and disciplines as serious objects of study. (2001: 546)

In this way, a key feature of PCK was its topic-specific nature. For science teacher researchers, this offered a unique and particular area of enquiry into exploring the professional knowledge of expert science teachers. Because the content of science can sometimes be abstract and conceptually difficult, particular attention to how learners make sense of it is of particular importance. Many science education researchers have taken up the construct of PCK as a serious and integral part of the knowledge base of science teachers (see also Abell 2007; Appleton 2002; Gess-Newsome & Lederman 1999; Loughran *et al.* 2006; van Driel 2008; van Driel, de Jong and Verloop 2002).

So what does PCK look like? This simple anecdote attempts to demonstrate the difference between having separate knowledge of teaching and knowledge of content, as opposed to the amalgam that is PCK:

> Helen is a science teacher who has been teaching for a few years now. She has excellent knowledge of the subject-matter, having worked as a chemical engineer prior to entering teaching and she uses a range of pedagogical procedures that she has learned from her teaching degree. She has just finished a lesson on how to write chemical equations with her Year 10 Science students and she felt that the lesson went well.

Helen recounted that she began the lesson by introducing some simple steps on the whiteboard. She had her students copy down the steps into their workbooks. She then provided and worked through some examples on the board. Students were next given a worksheet with a list of different chemical reactions. Each reaction was missing various components and it was the students' task to fill these in. After some time, she stopped the class and asked the students to do a practical. The practical involved having students observe a chemical reaction. She said that this was a good lesson because everyone behaved themselves, they seemed to enjoy filling in the worksheet and that the practical got them involved in 'doing' Chemistry.

This anecdote highlights that the teacher had good content knowledge, and that she used a variety of pedagogical procedures (providing examples of how to do the work, using worksheets to consolidate and provide evidence of learning, and using practicals to provide "real" observations of a chemical reaction).

But how did the teacher know that her students actually learned the intended content to be learnt? What gauge did she use? Yes, the lesson went well in terms of her expectations of student "on-task" behaviour but did the lesson go well in terms of developing students' understanding? Her reasons in this regard were not provided. Her pedagogical procedures were chosen (perhaps subconsciously) on the basis of student management. Also, the practical added nothing to students' understanding on how to write a chemical reaction – perhaps it was only added to the lesson as a "wow" factor. The point of the above anecdote was to illustrate that the teacher had no obvious PCK. She may have had good content knowledge and adequate pedagogical knowledge, but her reasons for using the pedagogical procedures were an ulterior motive (student management) rather than enhancing her students' understanding. The purpose of the above example was to demonstrate that it is not enough for a teacher to possess these two domains of knowledge alone. And it is at this point that pedagogical content knowledge (PCK) becomes an important part of an expert teacher's knowledge. PCK represents the amalgam of content and pedagogy which powerfully combine to enhance student engagement with learning.

Given the significance of PCK in science teachers' professional knowledge of practice, it becomes an important area for researchers to investigate. However, this form of knowledge is so unique to the individual teacher and specific to their understanding of content and pedagogy, that it is often tacit or intrinsic in their practice. For the teacher, their PCK is often therefore quite elusive and difficult for them to articulate (Loughran *et al.* 2006).

The Framework of CoRes

Science education researchers, Loughran and colleagues (Loughran *et al.* 2006), developed a framework of Content Representations (CoRes), which they believed would be able to articulate and portray science teachers' PCK. In so doing, they hoped that teachers could begin to recognise and develop their PCK in ways which would enhance their professional knowledge of practice.

CoRes are offered as a blank table and are designed to represent the content of a whole topic. Across the top row, teachers are required to tabulate the "Big Ideas" or concepts within that particular topic. Down the left-most column are the CoRe's prompts. These prompts or questions ask teachers to consider their thinking and reasoning behind the content of the particular science topic and their decision-making around their choice of pedagogical activities for their specific students. See Figure 1 as an example of a completed CoRe ("CoRe" refers to a singular Content Representation) template. In this way, CoRes were intended to capture instances of teachers' PCK and explicitly reveal their specialist knowledge of practice. In so doing, the theoretical construct hopefully becomes meaningful, powerful, recognised and valued as part of their professional knowledge, and provides a new discourse of teacher professional language.

	Important science ideas / concepts			
	Big idea A Earth, sun & moon	**Big idea B** Night & day	**Big idea C** The seasons	**Big idea D** Bringing it all together
What do you intend the students to learn about this idea?	That the Earth is on a tilt and orbits around the sun, and the moon is a natural satellite that orbits the Earth. 1 rotation of the Earth is approximately 1 day. 1 orbit of the sun is approximately 1 year 1 full orbit of the moon and the different phases of the moon occur in approximately 1 month.	To understand and explain the relationship between day and night and the rotation of the Earth.	To understand that the sun, the tilt of the Earth and its orbit around the Sun influences and determines the seasons.	Pull it all together, make connections. Reflect upon what they have learned.

	Features of the sun, Earth and moon such as surface, temperature and gravitational pull. We also slightly discuss stars, constellations, locations and their appearance.			
Why is it important for students to know this?	This introduction will help give them an insight in features of the sun, moon and Earth, and also build the foundation to understanding the next concepts of night and day and the seasons.	To answer their queries about the natural world, such as day becoming night, and learn to use scientific vocabulary in place of everyday language to describe and explain their research, observations and measurements.	To understand the seasons, weather and why some countries are hotter or colder than others. We wanted the children to understand that it is something that we cannot actually control. We also lightly discuss the human impact on the ozone layer so that they could understand that there was something that we can do to help the situation.	We want the children to understand the role that the Earth, the sun and the moon have on our planet in regards to day and night and the seasons. We hope that the unit will promote their thinking about their environment and how it connects to their life. We hope that they can make connections between the unit and the real world.
What else do you know about this idea (that you do not intend students to know yet)?	The position of other planets in the solar system (this is a major focus in the level 4 curriculum).			
What are the difficulties/ limitations connected with teaching this idea?	Some children are confused by the Earth orbiting the Sun and the Earth also spinning on its axis. They often think they are the same thing. Equipment such as three different-sized polystyrene balls, skewers and pastels will be required for the model.	Some children have the misconception that it is night-time at the same time all around the world. Equipment such as a computer, data projector, torch and world globe will be required to give the children a visual representation of the concept.	I found it difficult to teach this component as I didn't fully understand it either. However, after I did a bit more research, I was able to pass on my knowledge and the way I came to understand it, to them. I think that by being in this situation, I was able to understand how they were feeling. So we worked together to understand how it worked.	The booklet activity will be more beneficial for the Grade 3 children as some of the concepts may be too difficult for the prep children to understand. It will also be challenging for the children with special needs because they find it hard to cope with change and unfamiliar environments.

What is your knowledge about students' thinking that influences your teaching of these ideas?	We included a task for the students to construct a model of the sun, moon and Earth, as we knew that they would have trouble visualising the placement in space. This would also help them to gain an understanding of the size of the sun, moon and Earth in relation to each other.	Day and night is a difficult concept for some children to understand because they can't actually see it happening quickly, they just know it happens. Models using a globe and torch, and interactive programs on the computer are used to help these children who visually learn best.	They were really keen to learn about how the seasons come about, as this was a question asked by many of the children at the beginning on the wondering wall. Because they had leant about the Earth spinning on its axis and where the sun sits in relation to the Earth, they understood this concept much quicker than I anticipated. This enabled us to delve a little further into it by looking at what the seasons are like, what occurs during the seasons, what people wear, how they affect the land, and activities that people do. Again, we used some interactive programs to give the children visuals, and we also shared information during small group and whole class reading time.	Although the children were extremely excited to be mini-teachers to the prep children, they were also very nervous about their presentation so we rehearsed the presentation to the class first. We spoke of ways to present work, speak fluently and clearly, how to ask questions, not say "um", stand tall, maintain eye contact, etc. We will work through the test questions as a class because it is worded as a story (rather than explicitly asking the children to answer a question) and the children have had little experience doing a test like this and are likely to become confused about what they are actually being asked to do.
Are there any other factors that influence your teaching of these ideas?	The children were asked to bring in a tissue box to stick their model into because we are no longer able to use egg cartons due to allergies. I also had to break the skewers for the polystyrene balls as they were too sharp for the children's hands and many have caused splinters or cuts. They also needed a visual such as a world globe, when colouring-in their polystyrene ball to look like the Earth.	We planned lots of group-work for this concept as the children often feel lost on their own and are more likely to have a go at something challenging if working with others. The children in my class enjoy investigating and finding out the answer for themselves, rather than having me tell them.	We wanted the children to look further into the concept of the seasons, so rather than giving them a prescribed task of finding out the answers to questions devised by the teachers, we had them set their own questions up to try and give others an insight into their thinking about the seasons. This worked well as it gave the children some ownership of the task. They enjoy competition and they liked that it	When the children were selecting the content of their booklet, they were reminded to keep it fairly simple so that the prep children would be able to engage in their presentation and understand the concepts they were describing.

			would eventually be turned into a class quiz.	
	The whole level is extremely girl-heavy. Each Grade 3 class has only 7 or 8 boys, compared to 15 girls. The majority of staff is also female, so we wanted to try and give the boys some male interaction. We approached a Secondary College to provide some boys that would be able to help teach some aspects of the unit to small groups to try and engage the Grade 3 boys further.			
What are your teaching procedures (and particular reasons for using these to engage with this idea)?	We did a pre-test to find out what the children already knew and what misconceptions they had. We did this to find out what concepts we needed to cover in the unit and which misconceptions needed to be challenged. After being immersed in pictures, visuals and with stories, the children were asked to prove/ challenge their understandings. We did this to ensure that the children actually understood what they were saying and had reasons to explain their view. We also constructed a Wondering Wall whereby the children write down any questions (on paper bricks) that they have about the topic that have not yet been	Before any discussion of night and day, children worked in small groups to demonstrate their conception of how night and day occurs. They chose their method of presentation; this way it was relevant to their preferred learning style. They could do it as a poster, play, presentation, etc. Children were then placed into "Expert Groups" and were given information packs on night and day. They used a 4 Square Lotus Diagram to collate information and data on the Sun, Moon, Earth and Other (things that did not fit into a specific area – such as daylight savings). This promotes thinking skills and cooperative teamwork in addition to researching, selecting and	Starlab Incursion: we selected Starlab to give the children the experience of sitting beneath the stars. The Starlab staff are experienced in their field and were able to answer some of the children's difficult questions that the teachers struggled with. Seasons Brainstorm: the children described what they knew about the seasons, such as the water, air, land and living things in our area during each season. They looked at seasonal images from all over the world – we did this to give them an idea of how the seasons look in other countries, such as snow in winter. We also discussed the clothing people wear and the impacts of the seasons. A class chart was created	Prep booklet: we asked the children to prepare a booklet to present to a prep class. It was to include a summary of the things they had learnt in the unit. It could be a "Did you know?", collection of Quiz Questions, poster or booklet. We selected this activity so that the children could convey their learning to others and also improve presentation skills. What Happened Last Night?: This is a formal assessment task on the unit that will be assessed with a rubric. We selected this type of assessment as a concrete sample of what the children can do. It will be used in addition to all other assessment pieces to score the children for reporting purposes.

	answered. This activity gets them thinking about the topic on a broader scale. They are able to ask questions that they might believe are "silly" that in fact aren't, such as "Why do people float on the moon?" We viewed an interactive whiteboard program on the Earth and they answered a 20-question quiz to demonstrate their knowledge so far. The children constructed a teacher-directed model of the sun, Earth and moon. It was then used to demonstrate the orbit paths of the Earth and moon. We knew that the children would not be able to do this on their own; however, they would benefit from a visual of their placement in relation to each other. Year 10 Secondary students helped the children create a Planisphere. We selected this activity to allow the children to be taught from a different perspective. They enjoy guest speakers and learning from young people who can connect with them.	summarising. After several sessions, the children were then expected to report back their findings to the class and we discussed the correct explanation of how night and day occurs. We observed and recorded sunrise and sunset times for one week. The results were then graphed and discussed. This activity helped to connect part of the unit to the real world for them.	on each season We used the Thinkers Keys such as the "Prediction Key" to think what Vermont South would be like if it was always one season and the "What If Key". The children used an interactive program that explains how the seasons work. We chose this because the computers are engaging, and many of the children in the class are visual learners. In groups of 3, children used the Question Matrix to develop 3 quiz questions about the seasons and investigated the answers for them. All groups joined together at the end to have a class quiz. We selected this activity because our Action Learning Project for this year is engaging boys in learning, and research suggests that boys enjoy competition. The children viewed the interactive whiteboard program on the seasons and answered the 20-question quiz. Children worked in pairs to use a Venn Diagram to compare three seasons. We chose this to promote their thinking skills as the Thinking Curriculum is a major focus at our school.	The children viewed interactive whiteboard programs and quizzes on the sun and moon. Again, we selected this activity because the children really enjoy the other quizzes and like working with computers and seeing visuals. The boys particularly enjoy competition work.

Specific ways of ascertaining students' understanding or confusion around this idea (include a likely range of responses).	The whole unit is tested at the end by an activity that is written in story format whereby the students are asked questions and required to explain or draw their answer. Students' understanding would be tested and assessed via informal observation, anecdotal notes, work pieces and general discussion before progressing to the next concept. The student model was also used as a guide to ascertain the students' understanding.	Expert group presentation was assessed with feedback and discussion. The 20-question interactive quiz was also used to determine children's understandings. Students' understanding continued to be tested and assessed via informal observation, anecdotal notes, work pieces and general discussion before progressing to the next concept.	The 20-question interactive quiz was used to promote discussion about the seasons. The class quiz also promoted discussion and enabled us to view which concepts the children had grasped. Students' understandings continued to be tested and assessed via informal observation, anecdotal notes, work pieces and general discussion before progressing to the next concept.	Prep booklet. What Happened Last Night? Assessment. Sun, moon interactive whiteboard programs and quizzes.

Table 1. An example completed CoRe (created by Delta)

Year level: Grade 3 / 4; Content area: Space.

Since their development, CoRes have generally been recognised as a valid instrument in articulating science teachers' PCK in the science education literature (Kind 2009). However, there are few accounts of how they are valued by practicing science teachers. This chapter presents the findings of a study by Bertram (2010) which largely sought to validate this framework with practising science teachers and to test their applicability in the real world of teacher practice. In the study, the CoRe framework was presented to six practicing (primary and secondary) science teachers, whom developed their own CoRe as part of their practice. The two year study explored:

- how CoRes might be valued by these teachers;
- how the process of creating one and using it in their practice might, if at all, have influenced or developed their professional knowledge of practice;
- if they felt it captured or portrayed instances of their PCK; and finally,
- how their individual understanding of PCK might have developed as a consequence.

Research Design

The research study (see also Bertram 2010) was designed around a longitudinal, ethnographic methodology (see Wiersma 2000 for a full description of ethnographic research). Six practising science teachers were involved in an extensive interview process over two years. The first interview explored the teachers' pre-study views on teaching and learning so that a picture of their professional knowledge could be ascertained. The construct of PCK and the framework of CoRes were then explained. Participants were then expected to construct and develop their own CoRe based on a science unit that they would soon be teaching. Participants were interviewed on the process of making the CoRe and how this had, if at all, begun impacting on the way they understood their teaching and learning. In due course, participants taught the unit on which their CoRe had been based. A follow-up interview explored their views on the impact, if at all, that the CoRe might have had on their teaching and learning, their professional views on practice, and whether they could begin to recognise instances of their own PCK.

Approximately a year after using the CoRe in their practice, the participants were interviewed for their post-study views on teaching and learning. These views were compared to their pre-study views and the participants were asked if any changes might have been influenced by their use of their CoRe in their practice. This final interview also considered the participants views' on the long-term impact or influence which CoRes might have had on their professional practice, and in particular, how they might have, if at all, developed their own PCK.

The Participants

Of the six teachers who participated in the study, two were primary school generalists and four were secondary science teachers. At the time of the first interview, three (Rani, Julie, Samantha) of the four secondary teachers were teaching mostly middle school science (Years Seven through to Ten) as part of their teaching load. The fourth teacher (Jerry) was a senior specialist teaching Years Eleven and Twelve physics. All of these teachers were experienced, having between eight and twenty-five years of teaching experience. The remaining two volunteers of the six were both generalist primary school teachers in government, co-educational primary schools in Victoria. One (Delta) had taught for three years and the other (Gordon) had only been teaching for six months at the time of the first interview. All participants' names are pseudonyms. A summary table (see Figure 2) of the participants' background information is offered as a quick reference whilst also serving as a brief, initial introduction to each participant.

Participants	Background questions			
	Experience in teaching science (years)	Current school type	Current employment position	Grades/classes currently being taught
Julie	25 years	Independent, co-educational, Pre-prep to Year 12 college	High School Teacher of Science – Head of Science Faculty	Yrs 7, 8, 9, 10 Middle School Science
Rani	14 years	Independent, co-educational, Pre-prep to Year 12 college	High School Teacher of Science	Yrs 7, 9, 10 Middle School Science and Yr 11 Biology
Samantha	10 years	Independent, co-educational, Pre-prep to Year 12 college	High School Teacher of Science	Yrs 7, 8, 10 Middle School Science
Jerry	8 years	Independent, co-educational, Pre-prep to Year 12 college	High School Teacher of Physics and Information Technology	Yrs 11, 12 Physics and Yrs 7, 8, 9, 10 Information Technology
Delta	4 years	Government, co-educational, Primary school (Prep to Grade Six)	Generalist Primary School Teacher	Grade Three
Gordon	6 months	Government, co-educational, Primary school (Prep to Grade Six)	Generalist Primary School Teacher	Grade Five/Six composite class

Table 2. Summary of each participants' background

In the study, each participant contributed to creating one CoRe either individually or within a group. Delta and Gordon (each from different primary schools) completed individual CoRes. While both focused on Space as a topic, Delta's CoRe (which is the example CoRe offered as Figure 1) was aimed for Grade Three/Four students while Gordon's was for Grade Five/Six. Both Delta and Gordon had not taught this particular topic before in their teaching career. Jerry also worked individually on the topic of Interactions of Light and Matter for Year Twelve Physics – a topic which he had taught for the last three years. Julie, Rani and Samantha, who were all from the same school, worked together in creating a CoRe on the topic of Genetics for Year Ten Science. This was a topic that they all had a minimum of ten years' experience in teaching.

Analyses and Findings

All participating science teachers claimed and endorsed CoRes as being an effective instrument which helped them to better understand their professional knowledge of practice. On a general level, all participants believed that CoRes offered them a structured and meaningful means of reflection which forced them to reflect in a purposeful and deliberate manner.

Notably, their responses in the pre- and post-intervention interviews have clearly shown some changes in their ways of thinking about their professional knowledge. In fact, all participants claimed that at least one of their pre-intervention views on teaching and learning had been influenced, changed or developed as a consequence of this study. One such indicative response is provided by Gordon:

> [This study] influenced my view of teaching insofar as I think ... teachers need to actually think about what they've done and what they've done successfully or not, more often ... In terms of students, I suppose it's probably made me consider the enquiry-based learning aspects further and just different ways to make that interesting for students and to keep them involved in that process. (Gordon, post-intervention interview)

As a teacher of primary-school science, Gordon also indicated that CoRes improved the way he came to view and approach unfamiliar content:

> Looking at my [pre-intervention] views, I was quite intrigued to see the way that I had changed my perspective on science teaching ... – I'd said that there were some elements [of science content] which I found quite difficult to teach ... because I didn't have the knowledge about those things. But ... I've realised that's something that I need to push myself on and really work to develop because I've seen the merits of it, particularly in science-based programs, in enquiry-based learning. (Gordon, post-intervention interview)

Individually, though, the CoRe each brought out something different about the practice of each participant. A summary for each of the six participants follows.

Julie

Julie felt that this study (through CoRes) was "the best tool I have come across so far" in that it made her consciously reflect on her practice (Julie, final interview). She appreciated how it made her consider the "why" and "how" of her practice rather than just focusing on the "what". In this regard, she claimed that this way of thinking resonated with her and that it would become "entrenched into the bones" of her practice (Julie, final interview).

Julie's definition of PCK at the end of this study was strongly content-orientated (she felt that superior content knowledge was perhaps more important above anything else) and did not focus so much on the idea of how she understood her particular students. Yet, she had earlier described how "knowing the kids" was also an important part of PCK (Julie, mid-interview).

Of the CoRe, she felt that it was a "fantastic tool" which provided scaffolding in articulating meaningful thinking about her practice (Julie, final interview). She felt that CoRes provided an effective method for drawing out teachers' PCK. While she said that this study was "very important", she felt that teachers may be reluctant to undertake it willingly. She herself, however, claimed that it had influenced the way she thought about her teaching – "the importance of each little bit" (Julie, final interview) – and that it gave her a structure to reflect on – one which she claimed she would revisit regularly.

Rani

Rani felt that PCK was very important for teachers to know. Her definition of PCK married together knowledge of students with knowledge of content in ways that could produce effective teaching approaches to maximise students' understanding. She also claimed that CoRes provided a framework for meaningfully examining content and planning its delivery. She felt that teachers who had become stale in their approach or who were beginning teaching could benefit from the framework.

By raising awareness of PCK, Rani believed that this study had influenced her own practice. She explained that although she was already a "strong advocate of reflecting" (Rani, final interview), the venture had reinforced the importance of doing so. She also claimed that the study allowed her to view the content in more depth than she did before. While she stated that this was "an excellent study" because it provided insight into the purpose and delivery of content, it also "truly" affirmed her as a successful teacher (Rani, final interview).

Samantha

Samantha felt that PCK represented the knowledge of teaching and learning which constituted "good" practice, and she believed that "good" teachers intrinsically embodied a PCK philosophy (Samantha, final interview). By defining it by name, Samantha felt that it could be more easily identifiable and explored, particularly by beginning teachers. She claimed that it was "very important" and a useful construct in teachers' professional knowledge (Samantha, final interview). She felt that CoRes were effective in offering teachers a way of looking at their practice and in embodying PCK.

Samantha's definition of PCK lacked detail about the particular nature of content knowledge and the knowledge of specific and individual students. However, it did include an emphasis on knowing the content well and therefore using the most effective manner in which to present that content to students.

For Samantha, this study has revealed that some aspects of her practice have been influenced through CoRes – although she had claimed otherwise when she was explicitly asked. In some of her responses, she felt that she was more alert to knowing and catering to her differing students' needs, and that she would more consciously evaluate the effectiveness of her pedagogical approaches. This could be interpreted as evidence that an awareness of PCK through this study had actually impacted, to some extent, her current practice.

Jerry

Jerry had a clear understanding of what PCK entailed. His definition was aligned with that as defined in this study – that PCK was about the "teaching of content tailored to specific cohorts" (Jerry, final interview). It is "dynamic, effective, personalised teaching" (Jerry, final interview). In this way, Jerry hinted at the importance of knowing the content, knowing his students and knowing how to blend the two together to present effective pedagogical approaches to improve students' understanding.

In terms of the impact of this study, Jerry felt that he would remember the CoRe as a tool which allowed him to lay out and examine the content of a topic in detail – more so than might otherwise be the case. Overall, Jerry claimed that this study was "effective" and could offer greater insight into teachers' practice (Jerry, final interview).

Delta

It is reasonable to infer that Delta had formed a clear understanding of the definition of PCK as a result of this study. To her, PCK was how she understood her students, the content, and how to link them in a way which produced effective teaching approaches which would enhance students' understanding. She felt that PCK, as a construct, was "very important" for other teachers to incorporate into their practice (Delta, final interview). Interestingly, though, Delta claimed that this knowledge should already be an intrinsic part of successful teachers' practice anyway.

Delta believed that this study influenced her long-term views on teaching and learning. She claimed that she would remember many questions from the CoRe as she thought more meaningfully now about her practice. She also thought that CoRes drew out aspects of her PCK although she was concerned about how much time was needed to invest in producing and using them. Generally, however, Delta felt that through her involvement with CoRes, her practice might be enhanced because it had caused her to, in the very least, "definitely reflect more" (Delta, final interview).

Gordon

For Gordon, this study (as experienced through CoRes) offered a "methodology" through which teachers could meaningfully analyse their practice and develop it through reflection (Gordon, final interview). Gordon came to understand PCK as the melding of content knowledge with the knowledge of particular students to deliver optimal pedagogical approaches which improved student learning. Gordon thought that PCK was "important" because it could develop an awareness of a teacher's own philosophies and knowledge of practice, and he felt that beginning teachers would particularly benefit in this regard.

He believed that his thinking about teaching and learning had been influenced by this study, and he particularly thought the CoRe's prompts were "the most worthwhile" part of the study (Gordon, final interview). He stated that it provided him with a suitable structure from which to examine, question and plan the content and his approaches. He felt that it prompted him to think more deeply about the meaning behind teaching, his students, and how he would specifically cater to their particular needs. Gordon felt that the study was useful for teachers and he endorsed its use as part of regular teacher professional development.

General Summary of Findings

For three of the participants, they felt that it made them re-think their general understanding of what "teaching" and "learning" meant to them on a personal level. For three other participants, they claimed that the CoRe impacted the way they understood the term "student learning" and it caused them to think more carefully of how their particular students understood the content being taught.

All participants (none of which had an understanding of PCK prior to this study) agreed that the construct of PCK, as developed through their CoRe, offered teachers an important and useful construct for shaping their professional knowledge. For the participants themselves, they now possessed an instrument which had provided concrete forms of instances of their own PCK. All participants believed that by having an awareness of these instances, and in the process of making the CoRe – the deliberate questioning and reasoning about the content and the pedagogy forced by the CoRe's prompts – improved their understanding of teaching and learning, and impacted their long-term knowledge of practice. In this way, with enhanced engagement with their own teaching, it could be expected that student engagement would improve as a consequence.

The researcher also noticed that, at the post-intervention stage, the teachers had now begun to develop a shared language of communicating their PCK and ideas about teaching and learning with others.

While the participating science teachers' views of CoRes support that it is indeed an effective instrument in articulating and developing PCK, and that it would be extremely useful for the professional teacher, there was a major limitation to its design. All participants stated that an enormous investment of time was required for its production, and not one of the participants could see themselves using it in their own practice of their own volition. Two participants suggested that perhaps CoRes could be embedded into the curriculum practices of the school.

In sum, the overall findings of the study were:

- CoRes and PaP-eRs provided a means for helping participating science teachers communicate through a shared language;
- CoRes and PaP-eRs influenced participating science teachers' professional practice in meaningful ways;
- CoRes and PaP-eRs helped participating science teachers think differently about their practice;
- CoRes and PaP-eRs provided concrete examples and portrayals of participating science teachers' PCK;
- CoRes and PaP-eRs were shown to be effective in meaningfully developing participating science teachers' PCK; and,
- participating science teachers believed that CoRes and PaP-eRs were worthwhile and valid tools which improved their understanding of

their own practice and, in particular, how they came to understand and recognise their own PCK.

Implications for All Types of Educators

The findings from the study have shown that CoRes are a very useful heuristic for practising primary and secondary science teachers, which in turns engages them more actively in the teaching-learning process, and as a consequence, improves the quality of their teaching and, ultimately, student engagement. A call for further studies which link teachers' PCK (and indeed perhaps via the use of CoRes) with student engagement is advanced. Undoubtedly, a link (whether tacit or obvious) should exist between teachers who purposefully engage with their PCK and student engagement in learning.

In the opening to this chapter, the idea of its value for all educators (not just primary and secondary teachers or teachers of science) was floated. Can the framework of CoRes extend its use and applicability to early childhood educators, university lecturers and tutors, adult educators and other educators? The possibility certainly exists. The present work presented evidence that CoRes work for science teachers. This gives rise to the implication that perhaps CoRes offer value to teachers in different fields (not just science) and at all levels in the education spectrum. Of course, in relation to the applicability of CoRes in disciplines outside of science, some challenges would definitely be expected. How might CoRes represent the content in, say, a literature subject or a language subject or a subject where concrete facts do not dominate in the same way or form as they do in science? Can CoRes represent this type of content, or can they be modified somehow, in ways that still prompt the educator to engage with the content more so and improve their professional knowledge of practice? These possibilities beg exploration.

Conclusion

This chapter reported on a study that set out to explore how practising science teachers might value (or not value) the validity of CoRes as an effective framework at capturing and portraying science teachers' PCK. This study importantly advances the education research literature by testing for applicability the theoretical construct of PCK in the actual classroom. The findings provide evidence that CoRes are indeed valid instruments in prompting teachers to consider their practice beyond normal. Effectively, all participating science teachers claimed that CoRes positively influenced their understanding of PCK and that it developed this understanding in profound ways. They claimed that CoRes effectively captured and portrayed instances of their PCK, and that, in so doing, they could begin to explicitly recognise aspects of their knowledge about teaching and learning in more powerful ways. In turn, it would be expected that, as a consequence, student engagement is enhanced. Engagement then becomes genuine in and about learning, rather than being simply a grab-bag of tricks that entertains, usually at the surface level.

It is hoped that the use of CoRes might now be seen as being of benefit for all types of educators at all levels and in all domains (whether in an amended form or as is), and that this work prompts some further exploratory research into how this might look. An explicit awareness of the construct of PCK offers educators a lens in which to engage with their practice. Through this lens, it offers the possibilities to share insights, pedagogies and content knowledge with colleagues in ways that surely promote a sustainable professional body of knowledge for teaching.

References

Abell, S. 2007. 'Research on Science Teacher Knowledge'. In Abell, S. & Lederman, N. G. (ed.). *Handbook of Research on Science Education*. Mahwah: Lawrence Erlbaum Associates.

Appleton, K. 2002. 'Science Activities that Work: Perceptions of Primary School Teachers'. *Research in Science Education* 32(3): 393–410.

Bertram, A. 2010. *Enhancing Science Teachers' Knowledge of Practice by Explicitly Developing Pedagogical Content Knowledge*. Unpublished Ph.D. Thesis, Monash University, Clayton, Victoria, Australia.

Borko, H. & Putnam, R. T. 1996. 'Learning to teach'. In Berliner, D. C., and Calfee, R. C. (ed.). *Handbook of Educational Psychology*. New York: Macmillan.

Calderhead, J. 1996. 'Teachers: Beliefs and Knowledge'. In Berliner, D. C., and Calfee, R. C. (ed.). *Handbook of Educational Psychology*. New York: Macmillan.

Gess-Newsome, J. A. & Lederman, N. G. (ed.). 1999. *Examining Pedagogical Content Knowledge: The Construct and Its Implications for Science Education*. Dordrecht: Kluwer Academic Publishers.

Kind, V. 2009. 'Pedagogical Content Knowledge in Science Education: Perspectives and Potential for Progress'. *Studies in Science Education* 45(2): 169–204.

Loughran, J., Berry, A. & Mulhall, P. 2006. *Understanding and Developing Science Teachers' Pedagogical Content Knowledge*. Rotterdam: Sense Publishers.

Park, S. & Oliver, J. S. 2008. 'Revisiting the Conceptualisation of Pedagogical Content Knowledge (PCK): PCK as a Conceptual Tool to Understand Teachers as Professionals'. *Research in Science Education* 38: 261–284.

Seixas, P. 2001. 'Review of Research on Social Studies'. In V. Richardson (ed.). *Handbook of Research on Teaching*. Fourth ed. Washington: American Educational Research Association.

Shulman, L. S. 1986. 'Those Who Understand: Knowledge Growth in Teaching'. *Educational Research* 15(2): 4–14.

Shulman, L. S. 1987. 'Knowledge and Teaching: Foundations of the New Reform'. *Harvard Educational Review* 57: 1–22.
van Driel, J. H. 2008. 'Pedagogical Content Knowledge: The Central Element in Science Teachers' Knowledge Base'. Abstract of Contribution to Discussion Group no. 3: Teacher Training of the European Conference "Science Learning in the Europe of Knowledge". http://media.enseignementsup-recherche.gouv.fr/file/Conf_Grenoble_8_et_9_oct/61/3/resume_van_driel_41613.pdf (accessed 19 December 2012).
van Driel, J. H., de Jong, O. & Verloop, N. 2002. 'The Development of Preservice Chemistry Teachers' Pedagogical Content Knowledge'. *Science Education* 86: 572–590.
Wiersma, W. 2000. Research Methods in Education: An Introduction. Seventh ed. Needham Heights: Allyn & Bacon.

Chapter 7

Racial Behaviour Among Secondary School Students

Khalim Zainal, Johari Talib, Fazilah Idris, Mansor Bin Mohd. Noor, Norshidah Mohamad Salleh

Abstract

Schools can be considered a part of community and represent a smaller system of the community which reflect the real society of a nation. In schools, students are taught how to interact among themselves. Teachers play an important role by adopting equality for all students regardless of ethnicity and social status of the pupils. Should their teachers differentiate students based on ethnicity or social status, then students will also follow suit in their dealings with friends. This in turn will lead to a prolonged racism conflict within the classroom before spreading into the community. Racism, if left unchecked, will trigger a prolonged conflict because the students will become part of society, citizens and future leaders. In this paper, a study on racist behaviour amongst secondary school students in one of the states in Peninsular Malaysia will be discussed. This study is important since Malaysia is a country consisting of various ethnicities whereby harmony and peace are essential to her political stability, social and economical progress. The findings of the research show that the level of racial discrimination among high school students is quite low. However, this research found that racial discrimination occurs at a higher rate in rural schools compared to schools in the urban areas.

Introduction

Schools can be considered a part of community and represent a microcosm of society. This means that the school is a micro-reflection of the society and nation in which it is situated. In schools, students are taught how to interact and mingle among themselves. Students are first introduced to culture and differing social statuses as a result of their interactions with students from various backgrounds. Teachers in schools play an important role in this regard by adopting a position of equality before all students, regardless of the students' ethnicity and their social status (Larson & Ovando 2001). Students perceive teachers' behaviour towards them and even though teachers may be unaware of their influence, students will invariably follow their mannerisms in classrooms. Should teachers differentiate/discriminate students based on ethnicity or social status, then students will also follow suit in their dealings with other students. This, in turn, could lead to a prolonged conflict within the classroom before spreading into the community (Khalim 2004). This will only form racist behaviours among students. If left unchecked, racism may/will trigger prolonged conflict because students become part of society in terms of becoming citizens and even future leaders. In this section, a study on racist behaviour among secondary school students in one of the states in the Malay Peninsular will be discussed. The significance of such a study is patent, given that Malaysia is a country consisting of various ethnicities, whereby harmony and peace are essential to its political, social, and economical progress.

Malaysia's Pre- and Post-Independence Education System

Education plays an important role in all aspects of human life. Malaya and present-day Malaysia cannot deny the role played by education in terms of human development and physical development. Malaysia's citizens consist of various ethnicities, so it requires a mechanism that can bridge inter-ethnic relations and that mechanism is surely education. The history of education in Malaysia dates back to the spread of Islam in the Malay Peninsula and Malay Archipelago in the 14th Century. Education at that time was informal, whereby Arabian and Indian traders who were Muslims spread Islam to people in those places. They started the *pondok* schools in Perlis, Kedah, Melaka, Terengganu, Kelantan and Brunei. Similarly, the expansion of the Malacca Sultanate Empire also helped spread Islam and non-formal educational institutions in their colonies. Education was usually conducted in the *surau* and mosques during night-time and attended by male and female adults. The purpose of the education at the time was to instill good moral character, with the emphasis on religion while focusing on subjects that could be used for life. At the time, there were no diverse societies in Malaya like the kind witnessed during the British occupation, since colonialists were mainly responsible in bringing Chinese and Indians to the land, thus leading to the culmination of today's diverse society. The existence of a multicultural society adds to the complexity in administering education within this country, be it during colonisation or even post-independence (Khalim 2004).

Colonisation in Malaysia existed since the days of the Melaka Sultanate in the 16th Century, starting with the Portuguese and the Dutch in the 17th Century. In the 18th Century, it was the turn of the British, and after World War II, the Japanese occupied Malaya. Once the war ended in 1945, the British resumed control. This study focuses on the post-1945 British era. The British introduced an education system based on the Barnes Report of 1951, and one of its important facets was the concern to see unity among the various ethnicities. The rulers tried to change migrant behaviour by implementing bilingual Malay and English schools only. This meant that Chinese and Indian schools were to be abolished, which subsequently generated opposition from the two ethnicities, who claimed that their views were totally ignored. Thus came the Fenn-Wu Report which defended the need for Chinese education while maintaining that Chinese students will learn three languages, namely, Malay, English, and Chinese.

This new education system was to form a sense of national identity and the government was to train more local teachers while providing financial assistance to all schools involved. The Fenn-Wu Report also proposed that the Chinese be not too steeped in their traditions, since they were now citizens of Malaya. Furthermore, the Chinese were to eliminate the influence of external politics in Chinese schools, since it was not considered to contribute positively to the quality of education found in these schools. The Chinese community was also told to not interfere in the administration of the Chinese schools. In addition, Chinese schools in Malaya were to consist only of Chinese pupils, since only they knew and understood the problems of the Chinese. Afterwards, the British founded the Education Ordinance which was prepared by the Education Committee in 1952. The aim was to examine both the Barnes and Fenn-Wu Reports. The British proceeded to unite the two reports into one singular form called "Reports of Barnes on Malay Education and Fenn-Wu Report on Chinese Education". This Report was then to become the Education Ordinance of 1952 and was the first step towards the creation of the country's National Education Policy. Among the provisions in the Education Ordinance of 1952 were:

1. Malaya was to have two types of national schools, namely, one in the English language and one in the Malay language. Chinese and Tamil languages were to be taught if requested by the parents of pupils;
2. the Malay language was to be taught in English schools and English would be taught in Malay schools; and,
3. Tamil vernacular schools and Chinese vernacular schools were not accepted as part of the National School System.

After achieving independence in 1957, the Malaysian government sought to unite the various ethnic groups in Malaysia, its hard work producing the centralised education system. This system is very suitable for a variety of factors, including historical, geographical, economic, socio-political and educational. As Malaysians consisted of various races, religions, languages and culture, national unity was a major goal and, as such, it was asserted in the Education Act of 1961. Education's importance was also demonstrated during the implementation of the New Economic Policy, whereby education was seen as the tool to unite the people in order to abolish poverty. But after achieving independence, the tragic race riot which occurred on 13 May 1969 was regarded as a turning point for racial tensions in Malaysia. On the surface, the events of 13 May 1969 were a result of dissatisfaction among ethnicities, especially between the Malays and Chinese. On a deeper level, the race riot was an effect of the divide-and-rule economic policy of the British colonisation of the then Malaya. This is because ethnic groups were separated in terms of education, economy and settlement by the British during their occupation.

A comprehensive national education system at the time allowed for an able handling of the situation from becoming much worse. An understanding by the Malaysian people on the need for tolerance was still an important element that helped control the events of 13 May from becoming an even more serious tragedy. It is quite clear that only the education system could help change the mindset of the people, thus the events of 13 May propelled the government to further strengthen the education system and economy of the nation. The ethnic crisis fostered in the government an awareness of the need for national integration, since the event demonstrated that national unity was still fragile. In order to strengthen unity, concerted and serious efforts were made to further strengthen the education system. Furthermore, a national ideology called *Rukunegara* was introduced in order to provide the students with a solid foundation for national unity and love of the nation.

The 13 May riot may also be understood as a contributing factor in the formalisation of the *Rukunegara* in order to foster a sense of love for the country.

The Cabinet Committee Report of 1979 stated that Malaysia's education system could fully fulfil the nation's goal of creating a united society. This would allow for students to apply, test and understand the issues of morality and ethics. Malaysia's education system is spiritually-based which aims to lead to a balanced education. Thus, it aims to help foster in the student a balanced character in order to achieve his or her life goals. A spiritual foundation or axis to the education system also aims to avoid providing an overly materialistic education solely based on achieving material wealth as its final target. In order to strengthen the nation's education system, the National Education Philosophy (NEP) was also designed and approved by the Curriculum Centre on 14 December 1988. The NEP was designed based on the desire and ambition contained in the Razak and Rahman Talib Reports, the Education Act of 1961, the Cabinet Committee Report and the *Rukunegara*.

The Razak Report was submitted in 1956 by submitting a total of 17 recommendations aimed at forming a national education system for all ethnic groups through the use of the national language as the medium of instruction. Among others, the contents of the Razak Report are:

1. similar and equal syllabus for all schools in Malaysia;
2. that the Malay language be used as the national language and, thus, the medium of instruction;
3. that the National Language and English become compulsory for all primary and secondary schools;
4. for the National Type Schools, English/Chinese/ Tamil languages will be used as the medium of instruction;
5. the establishment of only one type of secondary school being opened to all races;
6. schools are to be run by the local authorities;
7. teachers of primary and secondary schools are to be qualified teachers;
8. the upper level education system consists of secondary schools, high schools and pre-university; and,
9. all teachers are placed under one professional service organisation, and he establishment of the Federal Inspectorate.

The Razak Report clearly prioritises national unity as the ultimate goal to be achieved. This means that the elements and values of solidarity were needed to be made the basis of the nation's education in order to ensure the welfare and interests of Malaysia's multi-ethnic society. Since Malaysia possesses such a diverse society, the concept of unity within the national context needs to be understood as a process that emphasises creating a sense of a united society which is in accordance with the principles of the *Rukunegara*. The creation of this unity must be of a kind that can combat the symptoms that can divide people. These symptoms are symptoms of racism, ethnicity and creed, religion, language, regional loyalties, and others. In order to achieve the said national unity through education, the Razak Report outlined two main criteria, namely: (i) the same school system for all; and, (ii) a school curriculum that is the same and is nationally-geared.

Another report followed, the Rahman Talib, which became the Education Act of 1961. Initially, it was committee-based and entrusted to review and to revise the National Education Policy found in the Razak Report. As such, the Rahman Talib suggested that:

1. free education is to be provided in primary schools;
2. primary schools will be National Schools and National Type Schools;
3. high schools will include students up to the age of 15 years old;
4. pupils are automatically elevated regardless of results;
5. general examinations in secondary schools are in the nation's official language;
6. Islamic education is to be provided for Muslim pupils and the number of students must be at least 15 students; and,
7. moral education needs to be taken seriously.

The National Education Philosophy (NEP) was approved by the Curriculum Centre on 14 December 1988. The NEP was designed based on the desire and aims of the Razak Report and Rahman Talib Report, the Education Act of 1961, the Cabinet Committee report and the *Rukunegara*. The NEP was designed with the purpose of producing citizens possessing good personalities plus a balanced intellect, spirituality, emotion and physique, while also believing and being obedient to God. In addition, citizens were aimed to be knowledgeable, creative-minded, rational, possessing good moral values, competent, able to contribute towards increasing the prosperity of the community and country, whilst being loyal and responsible in maintaining good and friendly relations among their fellow citizens (Ministry of Education Malaysia 1990).

The NEP clearly wanted the national education system to form well-balanced students. One of the ideas found within the NEP was the forming of a noble human. Thus, it is the responsibility of the national education system to provide the foundations for such a goal. The characteristics of these noble Malaysians were those acquainted with and able to differentiate between good and bad moral values; believing and practicing good behavior while also avoiding bad behavior; appreciating all noble values inclusive of spiritual, human and citizenship values; being able to contribute towards increasing the prosperity of the community and country; and being loyal and responsible in maintaining good and friendly relations among their fellow citizens (Ministry of Education Malaysia 1990). Thus, the essence of the NEP is geared towards fostering national unity among the nation's various ethnicities.

After gaining independence, the direction of Malaysia's education system was in line with the country's development. There was no denying the fact that the assertion of moral development was of immense importance. By possessing good character, all the desires and aims of the nation will be achievable in terms of physical and spiritual development. The NEP needed careful, focus, disciplinary management which was integrated in order for the general education system and, specifically, schools which were to produce students whom were capable of becoming useful citizens to society and the nation at large.

Malaysia's education system went through two distinct phases, that is, colonial British rule and post-independence. During the British occupation, more emphasis was made on the differing school and curriculum systems as per the various ethnicities at the time. Educational facilities were also limited, which limited the chances of one furthering his/her education to only those of the elite minority. In terms of its educational philosophy, the policy was to continue with the divide-and-rule process towards Malayans, with the intentions of consolidating the British colonisation of Malaya. Education was mainly to further sustain the ethnic identities among the many ethnics. However, post-independence, the education system was designed more towards racial integration and the creation of a united nation consisting of the various ethnicities. This was implemented through an emphasis on national – rather than ethnic – identity, with the introduction of the *Rukunegara* being one example. Education was also aimed at enlightening the people on the need for economic stability as a means of guaranteeing the nation's security. Hence, education during this phase was focused towards providing an understanding on the New Economic Policy so that the people understood the government's actions in securing the interests of the Indigenous people whilst not neglecting the interests of the other ethnicities. Such a goal could only be achievable via the creation of a comprehensive education system. Thus, during this phase, education was seen as a tool for nation-building and development, whilst stating the rights of each and every ethnicity in Malaysia. In other words, it was an effort towards achieving the national aspirations of unity, development and the creation of the ideal citizen.

The national education system emphasised national solidarity as well as development. Recognising the importance of education in building the character of the students, the present study has been undertaken in order to evaluate the effectiveness of the nation's education system in fostering national unity. This work is significant since it will influence the reception of the idea of "One Malaysia", as espoused by the government. It must be acknowledged that Malaysia is a multi-racial country wherein the difference is seen not only in ethnic terms but also in economic, cultural, and religious terms. Given that one cannot change one's ethnicity, the governed has focused on the economic structure, culture, and education as catalysts for national unity (Zara 2005). In addition, Ting Chew Pen (1987) also states that education plays a variety of functions. Besides simply delivering knowledge, skills and values that are essential for the survival of a society, education also serves as a tool to promote integration.

Disciplinary and behavioral problems in schools are worrying to parents and society at large. Problematic behaviour among students would worsen should it venture into inter-ethnic issues. This will cause schools to be places that are not conducive for the teaching and learning process to take place. Based on numerous data collected by the National Unity Department regarding incidents of social conflict from 1998 to 2004, although social conflict incidents only account for roughly 1% of all conflicts, the fact remains that other than incidents stemming from issues involving the social, religious, security, political and economic, it also involves many factors or perpetrators from various ethnicities (Kamarulzaman 2007). What could be understood from this is that even though the amount of social conflict issues is only approximately 1%, if it is not curbed, then it will only continue to grow and become a bigger problem for society – more so for societies composed of diverse ethnicities.

Therefore, the present study is conducted on the basis of identifying whether racist behaviours among adolescents occur in schools. Effective measures need to be taken in order to solve the problems posed by students and it should be noted that facing the challenges of racism is never easy. Various efforts have been made, including the establishment of the Department of National Unity and National Integration in the early 1970s in order to introduce programs that emphasises on forging unity within the community. Among the programs introduced were the National Integration Plan, the Pupil Integration for Unity Plan (RIMUP), the establishment of Vision Schools, National Service programs, 1Malaysia programs and various others that strive to promote unity and the understanding of cultural differences found in Malaysia.

Research Theoretical Framework

As has been mentioned previously, Malaysia is a country composed of various ethnics groups since the British colonial period. The divide-and-rule policy of the colonialists started the segregation of the various ethnicities to the point that they were geographically settled according to their settlements and their economic status. Not much was done by the British in uniting the various ethnic groups due to their desire to simply profit from the raw materials found in Malaya at the time. It was the intention of the British to see to it that the major ethnicities – Malays, Chinese, and Indians – did not unite so that the British desire to profit from the raw materials was smoothly realised. After gaining independence, the burden of creating a united society was a very serious issue, since, without national unity, it was to be difficult for a nation to achieve social and political stability. Instability, in turn, would hinder economic progress. Thus, one of the most common theories discussed by researchers when analysing societies made up of various ethnicities is assimilation theory. Assimilation theory – sometimes known as integration or incorporation – is the process by which the characteristics of members of immigrant groups and host societies come to resemble one another. This process, which has both economic and socio-cultural dimensions, begins with the immigrant generation and continues with the second generation and beyond (Brown & Bean 2006).

According to assimilation theory, whichever ethnicity migrates to the country of another ethnicity should adjust and adapt to the native ethnicity of the country. In Malaysia, the native ethnic group was the Malays, while the Chinese and Indians mostly came to Malaya on their on initiative or were brought by the British during the latter's occupation of Malaya. The British should have encouraged the Chinese and the Indians to adjust themselves with the ethnic Malays at the time, but given the colonial power's agenda to divide and rule the country, they did not encourage the assimilation process. Hence, after the gaining of independence from Britain in 1957, the government took steps to implement the assimilation process of the Chinese and Indians into native Malay society. Education is the main medium in order to ensure the success of the assimilation process. This resulted in all three ethnic groups together forming a political group. The Alliance Party, which was successful in Malaya's first election, was the coming together of leaders from the ethnic Malay, Chinese, and Indian communities. The drive for independence was a joint effort between the three ethnic groups as well. After the gaining of independence, the three ethnicities governed Malaysia and the efforts of the Chinese and Indians in assimilating with the ethnic Malays were also significant. The use of Malay as the official language served as the backbone in fostering the three ethnic groups as one Malaysian race. Via the Malay language as a medium of communication, the three ethnic groups began to be incorporated into every aspect of life. In 1963, the entry of Sabah and Sarawak into Malaysia saw the number of ethnic groups increase to approximately two hundred.

The assimilation process was further encouraged to the extent that all the leaders of the various ethnicities often reminded the people of the need to move together as one. Thus, the concept of "One Malaysia" was advanced by the current Prime Minister of Malaysia. This can be seen as the culmination of the assimilation process that occurred in the 21st Century which sees to it that national integration and unity among the various ethnicities was reflected via the celebration of religious festivals, cultures, and way of life as one nation race – Malaysians. The assimilation process is probably the only way to be able to bridge the gaps and barriers that separate the various ethnic groups in Malaysia. It is therefore necessary to conduct a study in order to see whether, after 55 years of independence, the assimilation process has been successful in building a generation of students that epitomises the spirit of a united Malaysian society.

This study was undertaken in order to determine the existence or extent of racism in the form of behaviour among the school adolescents. Questions that inform this study include: (1) What is the level of racism found among school-attending adolescents? (2) What are the factors that cause the outbreak of racism among school-attending adolescents?

Research Objectives

The research objectives of this work are: (1) Identify the level of racism in the behaviours of the school adolescents; (2) Identify the factors fostering racism in school-attending adolescents' behaviours.

Research Location

This research was conducted in schools across Negeri Sembilan. The choice of Negeri Sembilan was due to its social demography and economics. It is clearly rapidly developing its industry-based urban and rural areas. It is also situated between two developed states, namely, Selangor and Melaka. Negeri Sembilan covers 6643 square kilometers with a population of nearly one million people ranging from the three main ethnicities, Malay, Chinese, and Indians. Thuis, Negeri Sembilam reflects Malaysia's demographic reality, which is composed of 53% Malays, 30% Chinese, and the other 17% is constituted by Indians and other minorities.

Negeri Sembilan has a total of 86 secondary schools which are located in urban, suburban and rural areas. Most of the rural schools are dominated by Malay students, while the urban and suburban schools feature a diverse group of ethnicities. The sample consisted of 15 schools. The choice of schools is based on the location and the number of students in terms of representing a diverse ethnic group. Participating schools are divided into three categories, namely 5 schools with a majority of Malay students, 3 schools with a majority of Chinese students, and the remaining 7 are schools with a diverse yet balanced number of an ethnic student population of Malay, Chinese and Indian. The three schools that possess a majority of Chinese students are Sekolah Kebangsaan Wa Chan, Sekolah Kebangsaan Chi Wen, and Sekolah Kebangsaan Chung Hua. These schools were once private schools but now are schools assimilated into the government school system. (All of this information was obtained from the Negeri Sembilan Education Department.) The samples chosen consist of high school students. A total of 600 samples were used, consisting of 250 Malays, 250 Chinese, and 100 Indians. The respondents range across Form 4 and Lower Form 6 students, since they are considered mature to be involved in the study. They are also not being involved in any important examinations. The sample was chosen randomly.

Findings

Hypothesis 1: There is no significant difference between the index of racist behaviours among school adolescents in urban and rural areas.

School location	N	Mean	Standard deviation	Standard error for mean
Rural	311	2.2270	1.28978	0.07314
Urban	339	1.9304	1.12439	0.06107

Table 1.1. Description of racist behaviour by school location

		Levene's variance equality test		Mean equality test				
		F	Significance	T	df	Significance (2-tailed)	Mean differential	Standard error for mean
Behaviour according to school	Same variance	16.258	0	3.132	648	0.002	0.29663	0.09472
	Different variance			3.113	617.611	0.002	0.29663	0.09528

Table 1.2. Analysis of differences in racist behaviours according to school location

Based on Table 1.1, it was found that the $p=0.00 < α=0.05$. Thus, hypothesis 1 can be rejected. There are significant differences between racial behaviours found in urban and rural areas. It may be concluded that racist behaviours among school adolescents in rural and urban areas are statistically significantly different.

Hypothesis 2: There is no significant difference between the index of racist behaviours among adolescent school boys and girls.

School location	N	Mean	Standard deviation	Standard mean error
Boys	240	2.53	1.31338	0.08478
Girls	410	1.8044	1.06662	0.05268

Table 2.1. Descriptive of racist behaviours by gender

		Levene's variance equality test		Mean equality test				
		F	Significance	t	df	Significance (2-tailed)	Mean differential	Standard error for mean
Behaviour by gander	Same variance	28.530	0.000	7.672	648	0.000	0.72561	28.530
	Different variance			7.270	422.378	0.000	0.72561	

Table 2.2. Analysis on differences of racial behaviours according to gender

Based on Table 2.2, it was found that the p-value =0.00 < α=0.05. Thus, hypothesis 2 is rejected. There are significant differences in racial behaviours for school boys and girls. It may be concluded that the racist behaviour among school adolescents for boys and girls are statistically significantly different. Hypothesis 3: There is no significant correlation between the racial index behaviour among urban and rural school adolescents.

		School location	Behavioural mean
School location	Pearson correlation	1	-.122**
	Significance (2-tailed)		0.002
	N	650	650
Behavioural min	Pearson correlation	-0.122**	1
	Significance (2-tailed)	0.002	
	N	650	650

Table 3. Correlation between racial behaviour and location of school

** Correlation means at the level of 0.01 (2-tailed).

Based on Table 3, r = -0.122 is significant at α = 0.01 level. This means that hypothesis 3 is rejected because there was a significant relationship between the mean of racial behaviour and the school location. This goes to show that there is a relationship between racial behaviour mean and that of the school location. The correlation coefficient value of r=-0.122 means that there is a very weak negative relationship between racist behaviour and school location. This shows that even though there is a significant difference between the school location and the racial behaviour's mean, the relationship between the schools' locations does exist and that both indicate that they do not entirely agree with the racist behaviours found in schools.

Hypothesis 4: There is no significant correlation between the index of racist behaviour among adolescent school boys and girls.

	Correlation	
	Gender	Mean of behaviour
Pearson correlation	1	-.289**
Significance (2-tailed)		0
N	650	650
Pearson correlation	-.289**	1
Significance (2-tailed)	0	
N	650	650

Table 4. Correlation between racial discrimination and gender

** Correlation means at the level 0.01 (2-tailed).

Based on Table 4, r=-0.289 is significant at the level of α=0.01. This means that hypothesis 4 is rejected because there was a significant relationship between racial discrimination and that of gender. This goes to indicate that there exists a relationship between the mean of racial discrimination and gender. The value of the correlation coefficient r = -0.289 means that there is a weak negative correlation between racial discrimination and gender. This goes to show that although there are significant differences between gender and the racial discrimination index, the relationship in terms of school boys' and girls' opinions on racial discrimination strongly contradicts with the occurrence of racial discrimination among teenagers in schools.

Discussion

The findings of the research show that the level of racial discrimination among high school students is quite low. However, this research found that racial discrimination occurs at a higher rate in rural schools compared to schools in the urban areas. This is associated with the level of parental education whereby highly educated parents can be considered to be more open-minded and often encourage their children to mix more freely with other ethnicities. This is most likely normal since the parents interacted openly with other ethnic groups some time ago. This contrasts with parents from rural areas, as they do not possess a high level of education, which most likely limited their interactions with other ethnicities. This affects the way they educate their offspring. While we acknowledge that the education system creates the opportunity to change the mindsets of the students, the fact remains that students spend a significant proportion of their time at home with their families.

The research findings also indicate that there are differences of perspective when it comes to racial discrimination among adolescent school boys and girls. This is more so due to male students preferring to show their level of aggression compared to their female counterparts. This causes a lot of the former to experience behavioural problems compared with female students (Khalim 2004). However, the results show that problems of racial discrimination among both sexes as a whole is still low and can be deemed insignificant. The results state that racial discrimination among students in schools as being at a low level. This proves that the education system in Malaysia has been successful in creating unity amid students of various ethnic groups. Post-independence, the government had taken steps to build more schools and to further gradually strengthen the facilities in schools, since only via a comprehensive education will the nation be able to experience progress. In addition to that, the application of moral values in line with the National Education Philosophy (NEP) helped achieve the aim of unity through education. This can also create a sense of tolerance across the younger generation, thus enabling students to be considerate in their future actions. The introduction of a syllabus designed for specific subjects such as Moral and Civil Education by the Ministry of Education, for the purpose of providing basic knowledge on religious matters and cultural diversity of the various ethnic groups in Malaysia, can only have helped lessen racial prejudices and suspicion towards other ethnicities. This also contributed in achieving national unity by way of education.

As mentioned earlier, after gaining independence, the Malaysian government sought to mix the population, since British colonisation implemented a divide-and-rule policy. This had caused the main ethnicities of Malaya at the time to live in segregated ways according to their economic activities: ethnic Malays lived in rural and coastal areas, working as farmers and fishermen; ethnic Chinese lived around the mines and the cities as miners and traders; ethnic Indians lived on rubber plantations, working as farm labourers. These segregations did little for inter-ethnic socialising and, as such, made it difficult to achieve unity among the various ethnic groups. After independence, however, amidst difficult conditions, concerted efforts were made as the government strove to eliminate the ethnic-based economic system and settlements. The government initiated various measures to encourage the Malays to migrate to urban areas so as to achieve a sense of balance between the ethnic groups. The effects can still be seen today, as the style of living in clusters can be seen in rural areas compared to the cities. The latter limits inter-ethnic integration to occur in a more open manner.

The introduction of the New Economic Policy (DEB) in 1981 was aimed at countering the economic imbalance among ethnicities so that the gap could be narrowed, while, at the same time, eradicating poverty across society. This would also help in lessening the feelings of jealousy and distrust that could trigger potentially deadly inter-ethnic conflicts. The DEB failed to achieve its aims as a whole, but, at the very least, it helped create awareness of the need for tolerance, while also garnering a respect for the Constitution of Malaysia as the nation's supreme law. Today, another effort to maintain national harmony is being made in the shape of the New Malaysia Economic Model so that all ethnic groups will benefit from the government's efforts. All this can be clearly understood if the Malaysia education system achieves its aim of providing all Malaysian citizens a fully comprehensive education.

From its very inception, the Malaysian national education system's serious paying of attention towards national unity has clearly helped in uniting Malaysia's various ethnic groups. The post-Independence education system had successfully created a tolerant relationship between the groups. Starting with the Razak Report of 1956, which stressed the use of the National Language as the medium of instruction in the national education system, a common ground was found for all the ethnic groups to move together as one. This helped in establishing a sense of tolerance by using the same language of communication understood by the majority. The national education system in Malaysia was continuously monitored, and changes were made depending on the necessity which resulted in a higher level of tolerance and understanding between the ethnic groups. Various programs were also implemented within the education system, such as the Pupil Integration for Unity Plan, whereby each sports club and societies' activities were directed to involve inter-ethnic integration. In this way, the students would mix with one another and became familiar and comfortable with other ethnic groups. The same can be said of the *Rukunegara*: when it was introduced, the students had to appreciate the essence of the *Rukunegara* so that a national identity is developed within the student body, thus producing students with a love for the nation, irrespective of creed or religion. In addition to that, when the Ministry of Education ruled that all students undergoing the Malaysian Certificate of Education (commonly known as the *Sijil Pelajaran Malaysia*) were required to pass the Malay language subject as a prerequisite for certification and employment in the public sector, the students' focus towards the subject heightened dramatically. This helped all students – irrespective of ethnicity – to start mastering the Malay language as the main medium of communication. This helped narrow the communication gap between students from various ethnic groups.

Conclusion

This study shows that a strong education system is able to curb negative incidents such as racial prejudice and help avoid inter-ethnic conflicts while creating peace and a sense of love towards a country – even in a diverse country such as Malaysia. Although Malaysia gained independence 55 years ago, it is still considered a relatively new independent nation, so the success in building a harmonious country is commendable. The success of the assimilation process was effectively implemented via various closely-monitored programs. Nonetheless, more hard work needs to be maintained and advanced so that inter-ethnic programs focusing on national solidarity can consistently be implemented for the sake of political, social, and economical stability in the long run.

References

Askandar, K. 2007. *Ethnic Harmony and Unity*. Pulau Pinang: Universiti Sains Malaysia.
Azra. 2005. *Implementation of One National Type Schools Fosters Unity*. Perak: Kerian Education Community Portal.
Baker, T. L. 1994. *Doing Social Research*. Second ed. New York: McGraw-Hill Inc.
Blake, J. A., & Champion, D. J. 1976. *Method and Issues in Social Research*. New York: John Wiley & Sons.
Brown, S. K., & Bean, F. D. 2006. 'Assimilation Models, Old and New: Explaining a Long-Term Process'. http://www.migrationinformation.org/feature/display.cfm?id=442 (accessed 7 September 2009).
Connoly, P., & Keenan, M. 2002. 'Racist Harassment in the White Hinterlands: Minority Ethnic Children and Parents' Experiences of Schooling in Northern Ireland'. *British Journal of Sociology of Education* 23(3): 341–355.
Ghafar, M. N. A. 2003. *Questionnaire Design on Educational Surveys*. Skudai: Penerbit Universiti Teknologi Malaysia.
Konting, M. M. 2000. *Methods of the Education Research*. Kuala Lumpur: Dewan Bahasa dan Pustaka.
Polit, D. F., Beck, C. T., & Hungler, B. P. 2001. *Essentials of Nursing Research: Methods, Appraisal and Utilization*. Fifth ed. Philadelphia: Lippincott Williams & Wilkins.

Rokeach, M., & Mezei, L. 1966. 'Race and Shared Beliefs as Factors in Social Choice'. *Science* 151: 167–172.

Skager, R. E., & Weinberd, D. 1979. *Research Methods in Education: A Practical Guide.* New Jersey: Englewood Cliffs.

Tamam, E., Idris, F., Tien, W. Y. M., Hamzah, A., & Hamzah, R. 2006. 'News Media Socialization And Ethnic Tolerance Among Youth In Malaysia'. Paper presented at the 15th AMIC Annual Conference organized by The Asian Media Information And Communication Center, 17–20 July. Penang, Malaysia.

Ting, C. P. 1987. *Ethnic and Racial Relations: A Commentary.* Kuala Lumpur: Pustaka Dimensi.

Tuckmen, B. W. 1978. *Conducting Educational Research.* Third ed. New York: Harcourt Brace Jovanovich.

Chapter 8

Investigating a Win-Win Situation

Delivering Quality Swimming Experiences for Children in Local Primary Schools within the Gippsland Region, via Teacher Education

Timothy Lynch

Abstract

The purpose of this chapter is to reflect on the "commitment to action" designed by ministers of education, which act as stepping stones during implementation of the Melbourne Declaration on Educational Goals for Young Australians. The reflection conceptualises what these goals look like in practice within the Health and Physical Education (HPE) key learning area. "Swimming and water safety" for both pre-service teachers and children in Primary schools was implemented, which in hindsight provided a win-win situation. Furthermore, a framework enabling sustainable swimming education within the Gippsland rural community was developed.

There were barriers to be overcome and amendments identified for possible future improvements; however, the project is strongly supported by the Department of Education and Early Childhood Development (DEECD) Discussion Paper "A Tertiary Education Plan for Gippsland, Victoria". The pathway involving collaboration of various stakeholders has begun, a process that can now be reflected upon, reassessed, amendments made and relationships strengthened for the sustainability of swimming and water safety within local rural primary schools in the Gippsland region.

Introduction

The Melbourne Declaration on Educational Goals for Young Australians was established by the Ministerial Council for Education, Early Childhood

Development and Youth Affairs (MCEEDYA) in December, 2008. Goals included: Goal 1 – Australian schooling promotes equity and excellence; Goal 2 – All young Australians become successful learners, confident and creative individuals, and active and informed citizens. These Goals for Young Australians have driven the present National Curriculum reform; they are supported by socio-critical pedagogy in education and underpinned by a socio-cultural perspective. According to Professor Robyn Ewing, an education academic from Sydney University, the goals are "about equity and social justice and improved learning outcomes for our most disadvantaged and isolated students" (2010: 127). Such an educational policy reads well, Ministers state collaborative intent and identify possible improvements within Australian education, but how do the goals make a difference for children in classrooms? That is, what does goal implementation look like in practice?

The ministers of education designed a commitment to action, which act as stepping stones in goal implementation, they include:

- Developing stronger partnerships;
- Supporting quality teaching and school leadership;
- Strengthening early childhood education;
- Enhancing middle years development;
- Supporting senior years of schooling and youth transitions;
- Promoting world-class curriculum and assessment;
- Improving educational outcomes for Indigenous youth and disadvantaged young Australians, especially those from low socioeconomic backgrounds;
- Strengthening accountability and transparency.

This chapter reflects on the "commitment to action" during implementation of the Melbourne Declaration on Educational Goals for Young Australians, in an effort to conceptualise what these goals may look like in practice within the Health and Physical Education key learning area. The tangible educational content implemented was "Swimming and water safety" for both education students at Tertiary level and for children in Primary schools, which in hindsight appeared to be advantageous for both stakeholders – a win-win situation. A framework enabling sustainable swimming education within the Gippsland rural community was developed. There were barriers to be overcome and amendments identified for possible future improvements; however, the project is strongly supported by the Department of Education and Early Childhood Development (DEECD) Discussion Paper "A Tertiary

Education Plan for Gippsland, Victoria" which was released in August later in the year (2011). The Discussion Paper was encouraging and offered value to such pathways, shedding light on the difficulties faced by many stakeholders in the process. This chapter comprises a narrative memoir by the author of his involvement at tertiary education to implement swimming and water safety lessons in local primary schools.

Swimming Education Subject Content

Within the Bachelor of Primary Education course at Monash University, education students choosing the Physical Education major stream or selecting EDF2611 "Experiencing Aquatic Environments" as an elective, are required to hold a current teacher of swimming and water safety qualification by unit completion. This is a requirement mandated by the Victorian Institute of Teaching (VIT) (VIT 2008) for teacher registration as a Primary school Physical Education teacher. It was decided that a pathway be created to achieve these national ideals and goals through the implementation of swimming and water safety education. The unit at the Gippsland campus previously required that students complete swimming and water safety accreditation during their own time and present evidence of the qualification. The unit workshop program (two hours per week) was carefully redesigned to create a pathway between the university unit objectives and Registered Training Organisations (RTOs) swimming and water safety course units of competency.

There were two suitable programs offered by providers, associated with courses and qualifications for teaching Swimming and water safety: (1) Australian Swimming Coaches and Teachers Association (ASCTA) Swim Australia Teacher; and (2) Austswim training of teachers of swimming and water safety. Swim Australia (Australian Swimming Coaches and Teachers Association) was:

> launched in 1997 by the Federal Minister for Sport and Recreation to assist develop the Learn to Swim program in Australia to its full potential. ASCTA is a not for profit, membership based organisation that strives to achieve the World's best swimming and water safety Teachers and highest performing swimming Coaches. (ASCTA 2011)

Swim Australia's aim is for all Australians learning to swim and gaining water safety knowledge through safe, enjoyable and quality swimming lessons.

ASCTA is an Australian Registered Training Organisation (RTO) offering 35 units of competency, delivered in all states and territories (Australian Government 2011). Swim Australia Teacher courses include:

- Swim Australia Teacher (SAT) directed at 4–12 years;
- Swim Australia Teacher of Babies and Toddlers (SAT B & T) directed at 0–4 years;
- Swim Australia Teacher of Competitive Swimming (SAT CS) directed at 7–12 years;
- Swim Australia Teacher Adolescents and Adults (SAT AA) directed at 14 and above;
- Swim Australia Teacher Learners with Disability (SAT LWD); and,
- Swim Australia Teacher Culturally and Linguistically Diverse (SAT CALD). (ASCTA 2011)

Austswim has a close philosophical and working relationship with Swim Australia, the Royal Life Saving Society Australia (RLSSA) and Surf Life Saving Australia (SLSA) (Austswim 2009). Austswim programs for teaching swimming and water safety can be aligned with the units of competency in the corresponding Swim Australia Teacher courses. Austswim is also an Australian Registered Training Organisation (RTO), offering 18 units of competency but are not delivered within every Australian State and Territory (Australian Government 2011). Austswim courses include:

- Austswim Teacher of Swimming and water safety;
- Austswim Teacher of Infant and Preschool Aquatics;
- Austswim Teacher of Aquatics for People with a Disability;
- Austswim Teacher Towards Competitive Strokes; and,
- Austswim Teacher of Adults.

The third provider contacted was the RLSSA which is known in the state of Victoria as Lifesaving Victoria. Courses in relation to swimming and water safety provided by Lifesaving Victoria include: Keep Watch, Swim and Survive, Bronze Medallion, Junior Lifeguard Club, and Grey Medallion.

Correspondence with providers was initiated and it was anticipated that they would share similar swimming and water safety educational aspirations with that of Monash Gippsland. The response from ASCTA and RLSSA was very optimistic and built the foundations for strong partnerships. It was evident that ASCTA and RLSSA clearly valued the opportunity to promote swimming and water safety, especially within the demographics of Gippsland. Staff were personable and understanding in their dealings with the author, moved hastily to recognise the author's recognised prior learning (RPL) and to have the courses fully prepared so that success for all stakeholders was optimised. Both organisations were flexible in their disposition and offered large discounts in courses so that they were affordable for the university students. It was axiomatic that both providers aimed to promote swimming and water safety to its full potential and in a professional manner. Prioritising "education" was a commonality of both RTOs which appeared to enable strong collaboration with Monash University's Faculty of Education.

The factors taken into consideration when choosing a swimming and water safety course included quality (safety, insurance, and registered accreditation), cost, and collaborative potential. While both SAT and Austswim courses are nationally registered, when the two options are juxtaposed and compared (Table 1), light is shed on the course advantages of ASCTA, which includes: international recognition; International Federation of Swim Teachers Association (IFTSTA), less than half the cost, and is valid for a longer period of time.

Registered Training Organisation (RTO)	Austswim	ASCTA (Australian Swimming Coaches and Teachers Association)
Course	Austswim Teacher of Swimming and water safety	Swim Australia Teacher (SAT)
Minimal cost required by provider	$215	$100
Cost for university students	$215	$100
Amount of time valid	3 years	4 years
National recognition	RTO 104975	RTO20948
International recognition	–	International Federation of Swim Teachers Association (IFTSTA)
Units of competency	SRC AQU 003B SRC AQU 008B SRC AQU 009B SRC AQU 0010B SRC AQU 0011B SRC AQU 013B SRC CRO 007B	SRC AQU 003B SRC AQU 008B SRC AQU 009B SRC AQU 0010B SRC AQU 0011B SRC AQU 013B SRC CRO 007B

Table 1. Comparison between providers
(Australian Government 2011)

Pathways created enabled the opportunity for the university students to obtain qualifications in Australian Swimming Coaches and Teachers Association (ASCTA) – Swim Australia Teacher (SAT), Royal Life Saving

Society Australia (RLSSA) Bronze Medallion (BM), and RLSSA Resuscitation (RE) courses. By becoming an endorsed service member with Lifesaving Victoria, the author was qualified to endorse the BM, RE, and Bronze Rescue (BR). The students were required to have current resuscitation accreditation to obtain a Swim Australia Teacher qualification, so this enabled a pathway within a pathway.

Meeting the Educational Goals for Young Australians' Commitment to Action

1. Developing Stronger Partnerships

The attempt to create what could be described as a logical pathway led to a process of events that although initially on the surface seemed quite simple, involved a complex process of social relationships. Creating pathways between RTOs, namely, ASCTA and RLSSA, was necessary to enable the implementation of swimming and water safety lessons for the primary school children, but was only one of three equally important collaborations required. The other collaborations were with the local health industry (local leisure and sports centre), which included establishing a working relationship with external swimming instructors employed at the venue, and collaboration with local primary schools. Relationships between Monash University and all stakeholders played a major role in enabling fruition of the pathways.

Contact was initially made through informal introductions with the centre leader at the local leisure and sports centre, followed by e-mail and phone calls, which culminated with a formal face-to-face meeting prior to the beginning of Semester 1 at the local leisure and sports centre. This meeting was productive as far as it ascertained each stakeholder's purpose of collaboration. The author was able to share his vision of involving local primary schools during the unit (at no cost) and the pathway he was creating, which was fully supported by the leader. Facilities, costs, equipment, insurance, access, and spaces were discussed and finalised (where applicable). The author was introduced to the swimming supervisor who also supported the pathways being created, although with caveat. It was collaboratively decided that the author would provide the dates and times for the primary schools' free lessons to be conducted by the university students. The swimming supervisor would then use the sports centre's contact with the schools, through upper school swimming lessons facilitated during the year, to organise the lessons for children where priority was to be given to year levels who would otherwise miss out on the opportunity. This collaboration reinforced a larger partnership established between Monash University, the local City Council, and the Australian Government, coinciding with the completion of the local leisure and sports centre redevelopment project which involved the swimming pool facility. Effective communication and effort was essential for this pathway to be created, which involved personal face-to-face relations within the local health industry.

2. Supporting Quality Teaching and School Leadership

Swimming and water safety for the local schools was being introduced to the children in the early year levels; hence, it involved a change in curriculum. For this change to be effectively implemented required teachers valuing their influence on children and believing the difference they can make in reducing drowning fatalities through swimming and water safety education. Thus, by teachers observing the university students conducting swimming lessons, it was anticipated that this could initiate teachers and education students to act collaboratively and cooperatively in promoting swimming and water safety. Data gathered in a recent study (Whipp, Hutton, Grove & Jackson 2011) found that teachers working collaboratively with external providers is associated with positive perceptions about the value of the physical activity, which enables teachers to develop confidence and is less stressful. Curriculum change and reform is a process that is associated with teacher stress, so this partnership was perceived as favourable.

As part of the swimming and water safety course, the university students provided quality lessons for the local primary school students in Years 2/3 and Years 3/4 (early to middle years) from the local public and Catholic schools respectively. It was envisaged that this collaboration of quality teaching would become an annual event.

3. Strengthening Early Childhood Education

The best time to prepare children for safe aquatic participation and provide the skills and knowledge needed to have a lifelong safe association with water is during childhood (Royal Life Saving Society Australia 2010). Hence, primary schools and, in particular, primary school teachers play a vital role in providing access to all children. This is supported by research which suggests that the best time for children to learn and refine their motor skills is the preschool and early primary school years (Branta, Haubenstricker & Seefeldt 1984; Commonwealth of Australia 1992; Espenschade & Eckert 1980), as these are also the most formative years to establish a healthy approach towards physical activity (Queensland Government 2003). This phase of child development has the advantage that it is aligned with the child's natural play structure and is likely to have fewer competing activities, therein allowing children more time to concentrate on developing their motor skills. The early detection of motor problems facilitates early intervention programs which can reduce many physical and related emotional problems (Arnheim & Sinclair 1979; Commonwealth of Australia 1992; Hardin & Garcia 1982; Haubensticker & Seefeldt 1974; Johnson & Rubinson 1983; Seefeldt 1975; Smoll 1974).

In Australia, children have traditionally received their swimming and water safety education during primary school. Within Australian education curriculum, swimming and water safety is closely aligned with the Health and Physical Education key learning area which consists of three strands: Health, Personal Development, and Physical Activities. It is axiomatic that the HPE key learning area be prioritised in today's education, as it is necessary for holistic lifelong health and well-being. This prioritisation is an issue greatly valued by governments responsible for costs involved with wellness of citizens, the influence of hypokinetic diseases, and the strong connection physical activity has with optimal health and quality of life (Corbin, Welk, Corbin & Welk 2011; Robbins, Powers & Burgess 2011; Mackenroth 2004; Howard 2004). However, the HPE learning area has had a history of barriers that have impeded quality delivery within all Australian primary schools, which Sloan suggests has also existed in schools internationally (2010). These issues still exist today (ACHPER 2011).

4. Enhancing Middle Years Development

Swimming and water safety can be used to enhance the middle years development but was not the purpose within this pathway.

5. Supporting Senior Years of Schooling and Youth Transitions

Senior years of schooling and youth transitions were not involved during this pathway.

6. Promoting World-Class Curriculum and Assessment

ASCTA is Australia's peak professional swimming body, and courses are recognised by the International Federation of Swim Teachers Association (IFTSTA), thus providing a world-class curriculum for all stakeholders. As part of the SAT swimming and water safety course, the university students provided low-ratio quality lessons: the most children for any student teacher was four and often it was as low as two. This provided world-class swimming and water safety curriculum and assessment lessons for the local primary school students (Years 2/3 and Years 3/4) over three weeks.

7. Improving Educational Outcomes for Indigenous Youth and Disadvantaged Young Australians, Especially Those from Low Socioeconomic Backgrounds

Monash University (Gippsland campus) is situated in Churchill, Latrobe Valley, located in central Gippsland, eastern Victoria. A large percentage of the Gippsland region is comprised of a socio-economically disadvantaged population (DEECD 2011). Via implementing "hands on" practical teaching and learning experiences for the university students, subsequently the workshops enabled the provision of quality lessons at no cost for local primary school children (from a disadvantaged socio-economic region), who otherwise would not have received swimming lessons. This was of particular benefit because even though a considerable amount of work has been attributed to educating the Australian public about swimming and water safety awareness in a commitment to reducing drowning fatalities, research suggests that rural and isolated schools find it most difficult to conduct aquatic activities (Peden, Franklin & Larsen 2009). Rural communities are defined by the National Centre for Vocational Education Research (NCVER) as "being not metropolitan; not major regional centres; not remote; and having a population within town boundaries of less than 10000" (Clayton, Blom, Bateman & Carden 2004: 6).

There were Austswim course negotiations prior to the arrival of the author (mid-January), involving the local leisure and sports centre's swimming supervisor and a Gippsland Austswim Presenter. This involved the university students completing the course externally to the university unit. Negotiations between the local leisure and sports centre's swimming supervisor, local Austswim Presenter and Monash University Faculty of Education administrative staff in late 2010 confirmed that there would be a minimum of 100 students, 30 students per course, and each student would be charged $280 rather than the recommended price of $365 (personal communication, 28 February 2011). Hence, both families with children in local primary schools and university students benefitted financially from the pathways created.

8. Strengthening Accountability and Transparency

By implementing "hands on" practical teaching and learning experiences for the university students, the workshops enabled the provision of quality transparent lessons in that they demonstrated the university students' course content and pedagogy knowledge to teachers, teacher assistants, and parents from the local schools. They were also conducted in a public swimming facility open for interested parties to witness. As mentioned earlier, teachers working collaboratively with external providers who are associated with positive perceptions about the value of the physical activity enables teachers to develop confidence and is less stressful. Hence, it can be argued that the same positive perceptions can be developed through the collaboration with the university students.

Transparency accentuated the importance of the education degree when implementing swimming and water safety. An example of good pedagogy was witnessed when a child in Year 2 did not want to participate in an aspect of the lesson. The education student was understanding and gently encouraged the child to have a rest before having another attempt when he felt comfortable. Later it was reinforced by the classroom teacher that the education student had managed the particular child very well and built a good rapport which was evidenced by the child's application. Robertson (2008: 19) suggests that even the next sequential qualification extending from the swimming instructor, the Certificate IV in Training and Assessment, "does not embed the opportunity to develop the suite of knowledge bases required for autonomous training in diverse and complex environments". Naturally, alignment of a tertiary education university degree with the industry course was not always flush, an argument that cannot be hidden nor ignored within the transparent environment.

It is envisaged that through identifying how the swimming pathway addresses the Ministers' of Education commitment to action, the education goals are illustrated in practice and the value of the pathway is accentuated.

Support from Department of Education and Early Childhood Development (DEECD)

The Discussion Paper "A Tertiary Education Plan for Gippsland, Victoria" was a pleasing reminder that the effort required in creating such pathways was necessary and imperative. Change is a by-product of the collaborative process involved in creating the swimming pathway within Gippsland's community. Change brought envisaged improvement for the university unit, subsequently benefitting the community (school children) and yet, within this context, change also brought competition within the health industry. Competition evolved between swimming and water safety course providers, Austswim and ASCTA. The ASCTA SAT course chosen and introduced by the author, who may have been perceived by local stakeholders as an "outsider", did appear to be somewhat of a threat to business for some people involved.

As collaboration involves a complex process of social relationships, it was important to maintain realistic expectations of what could be initially achieved. Furthermore, transformations often result in conflict, loss, and struggle which are fundamental to successful change (Fullan 1982). If the pathways were to succeed in developing "education for regional sustainability", it was vital that time and effort was afforded a period of transition. The issues of change, collaboration and barriers that impede such projects were acknowledged by the Department of Education and Early Childhood Development's (DEECD) Discussion Paper "A Tertiary Education Plan for Gippsland, Victoria". This was reassuring for the project and encouraging that impediments were to be expected; the paper recommended that such pathways were essential for sustainability of Gippsland's education. The discussion paper assisted during reflection and unit evaluation, reminding the author of the purpose of the pathway and the realisation that it was achieved.

Feedback from the primary schools and education students was very encouraging, and evidence that they found the pathways to be meaningful and valuable. The author was commended by the Chief Executive Officer (CEO) of Swim Australia (ASCTA) based on feedback the education student participants expressed in the SAT student evaluations summary (personal communication, 24 June 2011), which was reinforced in the university unit evaluation completed by the students, where the best aspects of the unit included:

> Learning how to teach swimming and the opportunity to teach kids how to swim in prac. All aspects that we learnt about related to teaching primary kids (which hasn't happened in the last 2 yrs of PE). The Unit co-ordinator's explanations and teaching was fantastic with the use of his prior experiences etc. and also his hard work to help us reach success in all tasks. (Personal communication, 2 September 2011)

The children from the local primary schools were excited to be taught by the education students during each of the three weeks. Parents came to support their children, and comments from teachers, teaching assistants, parents, and the children expressed their gratitude for the lessons provided. One teacher wrote:

> My kids had a ball with the swimming. They were disappointed that it was only for the extra two weeks (one week was a holiday for this school). Like I said to you then, any time you need children feel free to approach us. We are very willing to assist. (Personal communication, 23 July 2011)

Positive experiences for children and their families promotes swimming and water safety, and builds aquatic confidence for the primary school children, university students, and primary school teachers. Implementation of swimming and water safety into the school curriculum enables children to become aware of water safety, subsequently decreasing drowning fatalities in the short and long term. Furthermore, it builds an optimistic image of Monash University within the community. The discussion paper "A Tertiary Education Plan for Gippsland, Victoria" (DEECD) listed raising aspirations and improved awareness as a targeted strategy, specifically "school engagement/outreach programs addressing the perception of tertiary education in the primary and secondary school environment" (2011: 21). This was raised as a priority as "low aspirations and attitudes towards education in Gippsland are a major concern" (2011: 22).

It was always going to be difficult for arrangements to suit all stakeholders all of the time. An ideological prioritisation of "education" appeared to enable strong collaboration between stakeholders but it was not going to guarantee a smooth flow in the implementation process. The strategy recommended for overcoming differences is "flexibility" (Kilpatrick & Bell 1999), "without such flexibility the diverse needs of stakeholders cannot possibly be met" (Clayton et al. 2004). Flexibility involves content, delivery modes, location, recognition of prior learning, existing qualifications, and skills.

Impediments were evident within the web of relationships and flexibility was essential. Confirmation of which schools, classes, numbers, and ability groups attending the swimming and water safety classes were late, which proved to be difficult for the author and education students. Another barrier that caused initial damage to the collaborative pathway, and, as such, the ASCTA reputation, which was difficult to rebuild within the community, was the misinformation provided to the primary school community about the lessons. The first time the author met with the classroom teacher and teaching assistants, he needed to reassure them about the safety of the lessons and defend the Swim Australia Teacher Swimming and water safety program. While it is understood that the training market is a competitive one (Clayton et al. 2004), such consequences of competition is not consistent with the Austswim-proclaimed close philosophical and working relationship with Swim Australia (Austswim 2009).

DEECD's discussion paper describes an option for the future as being "Institutional possibilities, focussed on the role of tertiary education providers in responding to local need through partnerships and flexible governance arrangements" (2011: 12). At times within this pathway, it did appear to involve the university tailoring to the needs of local industry, more so than the local industry adjusting to the requirements of university standards.

"Current pathways between schools, TAFE institutes and universities are unclear and inaccessible. A coordinated approach is needed to improve pathways between education providers" (DEECD 2011: 23). This imbalance and inaccessibility was exemplified by the demands placed on the author for meeting the swimming course presenter requirements. This was necessary to grant the university students with the swimming and water safety qualification. A requirement for the Presenter of Swimming and water safety for any provider involved completion of a Certificate IV in Training and Assessment (TAE40110) (personal communication, 2 February 2011).

While this is the requirement for anyone wishing to become a Swimming and water safety presenter, it did seem somewhat of a paradox that a university lecturer with a number of education degrees, 15 years full-time teaching experience in primary and secondary schools, two years full-time teaching experience at tertiary and current teacher registration, in the attempt to create pathways between tertiary and industry is then required to complete further study to demonstrate that he can meet the unit of competencies for a Certificate IV in Training and Assessment.

As advised by the Lifesaving Victoria General Manager for Education and Training, the "RPL document for your Cert IV is a long process and it is probably easier just to go and sit the course" (personal communication, 3 February 2011). This course was a barrier to creating a pathway opportunity within the Gippsland region. However, with many trips to Melbourne and extra work on behalf of the author and the RTO, Innovative Business Training (RTO Number 3875), the Certificate IV in Training and Assessment was obtained in time for the semester so that the pathway for the education students was possible.

Another barrier lies within Monash University – Gippsland, Bachelor of Primary Education degree, specifically within the PE major stream where the unit EDF2611 Experiencing Aquatic Environments is only offered biennially. Having this unit offered only once every two years is not ideal with renewal of the unit co-ordinator's swimming qualifications and maintaining working relationships with local industry and primary schools. As revealed during the semester, it was not possible to conduct the unit annually due to university policy processes and the time necessary for course and unit amendments. A course design where swimming is offered annually has been proposed for the future as part of the present Faculty of Education course renewal.

Furthermore, it can be argued that when using externally-provided programs implemented by external swim instructors, some teachers will not be utilised during the students' swimming and water safety lesson. This is not to suggest that schools do not use outside agents for swimming instruction or diminish the expertise that swimming instructors encompass; however, teacher involvement could be one possible strategy for educating all children and reinforcing knowledge, skills, and understanding. This may involve teachers being in the water if they are comfortable with this, or it may be involvement from the side of the pool, offering feedback, acknowledging children's efforts and improvements. It also involves external instructors and teachers collaboratively and cooperatively promoting swimming and water safety. Increasing teacher participation during lessons was identified as an area of focus for the future.

The Discussion Paper offered support to the author who instigated and drove the pathway. He used details and acknowledgement of social politics in an effort to maintain realistic expectations, and awareness that struggles and even opposition were necessary for swimming and water safety curriculum change. It is essential that teachers have both the knowledge and confidence to implement swimming and water safety into the curriculum. As stated by the Australian Water Safety Council (2008); swimming and aquatic activity in Australia are part of the social makeup of the country. Inspiration for the project was empowered by present and future teachers valuing and believing in the process and the vital role they assume.

Conclusion

This chapter illustrates the implementation of Educational Goals for Young Australians within Health and Physical Education in primary schools: "swimming and water safety" lessons. Via addressing the MCEEDYA "commitment to action" which supports achievement of the Goals, the importance of the collaborative pathway created is illuminated. A narrative memoir is written by the author of his involvement at tertiary education (Monash University) in Semester 1, 2011.

By using swimming and water safety as the curriculum content, stronger partnerships were developed supporting quality teaching and, in particular within this context, strengthened early childhood education. By initiating pathways with ASCTA and RLSSA, the University's primary education students promoted a world-class curriculum and assessment which they implemented in local primary schools, subsequently improving educational outcomes for disadvantaged young Australians, especially those from low socioeconomic backgrounds, and strengthened accountability and transparency for various stakeholders.

The DEECD's Discussion Paper "A Tertiary Education Plan for Gippsland, Victoria", released in August (2011), supported such initiatives and endorsed that they were essential for educational sustainability within this rural area. Collaborations assisted in achieving the Educational Goals for Young Australians cited at the beginning of this paper (i.e., Australian schooling promotes equity and excellence; all young Australians become successful learners, confident and creative individuals, and active and informed citizens).

A conscious effort has been made by the author to be fair in the presentation of events and data gathered. The purpose is not to be conceited in reflection, but rather to delve below the surface of policy implementation to offer insight into the complexity and difficulties involved in such processes, and to illustrate their actualisation in practice. The pathway involving collaboration of various stakeholders has begun, a process that can now be reflected upon, reassessed, amendments made and relationships strengthened for the sustainability of swimming and water safety within local rural primary schools in the Gippsland region.

References

Arnheim, D. D., & Sinclair, W. A. 1979. *The Clumsy Child*. Second ed. London: C. V. Mosby.

Austswim Australian Council for the Teaching of Swimming and Water Safety. 2009. *Teaching Swimming and Water Safety the Australian Way*. Second ed. Sydney: Mosby.

Australian Council for Health, Physical Education and Recreation (ACHPER). 2011. 'ACHPER Supports AFL Statement on Need to Strengthen PE and Sport in Primary Schools'. http://www.achper.org.au/__files/f/27583/ACHPER%20Media%20Release%2027%2005%2011.pdf (accessed 2 December 2011).

Australian Government. 2011. 'Training.gov.au A Joint Initiative of Australian State and Territory Governments'. http://training.gov.au/Organisation/Details/ (accessed 2 December 2011).

Australian Swimming Coaches & Teachers Association. 2011. *Could This Be You? Swim Australia Swim for Life*. Brochure. Beerwah: Author.

Australian Water Safety Council. 2008. *A Guide to Water Safety Essentials for Local Governments*. Sydney: Australian Water Safety Council.

Branta, C., Haubenstricker, J., & Seefeldt, V. 1984. 'Age Changes in Motor Skills During Childhood and Adolescence'. *Exercise & Sport Sciences Reviews* 12: 467–520.

Clayton, B., Blom, K., Bateman, A., & Carden, P. 2004. *What Works Where You Are? The Implementation of Training Packages in Rural Australia*. Canberra: National Centre for Vocational Education Research.

Commonwealth of Australia. 1992. *Physical and Sport Education: A Report by the Senate Standing Committee on Environment, Recreation and the Arts*. Canberra: Senate Printing Unit.

Corbin, C. B., Welk, G. J., Corbin, W. R., & Welk, K. A. 2011. *Concepts of Fitness and Wellness*. Ninth ed. New York: McGraw Hill.

Department of Education and Early Childhood Development. 2011. *A Tertiary Education Plan for Gippsland, Victoria*. East Melbourne: Skills Victoria.

Espenschade, A. S., & Eckert, H. M. 1980. *Motor Development*. Second ed. Sydney: Merrill.
Ewing, R. 2010. *Curriculum and Assessment: A Narrative Approach*. South Melbourne: Oxford University Press.
Fullan, M. 1982. *The Meaning of Educational Change*. New York: Teachers College Press.
Hardin, D. H., & Garcia, M. J. 1982. 'Diagnostic Performance Tests for Elementary Children (Grades 1–4)'. *Journal of Physical Education, Recreation and Dance* 53(2): 48–49.
Haubenstricker, J. L., & Seefeldt, V. 1974. 'Sequential Progression in Fundamental Motor Skills of Children with Learning Disabilities'. Paper presented at the International Conference of the Association for Children with Learning Disabilities, March. Houston, Texas.
Howard, J. 2004. 'Building a Healthy, Active Australia. Transcript of the Launch by Prime Minister, John Howard'. Launceston, Tasmania. www.pm.gov.au/news/speeches/speech961.html (accessed 7 January 2005).
Johnson, R., & Rubinson, R. 1983. 'Physical Functioning Levels of Learning Disabled and Normal Children'. *American Corrective Therapy Journal* 37: 56–59.
Kilpatrick, S., & Bell, R. 1999. *Sharing the Driving Seat: Tackling the Hard Issues*. Launceston: Centre for Research and Learning in Regional Australia, University of Tasmania.
Mackenroth, T. 2004, June 11. *Public Letter from the Deputy Premier, Treasurer and Minister for Sport*. Brisbane: Queensland Government Printer.
Ministerial Council on Education, Employment, Training and Youth Affairs. 2008. 'Melbourne Declaration on Education Goals for Young Australians'. http://www.curriculum.edu.au/verve/_resources/National_Declaration_on_the_Educational_Goals_for_Young_Australians.pdf (accessed 2 December 2011).
Peden, A., Franklin, R., & Larsen, P. 2009. 'Survey of Primary Schools Across Australia: An Examination of Key Water Safety Issues'. *International Journal of Aquatic Research and Education* 2009 3(2): 197–208.
Queensland Government. 2003. *Get Active Queensland, Early Childhood Resources*. Brisbane: Queensland Government Printer.
Robbins, G, Powers, D., & Burgess, S. 2011. *A Wellness Way of Life*. Ninth ed. New York: McGraw Hill.
Robertson, I. 2008. 'VET teachers' Knowledge and Expertise (Vocational Education and Training) (Report)'. *International Journal of Training Research* 6(1): 1–22.
Royal Life Saving Society Australia (RLSSA). 2010. *The National Drowning Report 2010*. Canberra: RLSSA.
Seefeldt, V. 1975, March. *Critical Learning Periods and Programs of Early Intervention*. Paper presented at the AAPHER Convention, March. Atlantic City, New Jersey.
Sloan, S. 2010. 'The Continuing Development of Primary Sector Physical Education: Working Together to Raise Quality of Provision'. *European Physical Education Review* 16(3): 267–281.
Smoll, F. L. 1974. 'Motor Impairment and Social Development'. *American Corrective Therapy Journal* 28: 4–7.
Victorian Institute of Teaching. 2008. 'Victorian Institute of Teaching Specialist Area Guidelines'. http://www.vit.vic.edu.au/SiteCollectionDocuments/PDF/1672_Specialist-Area-Guidelines-Nov08.pdf (accessed 3 December 2011).
Whipp, P., Hutton, H., Grove, R., & Jackson, B. 2011. 'Outsourcing Physical Education in Primary Schools: Evaluating the Impact of Externally Provided Programmes on Generalist Teachers'. *Asia-Pacific Journal of Health, Sport and Physical Education* 2(2): 67–77.

Chapter 9

Education, Teaching Entrepreneurship and Indigenous Peoples

Dennis Foley

Abstract

This chapter questions the effectiveness of mainstream education programs when we look at the outcomes of empirical research by the author on some 660 Australian Aboriginal enterprise case studies and over 150 Hawaiian and Aotearoa case studies which revealed that education, be it in tertiary or workplace – industry training is a key factor in developing the human and social capital of successful Indigenous businesspeople. Yet formal education as we know it … as we teach it in Australia has failed, and is failing Indigenous children, as revealed to us by the plethora of research in this area. The present polemic debate therefore questions the need for alternative – effective – entrepreneurship education for Indigenous peoples. A global search by the author revealed an education system born from the slums of New York and Chicago with outstanding success in assisting minorities to achieve capacity building and worthwhile skills. Following further field investigation, when modified and applied to Irish youth from low socio-economic backgrounds, including Irish Travellers (Ireland's Indigenous minority), resulted in outstanding success. Additional field investigations in Aotearoa revealed that the same program which has been indigenised, targeting Māori by Ahikaa Entrepreneurship New Zealand Trust to help Māori from gang – substance abuse and other Māori from low socio-economic backgrounds, the program achieved entrepreneurial activity and increased self-esteem levels unheard of previously. This paper examines the need for effective education, based on case study analysis of successful Indigenous entrepreneurs in several countries, highlighting a mainstream education system that is failing its Indigenous youth, and illustrating an alternative pedagogy and program that looks at the Indigenous in Aotearoa. If applied to other Indigenous populations (such as Australia), such a pedagogy and program could dramatically alter the lives of Aboriginal children in a positive manner – children who are currently at risk within our education system. Ahikaa (a Wellington-based Indigenous organisation) is training future active participants of New Zealand society; in Australia, we perpetuate Aboriginal social disease by "the Indigenous education twitocracy ... the Sir Lesley Pattersons ministering to our state education departments" (Pearson 2011: 35). In Australia, we need to stop making excuses based on "an Aboriginal social-order deficit" (Pearson 2011: 34) and think about developing the "self" in the Aboriginal individual.

Introduction

Moving on from Noel Pearson's (2011) attack on the failure of the Australian state education systems to educate and train Aboriginal Australians to a similar standard as that of the white, Anglo-European settler or dominant society, this paper investigates effective entrepreneurship training for Indigenous peoples in education programs that provide not only socio-cultural applicability but also a pedagogical process that meets the necessary criteria to attain "academic legitimacy" (Kuratko 2005: 579). This inquiry is the end product and culmination of some fifteen years of work across several academic disciplines. This includes business/management, sociology, anthropology, history, and education disciplines utilising an Indigenous epistemology that has allowed the author to gain an appreciation of the conditions that have empowered and thwarted Indigenous entrepreneurs in Australia, North America, New Zealand, the wider Pacific and Ireland. The investigation has involved not only mainstream institutional entrepreneurship programs and their applicability to the minority marketplace and related minority-focused financial literacy education programs, this on-going research has also recently viewed Indigenous-run community-based enterprise development projects.

The dilemma for educators is that mainstream education does not necessarily work for Indigenous people, for the mainstream education "system" – via its general academic practice, curriculum and teaching strategies – seeks to impose its way of perceiving and understanding the world on minority people by inserting them into pre-existing academic discourse and pre-existing social orders. In so doing, it demands conformity. This frequently leads to minority students asking themselves the question: to what degree will I engage in learning and at what personal cost (Mann 2001; Hockman

2010)? It also often gives rise to Indigenous people having to repress their own sense of self, culture, voice and educational desires, which effectively works to "de-Aboriginalise Aboriginal people" (Heitmeyer 1998: 198) Education scholars concerned with such issues of minority alienation, engagement and empowerment are increasingly aware that Indigenous students need more than this from an education "system". Hocking (2010) is an advocate of "blended learning" that selectively integrates into the mainstream system social and cognitive elements that are meaningful to minority students and of an inclusionary pedagogy that embraces a range of differences and enables minorities to draw on their own knowledge bases to demonstrate that they are learning. Shepherd supports (not in an Indigenous context), a "pedagogy that more broadly addresses emotion and the management of emotions" and, more specifically, that author is concerned with the emotions and creativity that need to be engaged within successful entrepreneurial activity (2004: 283). The importance of holistic engagement and management of emotion is taken up again in this paper when it examines the different barriers that Indigenous students of entrepreneurship must face. This is a significant issue given the degree to which the pedagogy that underpins entrepreneurship and enterprise education varies across institutions (Gibb 1996; Pittaway & Cope 2007). For reasons of simplification, this inquiry (like others before it) questions pedagogical application and conflates enterprise and entrepreneurship as one and the same (Pittaway & Cope 2007).

An enormous increase in the development of entrepreneurship education and related research trends have combined to finally lay to rest the myth that entrepreneurs are born and not made (Katz 2003; Kuratko 2005). Debate has evolved beyond whether entrepreneurship might be encouraged through education or taught as an academic discipline to what precisely should be taught and precisely how should it should be taught remain unanswered questions (Drucker 1985; Katz 2003; Kuratko 2005; Ronstadt 1987). Previous research has revealed that minority entrepreneurs have emerged in unprecedented numbers. This phenomenon may be linked to the mainstream development of entrepreneurship education (Kuratko 2005) however Indigenous entrepreneurs face many obstacles and difficulties that other entrepreneurs do not (Chananti & Greene 2002; Foley 2005; Fredericks & Foley 2006; Greene *et al.* 2003; Gundry & Welsh 2001; Kuratko 2005).

While it is increasingly recognised that minority entrepreneurs are confronted by different obstacles, it is less appreciated that conventional entrepreneurship education discourses and praxis are:

> discriminatory, gender-based, [Euro] ethnocentrically determined, ideologically controlled, sustaining not only prevailing societal biases, but serving as a tapestry for unexamined and contradictory assumptions and knowledge about the reality of [Indigenous] entrepreneurs. (Ogbor 2000: 605)

Ogbor (2000) argues that the structuring principle in wider society similarly reflects and consolidates the privilege and power of dominant groups. Entrepreneurship scholars such as Katz (2003), Kuratko (2005), and Shepherd (2004) most likely are not mindful of this injustice, for issues such as inequality are not discussed in their writings and they are immersed in the power structure of the dominant group within entrepreneurial literature. Furthermore, entrepreneurship discourse, in the main, further entrenches divisions between socio-cultural groups on the basis of race, ethnicity, and gender through processes including classification and codification that are more often than not the privilege of Western-educated white men at the forefront of American entrepreneurship discourse (Foley 2005; Ogbor 2000).

Matters pertaining to Indigenous entrepreneurial education cannot be found within this discourse. For this specialist field of academic inquiry, researchers need to look elsewhere; the supporting methodological statement allows the reader an insight into how far the author stretched the boundaries of research and enquiry.

Research Methodology

The research methodology of this and the author's related papers is informed by a range of academic disciplines and a systematic review of academic literature (Tranfield, Denver & Smart 2003; Pittaway *et al.* 2004). Firstly, the research into successful Indigenous entrepreneurs (Foley 2000, 2005, 2006, 2008a, 2008b, 2009, 2010a, 2010b) is based on multiple qualitative case studies within independent research projects across various national contexts, using a standard semi-structured interview format to ensure conformity and rigour (Yin 2002; Eisenhardt 1989). Based on empirical evidence, these inquiries adopted a thematic approach to research that was both focused and unified (Thorpe *et al.* 2006). The soundness of the methodology supporting the case study analysis ensured that rigour was not sacrificed by emic approaches which can stifle the interpretation of data by using only one dimension of evaluation (Pelto & Pelto 1978). The etic method of behavioural observation, identifying systems and patterns of behaviour through qualitative analysis based on the cultural generalisations of the observed (rather than the cultural standards of the observer) was applied (Pelto & Pelto 1978). From the Indigenous standpoint, the researcher elicited the terminology, the cultural domains and the societal values of the individual being examined, and realises that these qualifications may be different for each and every Indigenous group encountered. However, research with Indigenous participants that possesses an Indigenous standpoint and applies a methodological approach of holistic observation and interaction has the potential to be a true reflection of the Indigenous situation without bias (Nakata 1998; Rigney 1999). Due diligence was exercised, as the complex nature of identity can also create divisions between the researcher and researched, even when they are "racially matched" (Connolly 1998). Arguably, the need for an Indigenous approach to the recording of Indigenous knowledge that is flexible and accurate in its application was required, and has been accepted by peer examination and review (Foley 2000, 2005, 2006, 2008a, 2008b, 2009, 2010a, 2010b). Substantive coding (open coding and constant comparative coding; Glaser 1992; Glaser & Strauss 1965) was used throughout the research process in the analysis of the interview data. Attention was given to recognising data and relevant underlying patterns of incidents of data, fixing attention on obvious patterns or common incidents in data (open coding). Once a category was established, the data was examined to discover any emergent properties by constantly coding and analysing the data (constant comparative coding; Glaser 1992).

Due to the polemic framework of the debate on education throughout this essay, the "given" and the "needed" within the subject matter is treated through successive approaches and generally by using methods or viewpoints that are put to the author's test. The confrontation of different approaches is an essential characteristic of the genre (Lits 1994), and in considering the polemical essay as a methodological approach, we are brought back to the analysis carried out by Dominique Maingueneau in *Sémantique de la polémique* (1983). Polemic constitutes a means for reinforcing its own enclosure by exposing itself to an imagined, threatening "other", which is Ahikaa (and to a lesser extent, "The Young American Indian Entrepreneur Program" at Fond du Lac College, University of Minnesota). The polemical approach of this essay operates in a discursive niche of confrontation, openness, and redefinition which the author believes is necessary in delivering such a wide academic analysis into a political recommendation. The author has also engaged participatory action research (Wadsworth 1998) in his longitudinal study over several years of Ahikaa in its development, application and successes.

Organisational and/or Institutional Research

The overarching purpose of this research was initially to gain insights into how entrepreneurship education might be better delivered to Aboriginal Australia. It sought to identify alternatives to dead-end "training" programs that are autocratic and top-down (Smyth 2005), searching instead for empowering programs that have the potential to enable Aboriginal Australians to recognise their talents, acquire new skills, unlock their entrepreneurial creativity and reach their potential.

Several American entrepreneurial organisations claiming successful outcomes were analysed that included but are not limited to:

- CAMBA: a Brooklyn-based multi-service non-profit agency, offering free business training and counsel to the community;
- RUPRI: the Center for Rural Entrepreneurship which strives to be the focal point for entrepreneurship development in rural America, working closely with Home Town Competitiveness (HTC), a comprehensive approach to long-term rural community sustainability;
- Accion USA: a private non-profit organisation that provides credit and business training to micro entrepreneurs, low and moderate income self-employed women and men;
- The Edge Connection: a nationally recognised leader in microenterprise training and development, offering entrepreneurial training for low-to-moderate income individuals;
- The Corporation for Enterprise Development: expands economic opportunity for people of all ages and communities of all sizes. The council runs the REAL (Rural Entrepreneurship through Action Learning) Entrepreneurship Training Institutes, which provide curricula, training, and resources to help rural America grow through hands-on entrepreneurship education that prepares active, self-sufficient, and productive citizens to contribute to their communities' social and economic development;
- The Ewing Marion Kaufmann Foundation: funds and provides resources on entrepreneurship opportunities for youth. The foundation cultivates entrepreneurship on college campuses across the nation through its Collegiate Entrepreneurship Resource Centre, and nurtures entrepreneurial interest among

young people through its Youth Entrepreneurship Awareness Program;
- The Small Business Administration (USA): sponsors a Teen Business Link to provide business tips and resources for teens who want to start their own business, including financial and legal advice and networking opportunities;
- Youth Venture: an organisation investing in young people, ages 12 to 20, who create, launch, and lead sustainable, community-benefiting clubs, businesses, and organisations. They provide resources and information on creating an action plan, budgeting, and sustaining businesses, for youth interested in starting their own business.

Although these organisations/programs had shortcomings or were not suitable in the Australian context, there is a plethora of organisations that have sprung up, many copy-catting the established organisations yet to be discussed, however before finalising my conclusion of the key organisation, on 14 January 2012, I interviewed Jean Ness and Bryan Jon Maciewski at the United States Small Business and Enterprise Conference in New Orleans. Ms Ness and Mr Maciewski work in "The Young American Indian Entrepreneur" (YAIE) program at the University of Minnesota. This program shares many of the same qualities as the Network for Teaching Entrepreneurship (NFTE) and Ahikaa program that I will discuss in depth in this essay. The modules, the design, the pedagogy aimed at the development of the Indian individual in that Program is simple, outstanding in its potential application and history of implementation, relevant and accurate in the indigenisation of business skill development within the cultural application of Indigenous entrepreneurial training at a tribal and community college level, the Fond du Lac Tribal and Community College.

Recent research has demonstrated that using a particular pedagogical approach (or learning style) will only be successful when broader cultural issues are taken into account – something that Pearson refuses to accept in his blaming of a system and the teacher (Pearson 2011). When cultural issues are taken into account – including the responsiveness of the educational institution to the needs and aspirations of the Indigenous student and, at the same time, understanding their personal development shortcomings such as a lack of social and human capital linking this all to a reciprocation within community input (Brough & Bond 2009) – then you have a successful pedagogy (Chodkiewicz, Widin & Yasukawa 2008; Donovan 2007; Mander & Fieldhouse 2009; Watson *et al.* 2006).

The YAIE at the Fond du Lac Tribal and Community College model is designed to increase competency and skills in challenging subject matter that includes mathematics and science in a culturally relevant manner, providing preparation and essential skills needed for life, designed to also address the content standards for entrepreneurship education. The pedagogy applied has followed a history of researchers who indicate that using learning style preferences that include active experimentation, balanced with concrete experience and abstract conceptualisation can enhance entrepreneurial propensity (Gorman, Hanlon and King 1997). The use of behavioural simulation is also relevant in teaching entrepreneurship (Stumpf, Dunbar & Mullen 1991). McMullan and Long (1987) proposed that entrepreneurship education should also include skill-building components, such as negotiation, leadership and creative thinking, exposure to technological innovation, and new product development. Vesper and McMullan (1988) argued that entrepreneurship programs should also teach skills in detecting and exploiting business opportunities, as well as incorporate detailed and long-term business planning. Plaschka and Welsch (1990) introduced the concept of transition stages of entrepreneurship education, suggesting programs geared towards creativity, multi-disciplinary and process-oriented approaches, and theory-based practical applications, while Gibb (1993) proposed a model of enterprise education that was also appropriate to primary and secondary school curricula. Critical elements of the model were the incorporation of enterprise into the classroom environment, a project management task structure, and an enterprising teaching mode. The combination of these elements was expected to stimulate enterprising behaviour, skills, and attributes in students. The Young American Indian Entrepreneur Program also added cultural pedagogy to this long list, allowing the participant the opportunity to develop feelings of self-confidence, self-worth, self-management, teamwork, and problem solving (Consortium for Entrepreneurship 2004).

In 2008, the author began looking at the success of the New York-based program founded in 1987 by Steve Mariotti, the NFTE. My interest was based on recommendations and teaching awards from published literature, as well as the opportunity to interview the founder during a visit to the USA (Mariotti 2010). The NFTE shares many of the qualities of YAIE (the NFTE is the older of the two programs). NFTE, however, is distinctly aimed at minorities, while YAIE is geared towards American First

Nations. NFTE has been studied and adapted by independent educators in Ireland and New Zealand and around ten other countries internationally. The New Zealand based research led by Sir Ngatata Love also investigated the ways in which the Wellington-based Indigenous organisation, Ahikaa, could fuse NFTE programs with Māori values and pedagogical traditions to deliver programs to a minority population that mainstream training organisations within New Zealand largely overlooked on the basis of a range of differences, including age, gender, poverty, gang affiliation and incarceration records. These are demographics that the dominant settler society generally classifies as socially dysfunctional attributes.

Entrepreneurial activity and success in commercial enterprise is one important means via which some of the world's millions of repressed, alienated and impoverished Indigenous minority peoples might attain social acceptance and financial independence. Previous research by the author (Foley 2000, 2005, 2008a, 2008b, 2009, 2010a, 2010b) has shown that successful Indigenous owner-operators of commercial enterprises have a relatively high rate of secondary or trade education, yet little or no entrepreneurial training. This is changing for some Indigenous groups in some countries. It would appear that the key to successful entrepreneurship education for Indigenous minority populations is the combination of an empowering pedagogical approach, relevant content, and a culturally sensitive means of program delivery like the YAIE program.

A Climate of Economic Crisis, Pedagogical Hegemony, and Silenced Minority Agency

This chapter explores the emerging global focus on Indigenous entrepreneurial education within its fraught historical context. As recently as 2009, the United Nation's World Economic Forum recognised the need for more inclusive entrepreneurship education and the role this might play in solving major challenges such as poverty and human suffering. Its report argued that:

> Entrepreneurship has never been more important than it is today in this time of financial crisis. At the same time, society faces massive global challenges that extend well beyond the economy. Innovation and entrepreneurship provide a way forward for solving the global challenges of the 21st Century, building sustainable development, creating jobs, generating renewed economic growth and advancing human welfare ... Entrepreneurship education can be a societal change

agent; a great enabler in all sectors … all members of society need to be more entrepreneurial … The time to act is now. (World Economic Forum and Global Education Initiative 2009)

While different schools of thought on entrepreneurship education do exist throughout the world today, it is clear that western academic thought and pedagogies dominate most entrepreneurship education models. The greater majority emphasise the need for competitiveness, rely on abstract reasoning, and tie linear models of teaching and business planning to western models of teaching, learning and business. Almost without exception, Western institutions tout these models as the essential frameworks for successful entrepreneurship.

By contrast, the role of traditional Indigenous entrepreneurship in both pre-colonial and postcolonial economies and societies is most often ignored. Recent adaptations by Indigenous people to their traditional modes of entrepreneurship are also too frequently overlooked or poorly understood by most western academics, governments, and business leaders. One unfortunate result of this is the nominal support received by Indigenous minorities for their own economic activity and their own entrepreneurial initiatives. Indigenous entrepreneurship – like histories of Indigenous resistance to and Indigenous negotiations of colonial power before it (Stanner 1968) – is statistically "silenced" from reportage of the development of Australian and New Zealand economies. Research undertaken by the author in Canada, North America, Japan, the Pacific, and Ireland all supports the same conclusion: Indigenous entrepreneurs are under-represented in national economic statistics (Foley 2010b).

It is widely recognised that there is a desire among many of the world's 300–500 million Indigenous people to rebuild their communities and/or to provide for their family (University of Minnesota 2003; Peredo *et al.* 2004). Moreover, empirical research has demonstrated a development that is not so well-known: Indigenous people are increasingly undertaking trade-based and/or structured education, and this is linked to rising levels of Indigenous entrepreneurial success (Foley 2009). Recent empirical case studies tell us that the dominant intrinsic motivator for both Māori and Australian Aboriginal entrepreneurs is the need to provide for their nuclear family: to put food on the table and a roof over their heads (Foley 2006, 2008a, 2008b; Fredericks and Foley 2006). These findings challenge earlier research that argued that Indigenous entrepreneurship was primarily motivated towards meeting community and heritage obligations (Lindsay 2005). Australian anthropologist, Lorraine Gibson, provides insights into the dilemma that many Indigenous entrepreneurs experience when engaging in the dominant western economy. She observes:

> [The] sense of self, for most, is not determined by engagement in the capitalist division of labour; indeed, the greater the engagement in the capitalist economy, the more problematic and fraught a sense of self and a belonging can become. (Gibson 2010: 137)

The tension between this diminution of the "sense of self" and the need to maintain a strong sense of self through connection to Indigenous cultural values and practises in order to creatively engage in learning and entrepreneurship is rarely well=understood by non-Indigenous scholars and governments. The New Zealand-based Indigenous entrepreneurship educator, Ahikaa, adopts a holistic vision. It seeks to develop and empower the individual, the family *and* the community. Its philosophy affirms the writer's wider research findings, which identify the discovery and the unlocking of the potentiality of the Indigenous "sense of self" as the foundational building block of Indigenous entrepreneurial success (Foley 2000, 2005; Ahikaa 2011). And, indeed, is this not what the Young American Indian Entrepreneur program is also instigating?

A glance at some sobering 21st Century educational statistics in New Zealand enables the researcher to more fully appreciate the importance of findings that connect increased Indigenous education to increased levels of Indigenous entrepreneurial success. A mere 28% of Māori aged fifteen years and over have a post-school educational qualification, and 40% of New Zealand's Māori population have no formal educations qualifications which are significantly higher than 25% for New Zealand as a whole without formal qualifications (Statistics New Zealand 2006). When these crucial statistics are combined, it becomes clear that nearly two in five members of the Māori population fifteen years and older (40%) have no formal educational qualifications. While some segments of the Māori population undoubtedly have achieved solid economic development since the late 20th Century, very high levels of unskilled Māori workers cyclically give rise to high levels of unemployment, poverty, overcrowded housing, reduced life opportunities for children, and increased levels of all of the following indicators of human suffering: poor diet, cardiovascular disease, diabetes, obesity, drug and alcohol abuse, mental and physical trauma, crime and incarceration, domestic violence, and so on (New Zealand Ministry of Health 2010). Poor education arguably and inevitably leads to poverty. This feeds a pattern of descent into welfare dependence and a raft of accompanying negative social and economic outcomes (Cotterill, Rosandich & Rosandich 2009). This reality is in stark contrast to the mischievous "myth" of Māori "privilege" that is regularly propagated and circulated by popular media and some politicians, most notably in the wake of individual Treaty of Waitangi settlements. (Treaty of Waitangi claims and settlements have been cause for social tension in postcolonial New Zealand race relations and politics since 1975. Throughout the past three decades, New Zealand governments have provided formal legal and political opportunities for Māori to seek redress for breaches by the Crown of the guarantees established in the Treaty of Waitangi since 1840 through the Waitangi Tribunal. While it has helped put to rest a number of significant longstanding grievances, the process has been subject to many criticisms, ranging from the position that the redress is insufficient as compensation for Māori losses to the stance that there is no value in revisiting painful and contentious historical issues.)

Despite these attempts by government to redress injustices towards Māori and Māori disadvantage, Māori remain statistically the most under-educated, most highly unemployed, poorest, least healthy, most under-housed, most over-jailed and youngest-dying social group in New Zealand (Statistics New Zealand 2006). An education program that assists even a small percentage of this marginalised population to take on the role of an active and productive participant in society is at the very least "economically cost effective" (New Zealand Government 2009).

It is anticipated that the reader assumes that Indigenous people around the globe are also tarnished with this kind of statistic. Māori circumstances for this minority are the subject of the case study analysis to follow. It should be noted that entrepreneurship education for Indigenous people is a specialist field; the following discussion provides insights into this emerging area of academic interest.

The Teaching and Learning of Indigenous Entrepreneurship

The core or foundation of the author's research has been 660 qualitative case study examinations of successful Australian Aboriginal enterprises, together with 150 Hawaiian and Aotearoa case studies which revealed that education, be it tertiary or workplace – industry training is a key factor in developing the human and social capital of successful Indigenous business people. This important finding provides an invaluable insight into Indigenous entrepreneurship in Australia, Hawaii and Aoeteroa, we can begin to understand the impact of education as human capital, and more importantly, the connection of networking in the development of social capital and how this connects to the Indigenous entrepreneur's business activities. Indeed, some of the latest scholarship both reminds us that entrepreneurial activity is complex, at times chaotic and lacks any notion of linearity, and revisits the perennial question: given all these pedagogical challenges, "can we teach it?" (Neck & Greene 2011). This paper has already endorsed the argument that entrepreneurship can indeed be taught (Katz 2003; Kuratko 2005). The teaching of entrepreneurship to Indigenous peoples, however, involves accepting responsibility to not only facilitate the discovery of latent individual talents and the development and implementation of skills so that students may creatively engage with and excel in highly uncertain environments (Neck & Greene 2011). It must also adopt an inclusive pedagogy, establish a balanced understanding of cross-cultural dimensions of relevant issues (Mackinlay & Barnley 2010), and foster blended learning.

A heavy investment of intellectual capabilities has focused on identifying entrepreneurial "traits" so that these can be taught in the classroom, beginning with the economic work of McClelland (1965). Around that time, Collins and Moore (1964) identified one core trait of entrepreneurs as the need for independence. Stephens and Jarillo (1990) later identified the psychological characteristics of individual entrepreneurs, and Brockhaus and Hiorwitz (1986) contributed a set of personality attributes: the need for achievement, an internal locus of control, a propensity for high risk-taking, and a tolerance for ambiguity. As business schools grappled within MBA programs with the problem as to how to best teach such traits, researchers such as Milner (1996) codified the following personality patterns of entrepreneurs: the "personal advisor", the "empathetic super salesperson", the "real manager" and the "expert idea generator". The personality and psychological trait theory of entrepreneurs has since been expanded by researchers and educators. Despite extensive research, there remains no clear causal link between psychological traits research and entrepreneurial behaviour (Cooper, Dunkleberg & Woo 1988), thereby leaving open the question: are entrepreneurs born or made? There is little known evidence to suggest they are born. Rather, while some have traits, others obtain the necessary skills through a combination of education and skill acquisition (Mazzarol 2006). This paper works on the premise that entrepreneurs are not born; entrepreneurship skills are neither mysterious nor born of magic. Rather, entrepreneurship is an academic discipline that can be taught (Drucker

1985; Katz 2003; Kuratko 2005). This position then raises another question: how best might Indigenous entrepreneurship be taught and learned?

One particularly concerning aspect of entrepreneurial education content is that it was designed by and is still predominantly reflective of a white, male, bourgeois, Christian mentality. Like management education, it remains dominated by the masculine gender (Ely & Padavic 2007; Neck & Greene 2011). The pedagogical implications of entrepreneurial education until the late 1980s, was one of the potential entrepreneur having to fit into an "observe, describe and measure approach" that supported pre-existing "categorisations and correlations" (Christensen & Carlile 2009). With the growing realisation that entrepreneurship was indeed multidisciplinary, came the borrowing of analytical tools from other disciplines to further develop theory and interactive models. Theoretical refinements influenced teaching and research accordingly. The pursuit of academic rigour and legitimacy gave rise to preferred pedagogies, including case study analysis and business plan writing, which educational institutions widely deemed to be "safe" teaching methods. Entrepreneurial education thus became a linear process (Neck & Greene 2011). Pedagogical debate has centred on whether entrepreneurship education should advance in a predictive and linear process, or entail both the development of a toolkit of skills and techniques, and practiced experimentation that encourages creativity and innovation (Neck & Greene 2011). Neck and Greene observe that while entrepreneurship education is important, it remains constrained by outdated mainstream approaches. Together with other researchers, they argue that entrepreneurship education requires a new approach that is based on action and practice: a method that is people-dependent but not dependent on a given type of person. This philosophical approach must also incorporate a view of learning as a method and the method as being primary to specific content. They advocate that teachers need not teach a discipline but rather teach a method for the individual, to enable and empower "the self" to "navigate the discipline" (Neck & Greene 2011: 68).

Indigenous minorities with a low level of mainstream education and skill sets engage in the learning process in a discovery and exploration of "the self" – personal strengths, weaknesses, motivations and goals – and engagement with emotions and desires that are often neglected in "normal" educative processes (Savin-Badin 2000; hooks 1994). The Indigenous student demonstrates that the classroom need not be a restrictive, repressive and reductive experience that is predominantly shaped by their need to perform rituals and emotional responses that are valued by the dominant system of meaning and pedagogy (hooks 1994). After briefly reviewing recent developments in Australia and Britain, this paper outlines ways in which Neck and Greene's approach has been introduced into Indigenous entrepreneurship education by Ahikaa in New Zealand.

International Developments in Entrepreneurial Pedagogy: An Alternative for Indigenous Minorities

In Australia, the former national liberal government under the prime ministership of John Howard initiated a leadership/entrepreneurship training program known as the "Enterprise Learning for the 21st Century" project. This initiative was taken up by far too few schools: only forty-seven Australia wide (DEST 2007). One school that did have the foresight to implement this educational project during the 2004–2006 period was the Castlemaine Secondary School and adjoining Tertiary and Further Education (TAFE) College in rural Victoria. They accepted the Department of Education, Science and Training (DEST) funded project with very positive outcomes. When funding for the manager ceased, so too did the initiative. The Castlemaine program very likely became one of the more successful school "enterprises" due to the entrepreneurial drive and business expertise of the manager, which gave rise to numerous business ventures and industry consultations within the subject areas of Art, Mathematics, Science, Social Studies and English. For example, students established businesses such as: agricultural production, processing and retailing; book production and distribution; and advisory services to a local century-old iron foundry in business planning, modern methods and product diversification. Two Aboriginal students later proceeded from the DEST project to TAFE education. Had there been a more substantial level of Indigenous student participation, this case study would have been more informative (personal communication with Castlemaine Secondary School Staff 2006).

Enterprise gestation, the planting of the entrepreneurial seed and its propagation from within an educational setting, however, is not a novel concept. A decade or so earlier, the Judge Business School at the University of Cambridge in England implemented Social Enterprise teaching and research along similar lines. This produced positive work-based economic development in the Midlands District which targeted low socio-economic minority groups. It sought to empower minorities groups through training and instilling leadership qualities in individuals (Tracey, Phillips & Haugh 2005).

As previously mentioned, one outstanding organisation that seeks to motivate and empower troubled, economically-at-risk minority groups through teaching entrepreneurship – particularly youth living in difficult environments – is the New York-based Network for Teaching Entrepreneurship (NFTE). Founded by businessperson-turned-educator, Steve Mariotti, in 1987 (and who was awarded the 2010 USASBE Entrepreneurship Educator of the year), NFTE has since reached over 400,000 young people from low income communities, mostly from minority groups. Mariotti has expanded this non-profit educational operation across twenty-one American states and twelve countries, including New Zealand.

The Entrepreneurship New Zealand Trust delivers a set of NFTE-licensed educational programs that it modified to meet the special needs of local Indigenous people. It operates under the name of *Ahikaa*, which is a Māori word that means "keeping the home fires burning". This is a two-pronged reference: growing locally-based entrepreneurial spirit, skills and activity, and thus maintaining both Māori control of all things Māori, as well as Māori identity and well-being. Ahikaa programs primarily target Māori and other Indigenous Pacifica peoples with the aim of building self-confidence, self-motivation, visionary capabilities and entrepreneurial talents and abilities through education. It seeks to empower individuals, families and communities via providing youth with the necessary tools for fostering economic sustainability, enabling their full participation in local economies, and linking them to a broad range of networks and thus promoting the wider well-being of 'the self' and his/her family.

Ahikaa seeks to build upon the existing human capital of Māori youth, (who typically experience poor educational outcomes, akin to those experienced by Aboriginal Australian youth). The Ahikaa pedagogy often identifies unrecognised talents, skills and other resources within the person. It develops these and new skills to significantly increase the individual's social capital. Empirical research has shown that Indigenous human and social capital levels are frequently considerably less than those of members of mainstream settler society, which results in adverse environments for entrepreneurial interaction, including networking. This differential is often the product of not only colonial and postcolonial policies of forced social separation and segregation, forced de-Indigenisation and assimilation, and family disruption and dispersal through the forced removal and alienation of children. It is also the outcome of a series of draconian educational policies that in many cases continued until anti-discrimination legislation was introduced during the 1970s. Almost without exception, these policies gave rise to Indigenous minorities being trained only to a level suitable for unskilled manual labour (Foley 2008b, 2010a, 2010b). With the correct implementation and management, the Ahikaa program has enormous potential not only for Māori, but also for Indigenous Australians and other minority groups in Australia. This includes the growing refugee and asylum seeker population. The effectiveness of its successful delivery lies in the philosophy and pedagogy of the education program – and in the skilled educators who are purposefully trained in this innovative pedagogy.

After an extensive five-year international search for an appropriate educational program and pedagogy, leading Māori academic and educator, Professor Sir Ngatata Love, brought NFTE to New Zealand in 2005. After examining research conducted on the NFTE program outcomes by Harvard and Stanford Universities and Babson College, Love identified the NFTE program as highly credible and particularly suited to minority peoples. With generous public- and private-sector support during the initial stage – including that of Westpac Bank – Love formed an advisory team comprising academic, business and community (tribal/and pan-tribal) members, and commenced operations from Victoria University in Wellington. The team also established additional centres in collaboration with selected "grass-roots" organisations within target communities. From the outset, this advisory team and, later, a board of management, sought to establish educational pathways that embodied a fusion of NFTE entrepreneurship educational programs with the entrepreneurial traditions of Polynesia and the *tikanga* (socio-cultural values) of New Zealand Māori. The resulting vision of the Entrepreneurship New Zealand Trust is to provide people of all ages with the necessary skills to:

- first, recognise and capitalise on their strengths;
- second, utilise their existing resources most effectively;
- third, maximise their individual and group potentials; and,
- finally, develop and maintain their own businesses while maximising commercial opportunities.

Through its delivery of the NFTE-inspired Ahikaa programs, the Entrepreneurship New Zealand Trust is committed to both growing the skills of individuals, families and communities in financial literacy, and providing tools to enable them to actively participate in local, national and international economies. It works with and within its targeted communities and has built strong networks of Ahikaa graduates who regularly engage with each other, thereby continuing and sharing their learning while providing ongoing support to each other.

Until now, Ahikaa has directed most of its attention towards youth and families who are already disengaged from schools. These youth are the embodiment of current negative educational statistics that indicate that near to 50% of Māori leave the compulsory school system with no academic qualifications whatsoever. Working within community centres, *marae* (Māori meeting houses) and educational facilities in the poorest areas – often with third-generation gang families – Ahikaa has produced some impressive results. With a client group that has largely been "written off" by mainstream educators, research tells us that program graduates attain significant gains in self-confidence, self-motivation, and a clear sense of career direction. Furthermore, 60% of Ahikaa program graduates engage in further career-focused education within twelve months (Cocker & Love 2009).

In a similar vein to the former DEST-funded Enterprise Learning for the 21st Century project in Australia that sparked student enterprise initiatives from within the education system, Ahikaa is now targeting this study body. The Ahikaa curriculum has been aligned with the National Qualifications Framework in New Zealand, and Entrepreneurship New Zealand Trust is now partnering with mainstream educational organisations. Together, they are implementing school-based programs with the aim of lowering school attrition rates among Māori youth.

Based on the research undertaken by NFTE New York, young people in low-income neighbourhoods harbour similar desires to those of more advantaged young people. They, too, want a good education, to earn enough money to live well, and to make their family proud. Too few, however, have a clear pathway to get there. What is worse is that many feel that society expects them to fail. While 50% of minority youth in the United States drop out of High School, statistics are slightly higher in Australian and New Zealand at 54% (ABS 2008: 4; ABS 2004). It is noted that 81% of American students state they would not have dropped out if school programs were more relevant to their real life (NFTE 2007). During 2011, Mariotti (NFTE New York) published a list of twenty-four life skills that he believed every young person should know, and he argued that if these concepts are imparted in schools, this might help to reduce this negative attrition trend (Mariotti 2011). Ahikaa's school intervention program also seeks to reverse this trend. It aims to make high school more relevant to the preparation of minority (mainly but not exclusively Indigenous Māori) youth for their successful engagement in their local economy. While 20% of youth in the United States live in poverty, almost 60% percent – three times the American figure – of Aboriginal youth in Australia live in poverty (Hughes 2007). The statistics for New Zealand are similar for both Māori and wider Pacifica youth.

Ireland's Indigenous Minority: The Traveller or Pavee

Accomplished female entrepreneur, athlete and philanthropist Liavan Malin introduced the New York-based NFTE program to Ireland in 1987. NFTE Ireland is now running programs in Dublin, Limerick, Donegal and Belfast. It has plans to further expand its programs within Ireland in the near future (NFTE Ireland 2008) and has worked with Traveller groups – Ireland's Indigenous minority which is also less well-known as the Pavee – in West Belfast and elsewhere (Doherty 2011). Foroige took over Ireland's NFTE program in 2008. This National Youth Development Organisation engages over 50,000 youth annually. Like Ahikaa, Foroige is a community-based organisation. It has developed a unique and flexible pedagogy and is the leading youth organisation across both Northern and Southern Ireland. Research tells us that Foroige not only increases participants' business knowledge, but it also increases heightened education and career aspirations, and assists a significant number of young entrepreneurs to continue running their businesses (Doherty 2011).

The Republic of Ireland's 2006 census revealed that the unemployment rate for Travellers was 75% compared to only 9% of the general working-age population (Central Statistics Office 2007). After making some allowance for a cash economy among the Traveller population, the high levels of unemployment and of the seasonality or stagnation of a regular income creates severe socio-economic problems for Traveller families, particularly during the protracted winter period. More specifically, 63% of Traveller children under the age of fifteen had already left school (compared with only 13% of children nationally), and Traveller participation in higher education was less than 1% (compared with 30% of the Irish population nationally (Central Statistics Office 2007). On a transnational basis, 92% of Ireland's Indigenous Traveller peoples have no higher education qualifications, compared to 42% of Aboriginal Australians and 25% of Māori New Zealanders (Central Statistics Office 2007; ABS 2006; Statistics New Zealand 2006). Based on international statistics alone, there is undoubtedly an urgent need for NFTE-style educational programs tailored to meet the special pedagogical needs of Ireland's Indigenous Traveller community.

The Irish Traveller situation has been compounded by recent cutbacks in national educational programs by the Irish Republic. Its reduction of specialised teacher programs (Irish Traveller Movement 2011) is short-sighted and bordering on tactics of racial discrimination. When discussions are taken into account between the United Nations' advisory groups and the former Australian Human Rights Commissioner about the outcomes of similar exclusive practices, such developments in Ireland might be loosely classified as cultural genocide (Reyhner & Singh 2010). These cutbacks will undoubtedly give rise to a downward cycle in the short term of poorer educational attainment and increased poverty, as the uneducated become increasingly dependent on manual labour, overcrowded substandard housing, and an escalation of preventable diseases, reduced socio-economic standards, and early death. This pattern is visible across the greater majority of third-world countries, Aboriginal Australia and poorer regions of New Zealand. Recent research tells us that Travellers are invariably discriminated against within "settler" schools (IT Sligo 2011). It also highlights that the lack of attendance by Travellers at settler schools is not only due to ongoing discrimination (Cavailero 2011; Danaher, Kenney & Leder 2009). It is multi-faceted. Non-attendance can also be viewed as an assertion of Traveller identity when parents feel that such schools are disempowering for them and their wider minority community. Both the 1995 Task Force Report on the Travelling Community (1995) and a report by the Department of Education (2006) identify the needs for more inclusionary pedagogy and better-funded specialised education assistance. While Traveller teachers in the past had provided Traveller children with opportunities to enjoy their human right to meaningful education, this has since been withdrawn.

Speaking from Morning Ireland, the Ombudsman for Children, Emily Logan, identified these cutbacks in resource teachers as an example of a "poor choice in education", arguing that:

> the number of teachers cut in traveller education (773 out of 1200) was disproportionate and that with competing interests for resources,

we need to be careful about slashing or cutting budgets by a certain percentage and that more information should be gathered and a child impact analysis was needed. (Independent Irish Catholic News 2011)

This tragic loss of culturally-relevant formal education, general literacy and development of human capital will create a greater need for NFTE Ireland to develop and deliver their programs to minority Indigenous youth along the lines of Ahikaa. This raises the important question: who will fund these programs? Foroige have run specific programs for Traveller youth in Northern Ireland. They were, however, forced to cease them prematurely due to staffing problems. Early indicators tell us that Traveller youth engaged enthusiastically in the programs and that outcomes were promising Doherty 2011). During the second-half of 2011, the author interviewed twenty Travellers below the age of twenty five years who had all left school at the age of fifteen or sixteen. Eighteen of the twenty stated they would have liked to have continued to senior school or college with the aim of achieving employment or a better job. Based on the writer's preliminary investigations and as-yet-unpublished research findings, as well as other published reports (Department of Education 2006), there is an urgent need for Foroige to extend their operation in Ireland to cater for the specific educational requirements of Traveller communities.

Conclusion

Based on the author's research and observations, it is contended that the above-mentioned modified NFTE programs have become global leaders in providing entrepreneurship training, program resources, more inclusive pedagogies, and more socio-culturally relevant learning tools to low-income minority communities around the world. These resources have influenced and aligned with a number of national and international education and entrepreneurship education standards. As the parent organisation, NFTE has influenced private and public perceptions of the capability of youth to learn entrepreneurship concepts and to participate actively in business ownership. The success of this alternative approach is also supported by the unrelated development of the Young American Indian Entrepreneur program at the University of Minnesota. Multi-longitudinal research undertaken by Harvard's Graduate School of Education indicates very positive outcomes in general education and the capacity to develop business initiatives through these programs.

Ahikaa has incorporated into its education programs the concepts that cross-cultural educators teach more generally under the banner of "leadership". This might also be adopted in Australia to maintain Aboriginal forms of pedagogy. There is as yet no tertiary institution or organisation that is prepared to adapt this successful program to the specific needs for Aboriginal Australians.

Public intellectual, Aboriginal activist and anthropologist, Professor Marcia Langton, has recently identified a significant shortcoming in Australia:

> This problem has contributed to a relative absence of analysis of the economic history of Aboriginal Australians, fostering instead an approach that prioritises the political and cultural rights of indigenous people above the kinds of life-enhancing circumstances that are necessary for them to participate in the economy and create wealth. This kind of essentialism has also resulted in a disregard for the rights of indigenous people as individuals, rather than as communities seeking self-determination, especially with regard to the rights of women and children. (Langton 2011: 1)

Similar inabilities to apprehend the needs of Indigenous minorities also exist in New Zealand. Neck and Greene (2011) argue that Pakeha (non-Māori) are unable to analyse situations and act appropriately due to the inhibiting endurance of colonial paradigms and a general inability to accept "new" pedagogical approaches to learning. Ahikaa, however, is teaching a learning program that develops the Indigenous "self" and the Indigenous minority family and community. It is an innovative program that many mainstream and academic institutions have thus far been unable to fully comprehend and/or replicate.

Socio-economic advances by Indigenous minorities are not normally attained via large, sweeping programs that cost millions of dollars of public spending, driven by bureaucrats with little regard for the outcomes that Langton (2011) advocates. A current Australian Research Council-funded project undertaken by the author tells us that hundreds of thousands of dollars have been spent during the past three decades on uncoordinated financial literacy programs for Aboriginal Australians. Not only are these programs mostly uncoordinated and unnecessarily replicated across various states and national institutions, they lack credible methods of outcome measurement and public accountability. This includes the measurement of the effectiveness of financial literacy programs that too often succeed only in keeping a small army of predominantly non-Aboriginal consultants and bureaucrats employed and handsomely remunerated. Based on three years of research by the author, financial literacy education of Aboriginal Australians has been largely ineffective. Based on empirical evidence gathered to date within the western suburbs of Sydney, financial literacy for Indigenous Australians is an industry that employs many however it has been a failure. Qualitative case studies indicate that the mainstream education system places the blame for this failure on Aboriginal families. By contrast, Aboriginal families believe that the reason why their children have such poor literacy skills lies rather in the failure of insufficiently skilful educators and the education system more broadly.

NFTE programs delivered by community organisations Ahikaa and Foroige provide a promising alternative to mainstream education. The responsibility lies firmly within the entrepreneurship skilling program itself. NFTE-based programs have demonstrated that it is possible to engage the minds and hearts of Indigenous communities through blended pedagogies that are designed in collaboration with and work for Indigenous minorities.

The New York-based NFTE program initiated this educational development in 1987. New Zealand is delivering a purpose-designed program for Māori through Ahikaa. Ireland has shown that it can do likewise with Indigenous minorities. It remains to be seen if Australia can adapt an Ahikaa-type program for its Indigenous youth at risk rather than continue to pay small armies of consultants and bureaucrats to deliver largely-ineffective programs. As demonstrated, pre-existing mainstream educational programs too often give rise to alienated, under-educated and under-employed Indigenous minority youth who then get trapped in a downward spiral and regrettably many become social welfare statistics.

This is a complex issue and the author has attempted to provide the reader with a general understanding of the complexity of the research issues over many years to illustrate the need for educational programs such as NFTE, Ahikaa and the YAIE. Aboriginal Australia needs support in the development of its people within the financial and commercial sectors; it needs a NFTE-type education program to achieve this.

I take the opportunity of thanking all those involved in the development of this paper, including Dr. Catherine Love and Sir Ngatata Love, for their patience and investment in my understanding of their unique pedagogy, "*tēnā rawa atu koe*" – in my language, "*digerry-goor nygallia*".

References

Ahikaa. 2011. Ahikaa Vision, Ahikaa Philosophy. http://www.ahikaa.ac.nz (accessed 7 December 2011).

Australian Bureau of Statistics (ABS). 2004. '1301.10 Year Book Australia: Indigenous Education and Training, 2004'. http://www.abs.gov.au/AUSSTATS/abs@.nsf/Previousproducts/1301.0Feature%20Article162004?opendocument&tabname=Summary&prodno=1301.0&issue=2004&num=&view= (accessed 27 September 2007).

Australian Bureau of Statistics. 2006. '4713.0 – Population Characteristics, Aboriginal and Torres Strait Islander Australians, 2006' http://www.abs.gov.au/ausstats/abs@.nsf/mf/4713.0 (accessed 1 August 2011).

Australian Bureau of Statistics. 2008. 'Schools. 4221.0'. Canberra: Australian Government Printer.

Brockhaus, R. H. 1980. 'Entrepreneurial Folklore'. *Journal of Small Business Management* 25(1): 1–6.

Brockhaus, R., & Horwitz, P. 1986. 'The Psychology of the Entrepreneur'. In Sexton, D., and Smilor, R. (ed.). *The Art and Science of Entrepreneurship*. Cambridge: Ballinger.

Brough, M., & Chelsea, B. 2009. 'Little Theory, Big Plans: Social Capital and Community Building in Aboriginal Australia'. In Woolcock, G., & Manderson, L. (ed.). *Social Capital and Social Justice: Critical Australian Perspectives*. Darwin: Charles Darwin University Press.

Castlemaine Secondary College School Staff. 2006. Personal conversation with senior staff. 12 June. Castlemaine Secondary College.

Central Statistics Office. 2007. *Census 2006, Vol. 5: Ethnic or Cultural Background* (including the Irish Traveller Community). Dublin: The Stationary Office.

Chaganti, R., & Greene, P. 2002. 'Who are Ethnic Entrepreneurs? A Study of Entrepreneurs' Ethnic Involvement and Business Characteristics'. *Journal of Small Business Management* 40(2): 126–143.

Chodkiewicz, A., Widin, J. & Yasukawa, K. 2008. 'Engaging Aboriginal Families to Support Student and Community Learning'. *Diaspora, Indigenous and Minority Education* 2(1): 64–81.

Christensen, C., & Carlile, P. 2009. 'Course Research: Using the Case Method to Build and Teach Management Theory'. *Academy of Management Learning & Education* 8(2): 240–251.

Cocker, M. & Love, C. 2009. 'NFTE Pilot Follow-Up'. Unpublished Report to the Hui Taumata Trust.

Collins, O., & Moore, D. 1964. *The Enterprising Man*. East Lansing: Michigan State University.

Connolly, P. 1998. 'Researching Racism in Education: Politics, Theory and Practice'. Connolly, P., & Troyna, B. (ed.) Bristol: Open University Press.

Connolly, P., & Keenan, M. 2002. *Tackling Racial Inequalities in Northern Island*. Belfast: Northern Ireland Statistics and Research Agency (NISRA).

Consortium for Entrepreneurs. 2004. 'The Consortium for Entrepreneurship Education'. Columbus, Ohio. http://www.entre-ed.org/_arc/i-ref1.htm#i9 (accessed 1 November 2012).

Cooper, A. C., Dunkleberg, W. C., & Woo, C. Y. 1988. 'Survival and Failure: A Longitudinal Study'. Babson Park: Frontiers of Entrepreneurship Research, Babson College.

Cotterill, T., Rosandich, F., & Rosandich, J. 2009. 'Te Aho Takitoru – An Indigenous Social Work Framework'. Issue 1: http://www.outcome-network.org/paper/228:te_aho_takitoru_an_indigenous_social_work_framework (accessed 12 June 2011).

Danaher, P. A., Patrick., Kenny, M., & Leder, J. R. (eds.) 2009. *Traveller, Nomadic and Migrant Education*. New York: Routledge.
Department of Education. 2006. 'Report and Recommendations for a Traveller Education Strategy'. Dublin: The Stationary Store.
Department of Education, Science and Training. 2007. 'Enterprise Learning for the 21st Century Initiative'. http://www.dest.gov.au/NR/rdonlyres/C6FC86B2-6180-409E-9BDC-1B6AB75162FC/16697/Intro_001.pdf (accessed 1 April 2010).
Doherty, M. 2011. Email correspondence with author, 2 August.
Donovan, M. 2007. 'Can Information Technological Tools Be Used to Suit Aboriginal Learning Pedagogies?' In Dyson, L. E., Hendricks, M. A. N., & Grants, S. (ed.). *Information Technologies and Indigenous Peoples*. Sydney: Idea Group Inc.
Drucker, P. 1985. *Innovation and Entrepreneurship*. New York: Harper & Row.
Eisenhardt, K. M. 1989. 'Building Theories From Case Study Research'. *Academy of Management Review* 14(4): 532–550.
Ely, R., & Padavic, I. 2007. 'A Feminist Analysis of Organisational Research on Sex Differences'. *The Academy of Management Review* 32(4): 1121–1143.
Foley, D. 2000. 'Successful Indigenous Australian Entrepreneurs: A Case Study Analysis'. *Aboriginal and Torres Strait Islander Studies Unit Research Report Series*, vol. 4. Brisbane: Merino Lithographics.
Foley, D. 2005. Understanding Indigenous Entrepreneurs: A Case Study Analysis. Unpublished PhD Thesis. http://espace.library.uq.edu.au/view/UQ:179923 (accessed 4 July, 2011).
Foley, D. 2006. 'The Relationship Between Networking and Culture for Minority Entrepreneurs'. Third International Business Research Conference, Melbourne, 20–22 Nov.
Foley, D. 2008. 'What Determines the Bottom Line for Māori Tourism SMEs? Small Enterprise Research'. *The Journal of SEAANZ* 16(1): 86–97.
Foley, D. 2008b. 'Does Culture and Social Capital Impact on the Networking Attributes of Indigenous Entrepreneurs?'. *Journal of Enterprising Communities: People and Places in the Global Economy* 2(3): 204–224.
Foley, D. 2009. 'Does Education Compensate for the Absence of Social Capital Experienced by Indigenous Entrepreneurs?' Asia Pacific Symposium on Entrepreneurship & Innovation, 1–3 April, The University of Sydney.
Foley, D. 2010a. 'The Need to Understand the Interaction of Human and Social Capital on Indigenous Entrepreneurs'. *New Zealand Journal of Employment Relations.* 35(1): 65–88.
Foley, D. 2010b. 'Enterprise and Entrepreneurship are Not Un-Aboriginal'. *Journal of Australian Indigenous Issues* 13: 85–93.
Fredericks, H., & Foley, D. 2006. 'Indigenous Populations as Disadvantaged Entrepreneurs in Australia and New Zealand'. *International Indigenous Journal of Entrepreneurship, Advancement, Strategy & Education* 2(2): 34–49.
Gibb, A. 1993. 'Education for Enterprise: Training for Small Business Initiation – Some Contrasts'. *Journal of Small Business and Entrepreneurship* 4(3): 42–47.
Gibb, A. 1996. 'Entrepreneurship and Small Business Management: Can We Afford to Neglect Them in the Twenty-First Century Business School? *British Journal of Management* 7(4): 309–321.
Gibson, L. 2010. 'Who is You? Work and Identity in Aboriginal New South Wales'. In Keen, I. (ed.). *Indigenous Participation in Australian Economies: Historical and Anthropological Perspectives*. Canberra: ANU E Press.
Gorman, G., Hanlon, D., & King, W. 1997. Some Research Perspectives on Entrepreneurship Education, Enterprise Education and Education for Small

Business Management: A Ten-Year Literature Review'. *International Small Business Journal* 15(3): 56–79.

Greene, P., Hart, M., Gatewood, E., Brush, C., & Carter, N. 2003. 'Women Entrepreneurs: Moving Front and Center: An Overview of Research and Theory'. *Coleman White Paper Series* 3: 1–47.

Gundry, L., & Welsch, H. 2001. The Ambitious Entrepreneur: High Growth Strategies of Women-Owned Enterprises'. *Journal of Business Venturing* 16(5): 453–470.

Heitmeyer, D. 1998. 'The Issue is Not Black and White: Aboriginality and Education'. In Allen, J. (ed.). *Sociology of Education: Possibilities and Practice*. Katoomba: Social Science Press.

Hockings, C. 2010. 'The Artisan in Higher Education and the Craft of Inclusive Learning and Teaching'. Public lecture, 12 October, Adelaide.

hooks, bell. 1994. *Teaching to Transgress: Education as the Practice of Freedom*. New York: Routledge.

Hughes, Helen. 2007. *Lands of Shame: Aboriginal and Torres Strait Islander 'Homelands' in Transition*. St. Leonards: The Centre for Independent Studies Ltd.

Independent Irish Catholic News. 2011. 'Irish Priest Appeals Against Cuts in Traveller Education'. 2 June http://www.indcatholicnews.com/news.php?viewStory=18345 (accessed 3 August 2011).

Irish Traveller Movement. 2011. 'Cuts to Traveller Education'. Position Paper. April. Dublin: ITM Dublin.

IT Sligo. 2011. 'Research Highlights Discrimination Amongst Travellers'. http://itsligo.ie/2011/07/20/research-highlights-discrimination-amongst-travellers/ (accessed 22 July 2011).

Katz, J. A. 2003. 'The Chronology and Intellectual Trajectory of American Entrepreneurship Education 1876–1999'. *Journal of Business Venturing* 18: 283–300.

Kuratko, D. F. 2005. 'The Emergence of Entrepreneurship Education: Development, Trends, and Challenges'. *Entrepreneurship Theory & Practice* 29(5): 577–597.

Langton, M. 2011. 'Anthropology, Politics and the Changing World of Aboriginal Australians'. *Anthropological Forum* 21(1): 1–22.

Lindsay, N. J. 2005. 'Toward a Cultural Model of Indigenous Entrepreneurial Attitude'. *Journal of the Academy of Marketing Science* 5: 1–17.

Lits, M. 1984. *L'Essai*. Brussels: Hatier.

Mackinlay, E., & Barney, K. 2010. 'Transformative Learning in First Year Indigenous Australian Studies: Posing Problems, Asking Questions and Achieving Change. A Practice Report'. *The International Journal of the First Year in Higher Education* 1(1): 91–99.

Maingueneau, D. 1983. *Sémantique de la polémique: Discours religieux et ruptures idiologiques au XVIIE siècle*. Lausanne: L'Âge d'Homme.

Mann, S. J. 2001. 'Alternative Perspectives on the Student Experience: Alienation and Engagement'. *Studies in Higher Education* 26(1): 7–19.

Mariotti, S. 2010. Personal conversation, USASBE Conference, 15 January, Nashville, Tennessee.

Mariotti, S. 2011. '24 Concepts Every Young Person Should Know About Business'. *Huffington Post*. 6 June. http://www.huffingtonpost.com/steve-mariotti/ (accessed 16 August 2011).

Mazzarol, T. 2006. *Entrepreneurship & Innovation: A Managers Perspective*. Prahran: Tilde University Press.

McClelland, D. 1965. 'Need Achievement and Entrepreneurship: A Longitudinal Study'. *Journal of Personality and Social Psychology* 1: 389–392.

McCormick, B., & Gray, V. 2011. 'Message in a Bottle: Basic Business Lessons for Entrepreneurs Using Only a Soft Drink'. *Journal of Management Education* 35(2): 282–310.

McMullin, E., & Long, W. 1987. 'Entrepreneurship Education in the Nineties'. *Journal of Business Venturing* 2: 261–275.

Milner, J.B. 1996. *The 4 Routes to Entrepreneurial Success*. San Francisco: Berrett-Koehler.

Nakata, M. 1998. 'Anthropological Texts and Indigenous Standpoints'. *Australian Aboriginal Studies* 2: 3–12.

Neck, H, M., & Greene, P. G. 2011. 'Entrepreneurship Education: Known Worlds and New Frontiers'. *Journal of Small Business Management* 49(1): 55–70.

Network for Teaching Entrepreneurship (NFTE). 2007. "Network for Teaching Entrepreneurship Research Report'. New York.

New Zealand Government. 2009. 'Ngā Haeata Mātauranga – The Annual Report on Māori Education, Education Counts'. Education Information and Analysis Group / Group Māori. Wellington: Ministry of Education.

New Zealand Ministry of Health. 2010. 'Tatau Kahukura: Māori Health Chart Book 2010'. Second ed. June. http://www.maorihealth.govt.nz/moh.nsf/indexmh/tatau-kahukura-maori-health -chart-book-2010?Open (accessed 12 June 2011).

Ogbor, J. 2000. 'Mythicizing and Reification in Entrepreneurial Discourse: Ideology-Critique of Entrepreneurial Studies'. *Journal of Management Studies* 37(5): 605–635.

Pearson, N. 2011. *Radical Hope: Education & Equality in Australia*. Collingwood: Black Inc.

Pelto, P. J., & Pelto, G. H. 1978. *Anthropological Research: The Structure of Inquiry*. New York: Cambridge University Press.

Peredo, A. M., Anderson, R. B., Galbraith, C. S., Hoing, B., Dana, L. P. 2004. 'Towards a Theory on Indigenous Entrepreneurship'. *International Journal Entrepreneurship and Small Business* 1(1/2): 1–20.

Pittaway, L., & Cope, J. 2007. 'Entrepreneurship Education: A Systematic Review of the Evidence'. White Rose Centre for Excellence in Teaching and Learning of Enterprise: Working Paper 01/2007. The University of Sheffield. http://www.sheffieldcetle.ac.uk (accessed 15 August 2011).

Pittaway, L., Robertson, M., Munir, K., Denyer, D., & Neeley, A. 2004. 'Networking and Innovation: A Systematic Review of the Evidence'. *International Journal of Management Reviews* 5/6(3/4): 137–168.

Plaschka, G. R., & Welsch, H. P. 1990. 'Emerging Structures in Entrepreneurship Education: Curricular Designs and Strategies'. *Entrepreneurship Theory and Practice* 14(3): 55–71.

Reyhner, J., & Singh, N. K. 2010. 'Cultural Genocide in Australia, Canada, New Zealand, and the United States: The Destruction and Transformation of Indigenous Cultures'. *Indigenous Policy Journal* 11(3): 1–26.

Rigney, L-I. 1999. 'The First Perspective: Culturally Safe Research Practices On or With Indigenous Peoples'. 1999 Chacmool Conference Proceedings. Alberta: University of Calgary.

Rigney, L-I. 1999. 'Internationalisation of an Indigenous Anti-Colonial Cultural Critique of Research Methodologies: A Guide to Indigenist Research Methodology and Its Principles'. *Higher Education Research and Development in Higher Education* 20: 629–636.

Ronstadt, R. 1987. 'The Educated Entrepreneurs: A New Era of Entrepreneurial Education is Beginning'. *American Journal of Small Business* 11(4): 37–53.

Savin-Badin, M. 2000. *Problem-Based Learning in Higher Education: Untold Stories*. Buckingham: The Society for Research into Higher Education and Open University Press.

Shepherd, Dean. 2004. 'Educating Entrepreneurship Students About Emotion and Learning From Failure'. *Academy of Management Learning and Education* 3(3): 274–287.
Stanner, W. E. H. 1968. *The Great Australian Silence: After the Dreaming.* Sydney: Australian Broadcasting Commission.
Statistics New Zealand. 2006. *Census.* Quick Stats Rotorua District. http://www.stats.govt.nz/Census/2006CensusHomePage/QuickStats/AboutAPlace/SnapShot.aspx?type=ta&ParentID=1000003&tab=Education&id=2000024 (accessed 16 August 2010).
Stevenson, H., & Jarillo, J. 1990. 'A Paradigm of Entrepreneurship: Entrepreneurial Management'. *Strategic Management Journal* 11: 17–27.
Smyth, J. 2005. 'Modernizing the Australian Education Workplace: A Case of Failure to Deliver for Teachers of Young Disadvantaged Adolescents'. *Educational Review* 57(2): 221–233.
Stumpf, S. S. Dunbar, R. L., & Mullen, T. P. 1991. 'Simulations in Entrepreneurship Education: Oxymoron or Untapped Opportunity?' *Frontiers in Entrepreneurship Research* 681–694.
Task Force on the Travelling Community. 1995. 'Report of the Task Force on the Travelling Community'. Dublin: Stationery Office.
Thorpe, R., Holt, R., Pittaway, L., & Macpherson, A. 2006. 'Knowledge Within Small and Medium Sized Firms: A Systematic Review of the Evidence'. *International Journal of Management Reviews* 7(4): 257–281.
Tracey, P., Phillips, N., & Haugh, H. 2005. 'Beyond Philanthropy: Community Enterprise as a Basis for Corporate Citizenship'. *Journal of Business Ethics* 58: 327–344.
Tranfield, D. R., Denver, D., & Smart, P. 2003. Towards a Methodology for Developing Evidence-Informed Management Knowledge by Means of Systematic Review'. *British Journal of Management* 14: 207–222.
University of Minnesota. 2003. 'The Rights of Indigenous Peoples, Study Guide'. http://www1.umn.edu/humanrts/edumat/studyguides/indigenous.html (accessed 10 November 2006).
Vesper, K. H., & McMullan, W. E. 1988. 'Entrepreneurship: Today Courses, Tomorrow Degrees?' *Entrepreneurship Theory & Practice* 13(1): 7–13.
Wadsworth, Y. 1998. 'What is Participatory Action Research?' Action Research International, Paper 2.
Watson, P., Partington, G., Gray, J., & Mack, L. 2006. 'A Research Project Commissioned by the Aboriginal Education and Training Council of Western Australia'. Perth: Aboriginal Education and Training Council. www.etcwa.org.au/files/pdf/aboriginal_students_numeracy.pdf (accessed 4 July 2011).
World Economic Forum and Global Education Initiative. 2009. 'Educating the Next Wave of Entrepreneurs: Unlocking Entrepreneurial Capabilities to Meet the Global Challenges of the 21st Century'. A Report of the Global Education Initiative. https://members.weforum.org/pdf/GEI/2009/Entrepreneurship_Education_Report.pdf (accessed 1 June 2011).
Yin, R. K. 2002. *Case Study Research, Design and Methods.* Third ed. Newbury Park: Saga Publications.

Chapter 10

"Going to School on Our Country"

Expanding the Concept of Schooling in Semi-Sedentary Aboriginal and Sámi Communities in Australia and Sweden

Zane Ma Rhea

Abstract

Around the world, Indigenous and other traditionally-oriented peoples have asserted their *sui generis* right that they are the custodians of the lands and waters on which their ancestors have lived for centuries, despite the overlay of other claims and jurisdictions. Consideration of the implication of *"Going to School on Our Country"* for the engagement of Indigenous young people in formal national schooling involves an examination of the educational aspirations of Indigenous and other traditionally-oriented peoples alongside the socio-historical context of mainstream nation-states providing education for nomadic, semi-nomadic, and semi-sedentarised peoples. This paper focuses in particular on two traditionally-oriented communities, one in Australia and the other in Sweden, and makes a comparative analysis of the histories of education service provision in both places. It is, by now, well established that formal mainstream education systems that are provided by nation-states are designed to serve mainstream, culturally-dominant interests. What this study has revealed is that these Indigenous peoples are not necessarily opposed to mainstream schooling but rather aspire to an expanded provision of education that enables their young people to develop the skills that are necessary to succeed in mainstream society, be it Sweden or Australia, while also supporting these communities to create sustainable futures that enable them to grow and prosper in economically and socially viable, traditionally-oriented ways.

Introduction

> We just want what's best for our kids, you know. We want them to go to school on our country not some other peoples' country. That makes problem for us. We want them to have good jobs but we want our kids safe here with us. We don't let them speak English here. They get confused. The can speak English at school but not here at home. (Australian Indigenous traditional owner, Central Australia)

> The ice is melting and the seasons are changing. It's hard to make a living from reindeer anymore and we have to go higher up the mountains each year. I quit my work as a teacher so I could teach our young people about reindeer because that is their inheritance you know. They get so lost at school and who will they be if they don't know about reindeer herding? (Sámi Indigenous reindeer herder, Northern Sweden)

Around the world, Indigenous and other traditionally-oriented peoples have asserted their *sui generis* right that they are the custodians of the lands and waters on which their ancestors have lived for centuries despite the overlay of other claims and jurisdictions. Consideration of the implication of "Going to School on Our Country" for the engagement of Indigenous young people in formal national schooling involves an examination of the educational aspirations of Indigenous peoples alongside the socio-historical context of mainstream nation-states providing education for nomadic, semi-nomadic, and semi-sedentarised peoples. This paper focuses in particular on two communities, one in Australia and the other in Sweden, and makes a comparative analysis of the histories of education service provision in both places. It is, by now, well established that formal mainstream education systems that are provided by nation-states are designed to serve mainstream, culturally-dominant interests (Teasdale & Ma Rhea, 2000). What this study has revealed is that these traditionally-oriented peoples are not necessarily opposed to mainstream schooling but rather aspire to an expanded provision of education that enables their young people to develop the skills that are necessary to succeed in mainstream society, be it Sweden or Australia, while also supporting these communities to create sustainable futures that enable them to grow and prosper in economically and socially viable, traditionally-oriented ways.

The nation-state providers of education services to these remote places are in ongoing disagreement with Aboriginal and Torres Strait Islander and

Sámi peoples as to how best educate the young people of these communities. This paper argues that it is possible to develop an education service for nomadic or semi-nomadic, subsistence living people that takes into account the complex and sometimes competing demands being placed on its people. The biggest fear, as suggested by the quotes above, is that the Aboriginal and Sámi children are becoming confused, and are failing to learn the skills and knowledge to thrive in either mainstream society or on their traditional estates.

Background to the Study

The International Context

Around today's world, there are an estimated 370 million Indigenous people (UN Non-Government Liaison Service 2010). The United Nations' Working Group on Indigenous Populations has been using the following working definition (proposed by UN Special Rapporteur Martinez Cobo in 1986) to guide its work:

> Indigenous communities, peoples and nations are those which, having a historical continuity with pre-invasion and pre-colonial societies that developed on their territories, consider themselves distinct from other sectors of the societies now prevailing in those territories, or parts of them. They form at present non-dominant sectors of society and are determined to preserve, develop and transmit to future generations their ancestral territories, and their ethnic identity; as the basis of their continued existence as peoples, in accordance with their own cultural patterns, social institutions and legal systems. (Cobo 1986)

Many traditionally-oriented Indigenous, tribal, and minority peoples within nation-states continue to maintain aspects of their subsistence relationships to land and water, and issues of their ongoing food security are intimately tied to access to their traditional lands and resources. This chapter focuses on the Aboriginal and Sámi communities who live on their traditional estates, in places that are far from the administrative, often metropolitan, centres that govern their lives within the nation-state. While many of the issues facing these peoples are also common to more urbanised Indigenous and traditional peoples, this research seeks to understand the particular histories of remote- living peoples' experiences of mainstream, formal schooling, and its capacity to offer an expanded version in these contexts that achieves education "both ways". While nations, such as Israel, Egypt, Botswana, and India have directly considered the impacts of recent sedentarisation on Indigenous peoples, their entry into the cash economy from a subsistence level of life, ongoing semi-nomadism (sometimes also described as semi-sedentarisation or semi-sedentism), hunting and gathering, pastoralism, or a combination of such factors on the provision of formal schooling to their "at risk" populations (see, e.g., Golbman & Katz 1997; Kratli 2000; Shashahanil 1995; Salzman 1980; Swift *et al.* 1990; Tahir 1998; Tshireletso 2001; Vereecke 1989), scant research drawing on such historical data has been undertaken in either Australia or Sweden about these matters. In any remote community, people will tell you anecdotally about the high levels of non-attendance at school, of families suddenly moving without planning or preparation for transition of their school-age children to another school, of poor health, of poverty, about the lack of healthy relations between the school and the parents, and the failure of special programs, and so on. When these comments are considered in the light of international research findings (as above), it becomes apparent that these conditions are not particular to Aboriginal or Sámi people in remote communities in Australia or Sweden. They are experienced in common with other Indigenous and traditional peoples globally when they move from their traditional nomadic or semi-sedentary ways of life into sedentarisation.

Descriptors

Owing to the scope of this research, there are three types of interrelated literature (see, e.g., Stavenhagen 2004) that use a variety of descriptors for the attributes of people who fall under the broad category of traditionally-oriented "Indigenous" or other minorities who have been nomadic or semi-sedentary:

- descriptor based on how food is sourced: forager, sometimes including the refined descriptors hunter or gatherer, and pastoralist;
- descriptor based on mobility, usually on a continuum from nomadic to sedentary;
- descriptor based on economic engagement, usually on a continuum between subsistence to participation in the cash economy.

These descriptors offer insight into the factors that impact on the provision of schooling in remote communities, tensions between learning through the seasons about food and land and being in a school building every day;

learning the lessons of life in one's mother tongue and having to learn in a second or foreign language at school; travelling as opposed to sitting in one place; and living a subsistence life rather than one that requires money for basic necessities.

UN Declarations in General and Concerning Indigenous People

Within the last 30 years, Indigenous peoples have struggled both locally and internationally for recognition of their existence as peoples with rights. This is particularly complicated for nomadic and semi-sedentarised peoples whose ways of life are not the same as those Indigenous peoples living in more urbanised environments where they are now predominantly sedentary.

At the international level, there has been the creation of a wide range of international instruments and mechanisms aimed at securing the cultural and economic rights of Indigenous and other traditionally-oriented peoples. These conventions support rights consistent with the "educational aspirations" of Aboriginal and Sámi peoples but to date these rights have failed to be adequately translated into domestic law. As this study will show, the establishment of nation-state schooling was undertaken prior to many of the more recent declarations and agreements, and the conversion of these newer conventions into domestic law is proving to be a significant challenge in government policy and administrative practices in the education arena.

Adoption of the United Nations Declaration on the Rights of Indigenous Peoples: Responses from Sweden and Australia

The clearest international action to recognise and secure Indigenous rights was the UN Declaration on the Rights of Indigenous Peoples (2007). As can be seen from the following discussion, the endorsement of this Declaration has received cautious adoption in both Sweden and Australia. Sweden's response to the Declaration was given by Ulla Strom (UN General Assembly 2007; see full text in the Appendix). She announced after voting in the affirmative for the measure that:

> … her Government was pleased that the Assembly had finally adopted the Declaration. Sweden had supported the Declaration throughout the negotiation process, had voted in favour of the text and hoped that its implementation improved the situation of Indigenous peoples. At

the same time, the Declaration included several references to collective rights. While the Swedish Government had no difficulty in recognizing such rights outside the framework of international law, it was of the firm opinion that individual human rights prevailed over the collective rights mentioned in the Declaration.

Strom went on to say that the Sámi people were recognised as Indigenous by the Swedish Parliament, and the Government had based its relations with the Sámi on dialogue, partnership, and self-determination, with respect and responsibility for cultural identity. She affirmed that Sweden looked forward to discussing the implementation of the Declaration with Sámi representatives. She stressed that the political discussion on self-determination could not be separated from the question of land rights. She highlighted that the Sámi's relationship to the land was at the heart of the matter, and the Swedish Government must maintain a balance between competing interests of different groups living in the same areas in the north of the country.

Australia's response was given by Robert Hill (see full text in the Appendix). He announced after voting (together with Japan, New Zealand, the United States, and Canada) against the measure:

> The Australian Government had long expressed its dissatisfaction with the references to self-determination in the Declaration, he said. Self-determination applied to situations of decolonization and the break-up of States into smaller states with clearly defined population groups. It also applied where a particular group with a defined territory was disenfranchised and was denied political or civil rights. The Government supported and encouraged the full engagement of Indigenous peoples in the democratic decision-making process, but did not support a concept that could be construed as encouraging action that would impair, even in part, the territorial and political integrity of a State with a system of democratic representative Government.

On lands and resources, Hill said that the Declaration's provisions could be read to require recognition of Indigenous rights to lands without regard to other legal rights existing in land, both Indigenous and non-Indigenous. Any right to traditional lands must be subject to national laws, or the provisions would be both arbitrary and impossible to implement, with no recognition being given to the fact that ownership of land might lawfully vest in others. Australia would read the lands and resources provisions in line with its existing domestic laws, including the Native Title Act:

... while the Declaration would not be binding on Australia and other States as a matter of international law, he was aware that its aspirational contents would be relied on in setting standards by which States would be judged in their relations with Indigenous peoples. Accordingly, the Australian Government had been concerned throughout the negotiations to ensure that the Declaration was meaningful, was capable of implementation and enjoyed wide support in the international community. The Declaration failed in all those respects and Australia could not support it.

Unsurprisingly, the wariness of both governments in their responses to the Declaration has cascaded into domestic policy-making. In the last five years since the endorsement of the Declaration, remote-living Aboriginal and Sámi peoples have continued to move from their traditional estates and schools, whether by government intervention or through choice, for both peoples have continued to struggle to meet the education needs of these remote-living communities.

Comparative Perspectives on Indigenous Affairs: Sweden and Australia

Dow and Gardiner-Garden (1998) undertook a comparative study of Indigenous affairs that included both Australia and Sweden. While they note that "International comparisons in the area of Indigenous affairs are difficult to make" and that "The nature of the data available and the history of Indigenous-non-Indigenous relations vary greatly from country to country" (1998: 1), it is important to recognise the similarities internationally in the failure of mainstream formal schooling to address the education rights and needs of Indigenous and other traditionally-oriented populations (May 2001; May & Aikman 2003).

Dow and Gardiner-Garden (1998) also note that Indigenous people do not enjoy any constitutional or treaty recognition in either Australia or Sweden; that Australia has a poor history of Aboriginal and Torres Strait Islander representation in Federal Parliament, while Sweden has put in place a Sámi Parliament which, in addition to its political role, also performs the administrative functions of a department. The Sámi have thus been recognised as having limited rights with respect to land and resource use, while the Mabo decision, which recognised Aboriginal Native Title, has been undermined with the Wik decision and a raft of further amendments.

Dow and Gardiner-Garden (1998) further note that debates have evolved about land *use* rather than land *ownership* for both Indigenous groups.

There is scant research that has been conducted in either Australia or Sweden that compares historical provisions of education to Indigenous people, specifically examining the implications of community-controlled and state-controlled schooling. It is clear from the literature examined that, as Langton (2004: 1) states: "Despite few positive developments, the education status of the Australian Indigenous population is catastrophic." Dyer (2001) identifies the historical use of education as the main means for domesticating Indigenous populations, and examines the possibility of education having a development focus rather than a subjugating one. These rare foci in literature provided further impetus for the present study.

Australia: A Snapshot of Aboriginal and Torres Strait Islander Education in Remote Communities

In the early 1980s, the Australian government adopted an administrative definition of an Indigenous person as a "person of Aboriginal or Torres Strait Islander descent who identifies as an Aboriginal or Torres Strait Islander and is accepted as such by the community in which he lives" (Australian Government 2012; Dept. of Aboriginal Affairs 1981). There are some stark differences within the Australian Indigenous population that are of relevance to this paper. The first is that Aboriginal peoples living in remote areas are still struggling to obtain an education that meets their needs (Remoteness Area is a category of the Australian Standard Geographical Classification [ASGC]. The remoteness of a point is measured by its physical distance by road to the nearest urban centre. This paper, while including an overall perspective of Indigenous matters in Australia, is particularly focused on those communities classified as Remote and Very Remote [for further information see Chapter 8 of ABS ASGC July 2007]). The most recent statistics (from the 2011 Census) record that there were 548,370 Indigenous persons, being 2.5% of the total population who identified as Aboriginal or Torres Strait Islander. The Australian Bureau of Statistics (ABS) reports that, according to their analysis, many more Aboriginal and Torres Strait Islander people live in remote or very remote communities than non-Indigenous people (ABS 2010). In terms of the overall Indigenous population figure for Australia, nearly 32% live in major capital cities, nearly 43% in inner and outer regional places, and 25% in remote or very remote communities. From an analysis of the 2006 Census (ABS 2010: Table 3 [2011 statistics are not yet available for this discussion]), this translates to approximately 50,000 Aboriginal and Torres Strait Islander people living in remote locations, and approximately 82,000 people living in very remote locations.

Langton and Ma Rhea (2009) identify poverty as the most difficult issues facing Aboriginal and Torres Strait Islander people, particularly those living in remote and very remote locations, and they argue that the fact of poverty experienced by a significant proportion of Aboriginal and Torres Strait Islander families is having a direct impact on the ability of children from these families to take advantage of the opportunities promised by access to education. The poverty trap has become endemic because few Aboriginals and Torres Strait Islanders living in remote communities are sufficiently skilled to take up employment opportunities; instead, they are being clustered in the lower unskilled or under-skilled pool of labour in part-time positions, with lower pay, and in a small range of industries, such as public administration, health, and some trades. Those living in remote locations rely predominantly on government assistance, and the standards of literacy in English and numeracy are very poor among school children.

There are proportionally a small number of Australian Aboriginal and Torres Strait Islander children attending remote and very remote pre-schools, primary, and secondary schools as compared to the total Indigenous population – 1.1% and 0.3% respectively — with a proportionally higher presence in remote and very remote locations, unlike in metropolitan schools – 22% and 18.9% respectively (ABS 2006). This poses significant challenges in two ways. Systemic programs are predominantly designed to meet the needs of metropolitan and rural Indigenous students, given that they represent a much larger proportion of the Aboriginal and Torres Strait Islander students attending pre-schools and schools across the country. Second, Aboriginal and Torres Strait Islander students are more concentrated in remote and very remote communities, and their scholastic and cultural needs are distinct.

Historically, schooling designed to meet the needs of these remote communities was performed by missionaries and via funding by religious organisations. In more recent times, while the state has taken over schools in some of these communities, the standard of education available to many Aboriginal and Torres Strait Islander children has not been what most other Australians would have experienced. Brady (1997) argues that, historically, the majority of Aboriginal and Torres Strait Islander Australians have been excluded from the political, education, and employment systems. Even under such conditions, there are examples Australia-wide where Aboriginal communities have argued strongly for education opportunities and facilities for their children (see, e.g., Folds 1987; Harney 1957). Historical records highlight that the education system in general was delivered to ensure Aboriginal people were educated to be labourers, manual workers, or housekeepers. Despite recent significant financial investment by Australian Federal and State governments, high-level policy frameworks, national inquiries and taskforces, pilot education programs, and strong support from remote Aboriginal communities, the provision of formal schooling has not delivered the successful academic outcomes that had been set as the national priority goal for Aboriginal and Torres Strait Islander students.

Many people in remote communities continue to speak their mother tongue at home and in their day-to-day lives, and it is only in school that children are expected to speak English. The ABS reports: "Indigenous people living in Remote Areas are more likely to report higher levels of attachment to their culture as measured by their language spoken, participation in cultural events and identification with clan, tribe or language group' (2010: 2). The issue has been highly politicised in recent years, but the strongly articulated position in remote communities is that there is a preference for Aboriginal children to learn in their home language as well as in English. Even so, current Australian government policy leans towards monolingual English education, with some experimental programs funded at the local level for instruction in mother tongue. There are few qualified Aboriginal and Torres Strait Islander teachers nationally, and it is rare to find a qualified Aboriginal and Torres Strait Islander teacher in a remote school. More commonly, local Aboriginal and Torres Strait Islander men and women work in the school as teacher's aides, groundsmen, or cleaners.

Sweden: A Snapshot of Sámi Education in the Remote North

Education achievement for traditionally-oriented northern Sámi children is equally worrying. The Swedish government has been responsible for the provision of education for Sámi children since taking over from missionaries, similarly to Australia. Cohen (1976), Todal (2003), and Alerby (2006) among others have raised concerns about the persistent lack of improvements in education achievement of Sámi children, with fewer children accessing special Sámi schools each year. Correspondingly, the basis on which these communities are defined and historically have claimed special status, reindeer herding, is a shrinking industry.

In the northernmost part of Europe live the Sámi, an Indigenous people with their own culture and own language. They are numerically small, only approximately 70,000–80,000 across four nations: Norway, Sweden,

Finland, and Russia. Because formal census do not ask for people's ethnic origins, it is difficult to estimate the number of Sámi people. The territory in which the Sámi people live is called Sápmi, or Sámiland, and it is their land even though it is not recognised by these nation-states. In Sweden, there are estimated to be 17,000–20,000 Sámi people, approximately 0.2% of the total population (Darnell 1972; Darnell & Hoëm 1996; Alerby 2006). The Sámi language is divided into three main dialects: South Sámi, Central Sámi, and East Sámi. Within these dialects there are nine sub-dialects. North Sámi and Lule Sámi are the two largest dialects within the Central Sámi language. Because the differences between the dialects are so numerous, it is possible to consider them as three different languages. The Sámi language/group of languages belongs to the Finno-Ugric or Uralic family of languages (Demmert 1986; Sámi Board of Education 2006). In order for a Sámi person to register for the right to vote in elections for the Swedish Sámi Assembly, a person must define himself/herself as Sámi and either speak the Sámi language as a home language or have a parent or grandparent who spoke the language as a home language. To cater for those whose families had lost their language under assimilation pressures but who still think of themselves as Sámi, if the applicant's parents or grandparents did not speak Sámi but were registered to vote for the Sámi Assembly, the applicant can be registered (Sillanpaa 1997; Demmert & Keskitalo 1998).

Like the situation in Australia, *albeit* during an earlier period, missionaries in the 17th Century often forced Sámi children to attend missionary schools whether the children and parents wanted an education or not. In 1632, for example, a school for Sámi was established in Lycksele, Sweden. The hope was that the Sámi could learn Swedish, develop as Christians, and that some would serve as missionaries among their people throughout what was then known as Lappland (Nuwer 2002).

Sweden established so-called nomad schools in 1913. The aim was to provide a basic education while the children retained much of their own culture. There is ongoing provision in Sweden for Sámi children to attend a mainstream school or a Sámi School for the first six years of compulsory school. In the academic year 2008/09 there were a total of 139 pupils at the five schools where Sámi Schools were conducted (Statistics Sweden 2009). In addition to the usual subjects, the aim of the Sámi school provides education to safeguard and develop the Sámi language and cultural heritage (Demmert 1990). Teaching takes place in the Sámi language as well as in Swedish. In the secondary school years (compulsory for Years 7–9) there are no special provisions for schooling made but students can request to also study their language. The Swedish Language Act (2009) acknowledges that Sámi students have the right to mother tongue training, even if Sámi is not the primary language used in the home, and all Sámi students have the right to mother-tongue training regardless of the size of the group.

Background

In 2007, a research partnership developed between Australian Aboriginal people, Swedish Sámi, and academics from Monash University and Lulea University. They were awarded a three-year STINT Grant (from the Swedish Foundation for International Cooperation in Research and Higher Education) in order to develop the research relationship between education research communities in Sweden and Australia, offering opportunities for each nation to learn of the successes in improving education outcomes for Indigenous and traditionally-oriented peoples. Under this grant, a group from the Sámi and Lulea University team visited schools in Central Australia with Monash colleagues in December 2008 and in 2009; Ma Rhea undertook a period of research collaboration at Lulea University under the STINT grant which enabled the author to conduct research into the socio-historical development of Sámi education in northern Sweden, to visit schools offering education targeted at Sámi students, meet with parents, and spend time with Sámi traditional people. Late in 2009, on the invitation of a number of Australian Aboriginal and Torres Strait Islander families, under a Monash University Internationalisation grant and the STINT grant, Swedish academics travelled again to Central Australia with colleagues from Monash University to meet with families to discuss their ideas and the aspirations that they have for educating their children in order to achieve a sustainable future for their traditional way of life.

This paper reports on part of a larger research program. It focuses specifically on the comparative historical antecedents of mainstream schooling, interrogating the development of schools among recently sedentarised Indigenous populations in the settler states of Australia and Sweden.

Research Question

The focus of this paper is to compare and contrast the provision of education in two remote communities, Alice Springs, Central Australia, and Jokkmokk, Sweden, which while geographically disparate, have experienced both mainstream and Indigenous-controlled formal schooling within living memory. The key question of this paper is to ask: *What is the capacity of formal schooling to offer an expanded version in these contexts that achieves education "both ways"?*

The analysis has examined:

- how formal schooling in the two communities has been provided;
- in what ways the provision of schooling in these communities has been similar and different;
- how the children were educated in traditional ways during community-controlled periods;
- what assumptions are made in the delivery mode of education to these communities;
- the extent to which parents and the wider communities have been involved in the schooling of their children; and,
- what communities feel might be done to improve the standard of education for children.

The Methodological Approach

The conceptual framework for this research is embedded in the approach to the conduct of ethical research with Indigenous and traditionally-oriented peoples (AIATSIS 2002, 2012; Smith 1999; van Manen 1990; Umar & Tahir 2000), where it is identified that it is critical in the first instance to have clear partnership agreements with each community involved with this project within a collaborative research partnership framework (see Danaher, 2000; Ma Rhea and Rigney, 2002; Ma Rhea, 2011). Researchers from Monash and Lulea Universities had already established relationships with the two chosen communities, and this research has been informed by findings gained from previous collaborations. The evaluation findings of these other projects has revealed that the provision of schooling is greatly impacted by the effects of recent sedentarisation of the local Indigenous populations, and more attention must be given to involving the communities in the schooling of their children within the western education system (Alerby 2006; Ma Rhea & Atkinson, 2008).

Therefore, the aim of this part of the research has been to work with locally-based Aboriginal and Sámi research partners to seek the views of two groups of Aboriginal and Sámi peoples regarding their historical experiences of schooling and the potential for an expanded provision of schooling that might better suit their children. Overall, there were 27 Elders, parents and caregivers from various central Australian Anangu communities: Western Arrente, Luritja, Walpiri, and Central/Eastern Arrente speakers and associated school staff, and 25 Elders parents and caregivers from various Sámi communities living in and around Jokkmokk in Northern Sweden and associated school staff involved in meetings and discussions about the research questions. All interviews were undertaken by both locally-based Indigenous researchers and non-Indigenous university researchers, sometimes involving discussion across a variety of languages. The research approach used in this study has been socio-historical comparative, empirical, and interpretative, employing qualitative methods of data collection and analysis.

Data Collection

This study has employed two broad methods of data collection to foster an understanding of the history of the development of formal schooling in the two remote, recently sedentarised communities. Little research has been undertaken on this topic directly, so both fieldwork research and literature review methods have been employed. Some information was held electronically by organisations and communities, and other data was gathered in partnership with locally-based Aboriginal and Sámi educators who were partners of this research.

A close reading of archival, electronic, and other historical materials elicited both empirical and thematic detail. In the case of historical materials, primary sources have been consulted where available. Accounts of the development of formal schooling, descriptions and materials of relevance to each of the communities, anthropological accounts of the impact of the introduction of formal schooling (whether by missionaries or by the State), and sociological and education studies which further examine the provision of schooling in remote Aboriginal and Sámi communities have provided a picture of the provision of formal schooling.

Data Analysis

Following the analysis of the historical materials, the data gathered about local histories from the communities through interviews with people who have had "living memory" involvement with the provision of formal schooling have been analysed using grounded theory data analysis techniques (Strauss & Corbin 1990) and, triangulated with the official archival histories, found to reveal emergent themes. The data has begun to provide answers to the research questions outlined above, with a particular focus on what circumstances facilitated an understanding of what an expanded concept of "school" might be.

Ethical Considerations

All aspects of the research process for this project have been conducted within the already-established partnership agreements and have adhered to the *Guidelines for Ethical Research in Australian Indigenous Studies* (AIATSIS 2012) which clearly identifies eleven principles of ethical research that were followed in this project. Negotiations with key informants resulted in agreement for the conduct of this research project, established on the principles of good faith and free and informed consent (following AIATSIS 2000: 3–5). The research fieldwork was approved by Monash University Human Research Ethics CF09/2774 – 2009001589: Indigenous and Traditional People on Sustainable Futures in Education and by Lulea University, Sweden.

"Going to School on Our Country": Bridging the Policy-Implementation Gap

The findings from the discussions with both Central Australian Indigenous and northern Swedish Sámi participants, and examination of the historical, archival, and anthropological literatures suggest that improvements in the provision of formal schooling to these peoples is, at best, proceeding slowly. Equally, in both cases there has been limited success with attempts to incorporate culturally-relevant skills and knowledge into the development of pedagogical practices and curricula, even in those schools that have been designed to cater more appropriately to the needs of the children in these remote communities.

Voicing Indigenous Peoples' Visions of the Future within the Context of, and with Connection to, International Declarations and Agreements

By partnering with remote Indigenous communities, it has been possible to clearly identify the issues facing families as they attempt to send to, and encourage their children to stay at, school, such that schools can better take into account the needs of recently sedentarised remote populations. In both cases, the Indigenous school community spends considerable time trying to resolve the central dilemma facing them: how to operationalise high level, city-driven policy directives, while at the same time negotiating the myriad issues confronting each community "on the ground" as they try to preserve and maintain traditional approaches to education. Bauman (1999) theorises this sort of tension via his examination of culture as praxis. The informants in the research do not reject the modernising education project but refute that it has to encompass Western ideas and ideals or that it cannot be expanded to include both ways of education.

The communities who partner in this project are recognised as having lower education outcomes than the national average, being highly mobile or recently sedentarised, dealing with the complex issues of sedentarisation, including loss of access to traditional hunting and gathering lands, often forced entry into the cash economy from subsistence living, having a lack of skills for living in urbanised environments, experiencing poor health and often extreme poverty when compared to the average national Australian or Swedish household income.

Discussions with the key research partners of Aboriginal and Sámi teachers reinforced the work undertaken by Indigenous people to bring their education aspirations to the international table. As Battiste and Henderson (2000) argue, Indigenous and other traditionally-oriented peoples have been educating their children for centuries in nomadic or semi-sedentary subsistence conditions. As nation-states conquered and colonised, education was used to pacify nomadic populations throughout the world. In Sweden and Australia, commonly it was missionaries who provided the first formal schooling for Indigenous peoples in these remote locations. One informant described it thus:

> Them Christian fellas ... well they come to this country. They taught us about praying and told us to close our eyes and pray to God. When we closed our eyes we had the land and they had the bibles. When we opened our eyes again, we had the bibles and they had our land.

Over time, the provision of formal schooling to Indigenous and local communities was taken over by the nation-state. Interestingly, Sweden has not kept specific records of the Sámi population living within its borders. The stories told and existing records suggest that the nomadic Sámi population continued to move across imposed national boundaries between Russia, Finland, Norway, and Sweden for as long as it was possible to do so. As Sámi families have lost access to their traditional reindeer herding and hunting grounds because of encroachments by businesses (forestry and mining, in particular) and fishing in the coastal estates – as well as the impact of climatic change – many have become more sedentary. Sweden established special Sámi schools, one of which participated in the research for this study, but many Sámi families send their children to the mainstream school system. The families in this area send their children to school until they take the reindeer herds up to the mountains. The schools exert significant pressure on the families not to take the children out of school and, although the Sámi School has within its charter to support the preservation of Sámi cultural heritage, it too comes under significant pressure from the government to encourage the reindeer herders to allow their children to stay at school. The children of the reindeer herders are losing their inheritance, for without having an understanding and intimate relationship with the reindeer, a Sámi is not Sámi in the legally-recognised definition of the term (Keskitalo 1994; Kuokkamen 2003).

The Australian Aboriginal population in remote locations have also experienced a change from schools being run by missionaries to the government. Like the Swedish Sámi, most families send their children to mainstream government schools, and only a small percentage prefers instead to access Aboriginal-controlled schools. Like their Swedish Sámi counterparts, these families formerly cared for significant landholdings, moving around their estates so as to hunt and forage for food, performing rituals, and caring for country. As they have lost access to their lands, they have increasingly been forced into towns and town camps, and only a few families now live on their traditional estates with their title to do so. Even the families who continue to live outside of the towns are required to send their children to school, and it is a constant juggle between the two worlds to make sure that their children receive what they describe as "both ways learning". In comparative terms, the education achievements of these desert-dwelling children is still significantly lower than the national average, but they are, at least, still able to learn their cultural inheritance of language and country from their Elders.

Schooling in both Sweden and Australia is now increasingly shaped by centralised bureaucratic processes that are data-driven. Accounting methods are becoming more sophisticated and these methods are increasingly reaching into remote locations that have, up until the present, been located beyond the administrative reach of bureaucratic accountability. In order to access services, these nomadic peoples are increasingly becoming sedentarised, but the majority are seriously impoverished, without the range of skills required to engage in the capitalist cash economy. Schools are now required to report on the educational achievements of these children and the failure of the system in both countries is becoming more apparent. The tendency in both places had been to tighten the regulatory regimes in the local school systems to standardise conformity to the system. The findings of this research collaboration highlight the importance of involving the families and communities in the education of these children. The state cannot do this *in loco parentis*.

"Both Ways" Schooling

All the informants are living with the memories of their subsistence herding and hunting ways and skills but recognise that their children are increasingly being forced into the cash economy. Analysis of the discussions raised the following points for further investigation, echoing the rights-based approach favoured by the international Indigenous community towards the provision of education to Indigenous peoples:

> The children need to be available seasonally to learn from their elders how to feed themselves from their land. This should not compete with the need for them to attend school regularly to learn the knowledge required to function in mainstream society.

An Elder explains:

> The witchetty grubs don't wait for the school bell to ring … our kids need to be there with us when we look for them … the best time after the rains. They need to know lot of things that we can only teach them if they see it themselves … things like where to dig and … things like that. It's no good telling them about it afterwards.

A collaborative approach to educating young Indigenous children must seriously consider adapting the school year to the seasonal needs of the community. Given the environmental conditions of these communities, of snow and desert, it makes sense for the local education systems to adapt to their seasonal needs.

There is a need for people to move around their traditional estates in order to care for their lands and waterways, undertake rituals and ceremonies, and ensure that they are not over-harvesting the available resources such as foods, water, and wood. This should not compete with the requirement of administrative centres that people live in one place, attend one school, and have records that are maintained regarding their access to services in one place. It should not also be in competition with the growing need for younger people to go to mainstream school so that they can acquire the skills and knowledge necessary to engage in the cash economy in order for the family to have an economically-viable future. Usually this tension of having to choose has arisen because there have been encroachments onto the traditional lands of Indigenous subsistence-dependent cultures, and families have been forced into the cash economy because they can no longer feed themselves. The reach of globalisation into these remote communities through access to telecommunications opens up the consumer world, and these young nomads want what the children of the metropolis have: Nike runners, 50 Cent basketball shirts, Play Station, and the latest mobile phones complete with music apps and Facebook (Bauman 1998, 2001). Without strong partnership between schools and the families of these young people, there is a very clear danger that the youth will, as the informant in the opening quote so clearly stated, "be confused about who they are".

The solution to this issue could be found through two unrelated developments. Families who wished to take their children travelling with them would be supported to develop the skills to become home tutors while away from the local school. In parallel, for those families that seasonally travel to another community in another region, each child could be assigned a regional file number that allowed them to attend a school in another location and for the new school to be able to access their records. Most families mentioned that they only ever go to certain communities within their travels. With cooperation from families to establish such a system, it would not be difficult to realise.

Both Sámi and Aboriginal families returned consistently to the issue of first language rights. As one informant said:

> Young children need to be educated in their mother tongue first and then use their knowledge to learn other languages. This should not have to compete with learning the national language.

Historically, people in both communities were forced by missionaries and early school teachers to stop speaking their mother tongue, and many told stories of punishments they had received as young children. While Sweden appears to have belatedly adopted a rights-based approach to Sámi children being allowed to learn their language, within the context of the erosion of so many traditional Sámi rights, families are giving up on trying to get their children to learn the language. Informants said that often the Sámi school is the only place a child will hear Sámi language, as it is not spoken at home so much anymore.

In the Aboriginal context, it became evident in discussions that Aboriginal people continue to use their mother tongue as the *lingua franca* within their day-to-day interactions among one another, switching to English only when necessary. Informants told of how they actively discourage their children from speaking English at home. In the reverse of the Sámi experience, it is often only at school that an Aboriginal child hears English.

Conclusion

Given the well-documented, ongoing failure by nation-states to be able to deliver high quality education programs in remote and very remote communities, a more considered approach is required, based on sound research, drawing on the lessons of failed attempts as told by the past students of these communities, and also through historical materials regarding schooling of recently sedentarised Indigenous and other traditionally-oriented communities. Factors which lead to low academic achievement of Indigenous children in mainstream schools have been clearly recognised for some time as being: sporadic student attendance, low rates of both retention and completion of formal, mainstream schooling, and low levels of academic achievement among the adult population. In addition, issues of poverty, general transience of school staff and the local community, poor health, and negligible opportunity for local employment are factors that are known to have a significant effect on the interest of the community to engage with mainstream schooling.

There are no easy answers to these issues but the informants to this study are adamant that education is not working for their children in myriad ways. At the international level, this research validates the decision by both Australia and Sweden to ratify the Declaration on the Rights of Indigenous People, and encourages each nation to deliver on undertakings made through its signatory status to a number of other international protocols on the provision of education to Indigenous people and to human resource development more generally among their Indigenous populations. The findings indicate that the framework of the education approach developed through various UN mechanisms, for example, International Labour Organisation No. 169, concurs with the ideas and aspirations expressed in this study, and that each nation might give serious consideration to becoming a signatory to it.

At the national level, the findings of this foundational study are showing a pathway to bridging the gap between policy and implementation, enabling the Australian and Swedish governments to develop nuanced policy frameworks, and deliver more effective, expanded understandings of providing education services that address the pressing education challenges faced by these minority, semi-sedentary Indigenous populations and the education systems which are supposed to serve them.

At the community level, these peoples have experienced both community- and state-controlled education approaches, and they are seeking to find a way to expand the concept of schooling for their children, for education systems to recognise their right to be educated in the languages of their choice, the recognition of custodial responsibilities to lands and waterways, the right to live a nomadic or semi-sedentary life, and the right to learn about one's culture; and that these be recognised legally as their inalienable human rights that should not be quashed by administrative or pedagogical expediency.

Acknowledgements

The author would like to thank the Central Desert, the northern Sámi and other Indigenous people who are partners in this ongoing research collaboration. In particular, I would like to acknowledge Professor Henry Atkinson, Dr Barry Judd, Ms Bernadette Atkinson, Ms Rhonda Inkamala and family, and Ms Carina Sarri and family for their willingness to engage in the long-term development of this research partnership.

The author would also like to thank Professor Eva Alerby and her team at Lulea University for their hospitality, and to acknowledge the financial support from the Swedish Foundation for International Co-operation in Research and Higher Education (STINT http://www.stint.se/en/) for a program of research and collaboration called "Desert and Ice: Learning Without Boundaries" between researchers from the Faculties of Education, Lulea University, Sweden, and Monash University, Australia, from 2007–2010.

Thanks also to Monash University for their financial support from Engagement and Internationalisation grants to enable the engagement with, and participation of, academic and non-academic Indigenous researchers in this program of work. In particular, I would like to acknowledge Professor Adam Shoemaker and Professor Lynette Russell for their ongoing commitment to the development of Indigenous research leaders.

And, finally, thanks to colleagues at ANZCIES 2010 held in Melbourne for their critical responses to this paper.

Appendix

Full text of Sweden's response to the Declaration on the Rights of Indigenous People given by Ulla Strom (UN General Assembly 2007). She announced after voting in the affirmative for the instrument that:

> ... her Government was pleased that the Assembly had finally adopted the Declaration. Sweden had supported the Declaration throughout the negotiation process, had voted in favour of the text and hoped that its implementation improved the situation of Indigenous peoples. At the same time, the Declaration included several references to collective rights. While the Swedish Government had no difficulty in recognizing such rights outside the framework of international law, it was of the firm opinion that individual human rights prevailed over the collective rights mentioned in the Declaration.
>
> She went on to say that the Sámi people were recognized as Indigenous by the Swedish Parliament, and the Government had based its relations with the Sámi on dialogue, partnership and self-determination, with respect and responsibility for cultural identity. To that end, Sweden looked forward to discussing the implementation of the Declaration with Sámi representatives. She stressed that the political discussion on self-determination could not be separated from the question of land rights. The Sámi's relationship to the land was at the heart of the matter and the Swedish Government must maintain a balance between competing interests of different groups living in the same areas of the north of the country.
>
> She said that some clarification of her country's interpretation of the Declaration was necessary. For instance, the text's reference to self-determination should not be construed as authorizing or encouraging any action which would impair the territorial integrity or political unity of sovereign and independent States. She noted that a large part of the realization of the right to self-determination could be ensured through article 19 of the Declaration, which dealt with the duty of States to consult and cooperate with Indigenous peoples. In fact, that article could be implemented in different ways, including through a consultative process between institutions representing Indigenous peoples and Governments, and through participation in democratic systems, such as the current Swedish system. It did not entail a collective right of veto, she added.

Among other examples, she said that her Government interpreted references in the Declaration to ownership and control of land to apply to the traditional rights of the Sámi people. In Sweden, those rights were called reindeer herding rights and included the right to land and water for the maintenance of reindeer herds by Sámi herding communities, as well as the right to build fences and slaughterhouses for the reindeer and the right to hunt and fish in reindeer herd areas. Article 28 did not give Sámi people the right to redress for regular forestry by the forest owner.

The full text of Australia's response given by Robert Hill (UN General Assembly 2007). He announced after voting (together with Japan, New Zealand, the United States and Canada) against the instrument that:

> … speaking in explanation of vote before the vote, said Australia had actively worked to ensure the adoption of a meaningful declaration. Australia had worked hard to ensure that any declaration could become a tangible and ongoing standard of achievement that would be universally accepted, observed and upheld. The text of the Declaration failed to reach that high standard and Australia continued to have many concerns with the text. Australia had repeatedly called for a chance to participate in negotiations on the current text and was deeply disappointed that none had been convened.

> Regarding the nature of the Declaration, he said it was the clear intention of all States that it be an aspirational Declaration with political and moral force, but not legal force. The text contained recommendations regarding how States could promote the welfare of Indigenous peoples, but was not in itself legally binding nor reflective of international law. As the Declaration did not describe current State practice or actions that States considered themselves obliged to take as a matter of law, it could not be cited as evidence of the evolution of customary international law. The Declaration did not provide a proper basis for legal actions complaints, or other claims in any international, domestic or other proceedings.

> The Australian Government had long expressed its dissatisfaction with the references to self-determination in the Declaration, he said. Self-determination applied to situations of decolonization and the break-up of States into smaller states with clearly defined population groups. It also applied where a particular group with a defined territory was disenfranchised and was denied political or civil rights. The Government

supported and encouraged the full engagement of Indigenous peoples in the democratic decision-making process, but did not support a concept that could be construed as encouraging action that would impair, even in part, the territorial and political integrity of a State with a system of democratic representative Government.

On lands and resources, he said the Declaration's provisions could be read to require recognition of Indigenous rights to lands without regard to other legal rights existing in land, both Indigenous and non-Indigenous. Any right to traditional lands must be subject to national laws, or the provisions would be both arbitrary and impossible to implement, with no recognition being given to the fact that ownership of land might lawfully vest in others. Australia would read the lands and resources provisions in line with its existing domestic laws, including the Native Title Act.

Australia had concerns that the Declaration expanded any right to free, prior and informed consent too far, as the scope of that proposed right was too broad. It could mean that States were obliged to consult with Indigenous peoples about every aspect of law that might affect them. That would not only be unworkable, but would apply a standard for Indigenous peoples that did not apply to others in the population. Australia could not accept a right that allowed a particular sub-group of the population to be able to veto legitimate decisions of a democratic and representative Government. Australia also did not support the inclusion of intellectual property rights for Indigenous peoples.

On third party rights, he noted that, in seeking to give Indigenous people exclusive rights over property, both intellectual, real and cultural, the Declaration did not acknowledge the rights of third parties, in particular the rights of third parties to access Indigenous land, heritage and cultural objects where appropriate under national law. The Declaration also failed to consider the different types of ownership and use that could be accorded to Indigenous people and failed to consider the rights of third parties to property. Australia was also concerned that the Declaration placed Indigenous customary law in a superior position to national law. Customary law was not "law" in the sense that modern democracies used the term, but was based on culture and tradition. Australia would read the whole of the Declaration in accordance with domestic laws, as well as international human rights standards.

While the Declaration would not be binding on Australia and other States as a matter of international law, he was aware that its aspirational contents would be relied on in setting standards by which States would be judged in their relations with Indigenous peoples. Accordingly, the Australian Government had been concerned throughout the negotiations to ensure that the Declaration was meaningful, was capable of implementation and enjoyed wide support in the international community. The Declaration failed in all those respects and Australia could not support it.

References

Alerby, E. 2006. 'School – A Place for Health? Sámi Children's Experiences of School'. In. Kurtakko, K., & Ahonen, A. (ed.). *Arctic Children*. Rovaniemi: University of Lapland.

Australian Bureau of Statistics (ABS). 2002. '4102.0 – Australian Social Trends 2002 Education: Participation in Education – Education of Aboriginal and Torres Strait Islander Peoples'. http://www.abs.gov.au/ausstats/abs@.nsf/2f762f95845417aeca25 706c00834efa/e9edc3c77168a3d2ca2570ec000af328!OpenDocument (accessed 16 January 2012).

Australian Bureau of Statistics. 2004. '4102.0 – Australian Social Trends' Australian Bureau of Statistics. 2006. '1301.0 – Year Book Australia: Education and Training – Primary and Secondary Education'. http://www.abs.gov.au/ausstats/abs@.nsf/0/2 8C78111D9AF9E65CA2570DE0010CB64?opendocument (accessed 16 January 2012).

Australian Bureau of Statistics. 2007. '4221.0 – Schools Australia, 2006'. http://www.abs.gov.au/AUSSTATS/abs@.nsf/Lookup/4221.0Explanatory%20 Notes12006?OpenDocument (accessed 19 December 2012).

Australian Bureau of Statistics. 2008. '4714.0 – National Aboriginal and Torres Strait Islander Social Survey'. http://www.abs.gov.au/AUSSTATS/abs@.nsf/DetailsPage/ 4714.02008?OpenDocument (accessed 19 December 2012).

Australian Bureau of Statistics. 2010. '4102.0 – Australian Social Trends: The City and the Bush: Indigenous Wellbeing Across Remoteness Areas'. http://www.abs.gov. au/AUSSTATS/abs@.nsf/Lookup/4102.0Main+Features10Sep+2010 (accessed 19 December 2012).

Australian Bureau of Statistics. 2010. '4713.0.55.001 – Population Charateristics, Aboriginal and Torres Strat Islander Australians'.

Australian Government. 2012. 'Kinship and Identity: Definitions of Aboriginality'. http://www.alrc.gov.au/publications/36-kinship-and-identity/legal-definitions-aboriginality#_ftn16 (accessed 14 September 2012).

Australian Institute of Aboriginal and Torres Strait Islander Studies (AIATSIS). 2002. *Guidelines for Ethical Research in Indigenous Studies*. http://www.aiatsis.gov.au/__ data/assets/pdf_file/3512/EthicsGuideA4.pdf (accessed 16 January 2012).

Australian Institute of Aboriginal and Torres Strait Islander Studies. 2012. *Guidelines for Ethical Research in Australian Indigenous Studies*. http://www.aiatsis.gov.au/research/ ethical.html (accessed 30 April 2012).

Battiste, M. A., & Henderson, J. Y. 2000. *Protecting Indigenous Knowledge and Heritage: A Global Challenge*. Saskatchewan: Purich Publishing Ltd.

Bauman, Z. 1998. *Globalization: The Human Consequences*. Cambridge: Polity Press.
Bauman, Z. 1999. *Culture as Praxis*. Second ed. London: Routledge & Kegan Paul.
Bauman, Z. 2001. *Community: Seeking Safety in an Insecure World*. Cambridge: PolityPress.
Brady, W. 1997. 'Indigenous Australian Education and Globalisation'. *International Review of Education* 43(5–6): 413–422.
Cobo, J. M. 1986. *Study of the Problem of Discrimination against Indigenous Populations*. UN Doc.E/CN.4/Sub.2/1986/7/Add.4.
Cohen, R. W. 1976. 'An Educational Dilemma: the Lapps and the Swedish Schools'. *Comparative Education* 12(1): 37–43.
Danaher, P. 2000. 'Mapping International Diversity in Researching Traveller and Nomadic Education'. *International Journal of Educational Research* 33(3): 219–318.
Darnell, F. (ed.). 1972. *Education in the North: Selected Papers of the First International Conference on Cross-Cultural Education in the Circumpolar Nations and Related Articles*. Fairbanks: Arctic Institute of North America.
Darnell, F., & Hoëm, A. 1996. *Taken to Extremes: Education in the Far North*. Oslo: Scandinavian University Press.
Demmert, W. 1986. *Indigenous Peoples and Education in the Circumpolar* North. Juneau: University of Alaska.
Demmert, W. G. 1990. '*Strengthening Language: A Way to Improve School Performance*'. Umea, Education in Circumpolar North, 4th Annual Minorities of Education Conference, 12–14 June, Umea, Sweden.
Demmert, W., & Keskitalo, J. H. 1998. *Report from the International Steering Committee on Cross-Cultural Education in the North: Influencing Public Policy – Education in the Circumpolar North*. Equity & Excellence in Education 31(1): 81–83.
Department of Aboriginal Affairs. 1981. *Constitutional Section: Report on a Review of the Administration of the Working Definition of Aboriginal and Torres Strait Islander*. Canberra: Dept of Aboriginal Affairs.
Dow, C., and Gardiner-Garden, J. 1998. *Indigenous Affairs in Australia, New Zealand, Canada, United States of America, Norway and Sweden*. Commonwealth of Australia Background Paper 15, 1997–1998.
Dyer, C. 2001. 'Nomads and Education For All: Education for Development or Domestication?' *Comparative Education* 37(3): 315–327.
Folds, R. 1987. *Whitefella School: Education and Aboriginal Resistance*. Sydney: Allen & Unwin.
Gardiner-Garden, J. 2000. The Definition of Aboriginality: Research Note 18, 2000–01. Parliament of Australia.
Golbman, R. and Katz, Y. 1997. 'The Bedouin Community in the Negev: Educational – Community Characteristics'. Research Report No. 11. Israel: Institute for Education and Community Research, School of Education, Bar-Ilan University.
Gray, M., Hunter, B., & Schwab, R. G. 1998. *A Critical Survey of Indigenous Education Outcomes, 1986–96*. Centre for Aboriginal Economic Policy Research, ANU.
Harney, W. E. 1957. *Life Among the Aborigines*. London: Robert Hale.
Hunter, B., & Schwab, R. G. 1998. *The Determinants of Indigenous Educational Outcomes*. Centre for Aboriginal Economic Policy Research, ANU.
Hutchison, M. 2002. 'Australia'. In Marlow-Ferguson, R. (ed). *World Education Encyclopedia: A Survey of Educational Systems Worldwide*. Detroit: Gale Group.
International Labour Organisation (ILO). 1989. 'Convention No.169 (Concerning Indigenous and Tribal Peoples in Independent Countries)'. http://www.ilo.org/declaration/lang--en/index.htm (accessed 16 January 2012).

Keskitalo, J. H. 1994. 'The Case of the Sámi in Scandinavia'. *Education and Cultural Policies, Majority-Minority Relations*, 1: 50–56.

Kratli, S. 2000. 'Education Provision to Nomadic Pastoralists: A Review of the Literature'. Brighton: Institute of Development Studies.

Kuokkamen, R. 2003. 'Survivance' in Sámi and First Nations Boarding School Narratives'. *American Indian Quarterly* 27(3/4): 697–726.

Langton, M. 2004. 'Accelerated Education: Addressing Education Gaps and the "Whole of Life" Crisis Facing Australian Indigenous Youth'. *Australian Prospect* Easter: 1–24.

Langton, M. and Ma Rhea, Z. 2009. 'The right to the good life: indigenous education and the ladder to prosperity' in H. Sykes, (Ed) Perspectives. Sydney, Australia: Future Leaders, pp. 95–119.

Lee, R. B., & Daly, R. (ed.). 1999. *The Cambridge Encyclopaedia of Hunters and Gatherers*. Cambridge: Cambridge University Press.

Ma Rhea, Z. 2004. 'The preservation and maintenance of the knowledge of Indigenous peoples and local communities: the role of education' in *Journal of Australian Indigenous Issues*. 71, pp. 3–18.

Ma Rhea, Z. 2011. Partnership for Improving Outcomes in Indigenous Education: Relationship or Business? *Journal of Education Policy, 1–22.* DOI:10.1080/02680939.2011.621030.

Ma Rhea, Z & Atkinson, B. 2008. I'm Black ... Apart from that I Enjoy School: Aboriginal Children in Australia In Eva Alerby and Jill Brown (Eds) *Voices from the Margins: School Experiences of Indigenous, Refugee and Migrant Children*, pp.89–108, The Netherlands Sense Publishers.

Ma Rhea, Z. & Rigney, L.I. 2002. Researching with Respect: Supervising Aboriginal or Torres Strait Islander Students in J. Sillitoe et al. (Eds). *Assisting Beginning Research Students from Non-Traditional Backgrounds*, Higher Education, Research and Development, HERDSA.

Ma Rhea, Z. & Teasdale, G.R. 2000. 'A Dialogue between the Local and the Global' in G.R. Teasdale, and Z. Ma Rhea (Eds). *Local Knowledge and Wisdom in Higher Education*. UK, USA: Pergamon Elsevier, pp.1–14.

May, S. 2001. *Language and Minority Rights: Ethnicity, Nationalism and the Politics of Language*. London: Longman.

May, S., & Aikman, S. 2003. 'Indigenous Education: Addressing Current Issues and Developments'. *Comparative Education* 39(2): 139–145.

McRae, D., Ainsworth, G., Cumming, J., Hughes, P., Price, K., Rowland, M., Warhurst, J., Woods, D., & Zbar, V. 2000. *What Works? Explorations in Improving Outcomes for Indigenous Students*. Canberra: National Capital Printing.

Ministerial Council on Education, Employment, Training and Youth Affairs (MCEETYA). 2007. '*National Report on Schooling in Australia 2005, Preliminary Paper. National Benchmark Results Reading, Writing, and Numeracy Years 3, 5 and 7*'. Melbourne.

Ministerial Council on Education, Employment, Training and Youth Affairs. 2000. *Taskforce on Indigenous Education. Achieving Educational Equality for Australia's Aboriginal and Torres Strait Islander Peoples*. Canberra: Commonwealth of Australia.

Nuwer, H. 2002. 'Sweden'. In Marlow-Ferguson, R. (ed.). *World Education Encyclopedia: A Survey of Educational Systems Worldwide*. Detroit: Gale Group.

Pearson, N. and Kostakidis-Lianos, L. 2004. 'Building Indigenous Capital: Removing Obstacles to Participation in the Real Economy'. *Australian Prospect* Easter: 1–10.

Salzman, P. (Ed.). 1980. *When Nomads Settle: Processes of Sedentarization as Adaptation and Response*. New York: Praeger.

Sámi Education Board. 2006. 'Sameskolstyrelsen'. http://www.sameskolstyrelsen.se (accessed 16 January 2012).
Shashahanil, S. 1995. 'Tribal Schools of Iran: Sedentarization Through Education'. *Nomadic Peoples* 36/37: 145–156.
Sillanpaa, L. 1997. 'A Comparative Analysis of Indigenous Rights in Fennoscandia'. *Scandinavian Political Studies* 20(3): 197–217.
Smith, L. T. 1999. Decolonizing Methodologies: Research and Indigenous Peoples. London: Zed Books.
Statistics Sweden. 2009. 'Education in Sweden'. http://www.scb.se/statistik/_publikationer/UF0527_2009A01_BR_UF08BR0901.pdf (accessed 16 January 2012).
Stavenhagen, R. 2004. 'Indigenous Peoples in Comparative Perspective: Problems and Policies'. Occasional paper, United Nations Development Programme. http://hdr.undp.org/docs/publications/background_papers/2004/HDR2004_Rodolfo_Stavenhagen.pdf (accessed 16 January 2012).
Steering Committee for the Review of Government Service Provision (SCRGSP). 2009. *Overcoming Indigenous Disadvantage: Key Indicators*. Productivity Commission, Canberra.
Steering Committee for the Review of Government Service Provision. 2011. *Report on Government Services 2011*. Indigenous Compendium, Productivity Commission, Canberra.
Strauss, A. L., & Corbin, J. 1990. *Basics of Qualitative Research: Grounded Theory Procedures and Techniques*. Newbury Park: Sage Publications.
Swift, J., Toulmin, C., & Chatting, S. 1990. 'Providing Services to Nomadic People: A Review of the Literature and Annotated Bibliography'. *UNICEFF Staff Working Papers*, No. 8, New York: UNICEF.
Tahir, G. 1998. 'Nomadic Education in Nigeria: Issues, Problems and Prospects'. *Journal of Nomadic Studies* 11: 10–26.
Todal, J. 2003. 'The Sámi School System in Norway and International Cooperation'. *Comparative Education* 39(2): 185–192.
Tshireletso, L. 2001. 'Issues, Dilemmas, and Prospects of the State Provision of Education to Traditional Hunter Gatherer Societies of Botswana'. *Africa Studies Monographs* 26: 169–83.
Umar, A., & Tahir, G. 2000. 'Researching Nomadic Education: A Nigerian Perspective'. *International Journal of Educational Research* 33: 231–40.
United Nations. 1948. 'Universal Declaration on Human Rights'. http://www.un.org/en/documents/udhr/ (accessed 16 January 2012).
United Nations. 2000. 'We The Peoples' Millennium Forum Declaration and Agenda for Action: Strengthening the United Nations for the 21st Century'. http://www.kdun.org/en/documents/26-05-2000-MF.PDF?PHPSESSID=8eb5esquoealotdg7cprn43380 (accessed 16 January 2012).
United Nations. 2007. 'Declaration on the Rights of Indigenous People'. General Assembly GA/10612. http://www.un.org/News/Press/docs/2007/ga10612.doc.htm (accessed 16 January 2012).
United Nations Non-Government Liaison Service. 2010. 'General Assembly Adopts Declaration on the Rights of Indigenous People'. http://www.un-ngls.org/spip.php?page=article_s&id_article=343 (accessed 16 January 2012).
van Manen, M. 1990. *Researching Lived Experience: Human Science for an Action Sensitive Pedagogy*. Albany: State University of New York Press.
Vereecke, C. 1989. 'Nigeria's Experiment with a National Programme for Nomadic Education'. *ODI Pastoral Development Network* Paper No. 28d, London.

Chapter 11

The Koorie Footprints to Higher Education Program

An Analysis of Program Strengths and Challenges

Grania Sheehan, Tia Di Biase, and Kylie Clarke

Abstract

This paper informs the future evaluation of the *Koorie Footprints to Higher Education* (KFtHE) program based at the Churchill campus of Monash University in Gippsland, and provides an analysis of the program's strengths and challenges. The KFtHE program aims to encourage Indigenous students to aspire to higher education. The paper describes the way in which the program operated during the period February 2010 to February 2011 and the analysis presented is based on interviews conducted with program staff, program reports and presentations. The KFtHE program characteristics identified from this descriptive analysis are mapped onto the Design and Evaluation Matrix for University Outreach (DEMO) (Gale, Seller et al. 2010) to generate a qualitative estimate of the likelihood of program success in facilitating the transition of Indigenous students to higher education. The paper concludes by reviewing the use of DEMO in practice as a proscriptive tool for designing evaluation methodology for student aspiration programs.

Introduction

The *Koorie Footprints to Higher Education* (KFtHE) program was developed by Indigenous academics and staff at Monash University, Gippsland campus. The program involves Indigenous secondary students from Gippsland and the local Indigenous community. It aims to encourage local Indigenous students to aspire to higher education. This paper describes the operational aspects of the KFtHE program activities as they were conducted in the period February 2010 to February 2011, and is based on interviews conducted with program staff, program reports, and presentations. The program characteristics identified from this descriptive analysis are mapped onto the Design and Evaluation Matrix for University Outreach (DEMO) (Gale, Seller *et al*. 2010) to generate a qualitative estimate of the likelihood of program success in facilitating the transition of Indigenous students to higher education. DEMO was developed by Gale, Seller *et al*. (2010) to guide the review and development of established student outreach programs intended to increase the participation in higher education of students from disadvantaged socio-economic backgrounds. The application of DEMO as a proscriptive tool for informing an evaluation methodology which respects Indigenous community strengths and cultural practice is discussed.

Background

There has been rapid growth in the Indigenous youth population compared to Australian youth generally. More than half the Indigenous population (56.9%) in 2006 was aged less than 25 years, compared to a third (32.9%) of the non-Indigenous population (Biddle 2010; Australian Census 2006). This demographic difference underpins different foci in social and economic policy for the Indigenous and non-Indigenous populations. Whilst the policy focus for the latter is "increasingly concerned with the effects and implication of aging and retirement funding", the emphasis for Indigenous Australians "has remained and will remain fixed on the provision of education, training and entry into employment" (Biddle 2010: 4).

Increased access to and success in higher education for these young women and men are key to improving social and economic conditions in Indigenous communities, yet the participation of Aboriginal Australians in higher education nationwide lags well behind that of the general Australian population (Biddle 2010; Australian Census 2006). Population-based differences in education opportunity and achievement are evident across the education spectrum from patterns in Year 3 literacy and numeracy (DEEWR 2008), to participation in higher education (Gale, Tranter *et al*. 2010). More than three quarters (76.3%) of the Indigenous population aged 15 years and over had not completed either a degree or trade qualification – a rate 1.41 times greater than the rate for non-Indigenous Australians (54.1%) (Australian Census 2006). For Indigenous school leavers, vocational education and training is the prevailing alternative to school. An elevated proportion of Indigenous students, relative to non-Indigenous students, participate in the VET sector (Craven *et al.* 2005).

Indigenous men and women are participating in higher education, and increasingly so, although at a later stage in the life course (i.e., from the age of 33 onwards for females, and from the age of 40 onwards for males) (Biddle 2010), with mature-age Indigenous women participating in higher education at a greater rate than men (Biddle 2006). The challenge ahead lies in successfully preparing Indigenous school-leavers to participate in all levels of post-compulsory education, including the higher education sector. University-led programs that help to normalise higher education in Indigenous communities have an important role to play in the broader social and economic policy arena, yet to effect change, such programs must respect and reflect Indigenous community strengths and cultural practice (Lawrence 2007); this also applies to the evaluation methodology employed to review such programs.

The Koorie Footprints to Higher Education Program

The *Koorie Footprints to Higher Education* program (KFtHE) is located at the Monash University, Gippsland campus, with the aim of encouraging Indigenous students to aspire to higher education. The program involves Indigenous secondary-school students from schools throughout Gippsland and members of the local Indigenous community who participate in a series of activities. The program is grounded in research conducted by Robyn Heckenberg who created and established the program that was later co-ordinated by Kylie Clarke. The program is currently run under the auspices of the Gippsland Access and Participation (GAP) Project, which provides the financial and administrative support for core KFtHE program activities. GAP received funding from the Australian Government's Department of Education, Employment and Workplace Relations to increase participation of rural and Indigenous students in higher education (2009–2012).

This paper describes the operational aspects of the core KFtHE program activities as they were conducted in the period February 2010 to February 2011. The program began in 2001 and continues to operate in 2012. The descriptive analysis is based on discussions with GAP program staff who work on KFtHE program activities, the former KFtHE coordinator Kylie Clarke, and Robyn Heckenberg. Further material informing this analysis was drawn from the Monash University – Gippsland Campus website, presentations made about KFtHE program, and yearly reports about the program to the government funding body and Monash University. The characteristics of the program identified from this descriptive analysis are mapped onto the Design and Evaluation Matrix for University Outreach (DEMO).

The Design and Evaluation Matrix for University Outreach

The Design and Evaluation Matrix for University Outreach (DEMO) was developed by Gale, Seller *et al.* (2010) as a tool to review and develop established student outreach programs designed to increase the participation in higher education of students from disadvantaged socio-economic backgrounds (see, e.g., Austin & Heath 2010).

The DEMO, and the research which informed its development, is part of a Western research paradigm. The application of the DEMO to the operational characteristics of the KFtHE program likewise reflects this approach. This analysis has been used to advocate for research-based evaluation of the program, and to make albeit-tentative suggestions as to how such research could proceed. Recommendations with regard to methodology, control, and conduct of such an evaluation are within the purview of Indigenous scholars, program staff, and the Indigenous community (Martin 2003; Porsanger 2010; Rigney 1999), and hence beyond the scope of this paper.

DEMO was developed from multi-method empirical research conducted by Gale *et al.* in 2010. It is based on a national survey of programs run by universities in primary and secondary schools purposively designed to increase the participation in higher education of students from disadvantaged socio-economic backgrounds (Gale, Hattam *et al.* 2010). The primary focus of these programs designed to meet university equity obligations is raising students' aspirations for higher education (Gale, Hattam *et al.* 2010). Until recently, most of these programs have been focused on school students in Years 11 and 12, at a time when achievement and aspirations have been largely set (Gale, Hattam *et al.* 2010). Included in this survey were 59 programs from 26 universities that targeted pre-Year 11 students. Most of the programs sampled were aimed at Year 10 students, and the dominant focus of these programs is building student aspirations to attend university. Twenty percent of the programs sampled for this research targeted Indigenous students. The majority of programs used to develop DEMO share key characteristics with the KFtHE program – that is, it is predominantly an aspirations-based program targeting Indigenous students from Year 8 through to Year 12.

The research conducted by Gale, Tranter *et al.* (2010) included a review of literature describing pre-Year 11 outreach programs operating in Australia, Canada, the United States, the United Kingdom, and New Zealand. From this sample of university programs, Seller, Hattam *et al.* (2010) also identified seven as case studies. Drawing on the international research literature, the survey findings, and on these exemplars, Gale, Seller *et al.* (2010) were able to identify a number of characteristics, strategies, and perspectives that characterised successful programs and which constitute the DEMO. Gale, Seller *et al.* (2010) derived 10 characteristics (people-rich; financial support and/or incentives; early, long-term, sustained; collaboration; cohort-based; communication and information; familiarisation/site experiences; recognition of difference; enhanced academic curriculum; research driven; refer to the first four sub-sections of "KFtHE and the Ten Characteristics of Effective Programs" below for detail), four strategies (assembling resources; engaging learners; working together; building confidence; refer to the first four sub-sections of "KFtHE and the Ten Characteristics of Effective Programs" below for detail), and an equity orientation comprising three perspectives (unsettling deficit views; researching local knowledge and negotiating local programs; building capacity in communities, schools, and universities; refer to the sub-section "Equity Orientation" below for detail) that, in combination, were associated with effective pre-Year 11 outreach programs. "Effective" programs are defined as those most likely to increase the number of disadvantaged students going on to higher education than would otherwise be the case (Gale, Seller *et al.* 2010: 4). Such programs exhibit at least five characteristics, three strategies and two perspectives.

In this paper, DEMO is used as a tool to generate a qualitative estimate of the likelihood of KFtHE program success, and to provide background for the development of research to evaluate the *Koorie Footprints to Higher Education* program (KFtHE) program.

Fundamentals of the KFtHE Program Activities

The KFtHE program can best be described as an "Aspiration Program" (Gale, Seller *et al.* 2010) in that the program seeks to inspire aspiration for higher education within a collaborative network comprising the university, Gippsland schools, and the Indigenous community. In doing so, the program responds to a clear need on the part of Indigenous students (Craven 2005; James 2002; Alloway *et al.* 2004). Indigenous students have lower aspirations for careers, education, and training as compared to non-Indigenous students, and the factors that shape these aspirations can differ both in nature and intensity (Craven 2005). Their career choices and participation patterns in post-compulsory education reflect these differences. The program also adopts the classic strategy of programs aimed at raising aspirations for higher education which is to expose students to information about the university and its courses as well as vocations that require a university degree (Gale, Tranter *et al.* 2010).

The KFtHE program comprises three core activities that involve groups of Indigenous secondary school students:

- Print-Making Workshops;
- Monash University Gippsland Campus Camp; and
- School Visits.

At the time the data was collected, the program was supported by a full-time staff member based at the Gippsland campus who provided ongoing support for Indigenous university students, assisted in the recruitment of new university students, and coordinated the KFtHE program activities.

The three core activities described in this paper are those which are conducted under the auspices of the GAP project, with the exception of the school visits which are variously carried out in collaboration with Monash University Marketing ("The Discovery Club"), the Smith Family, and Catholic Education. The work of the coordinator and the support services provided on campus for Indigenous students are broader than the KFtHE program. Table 1 presents the number of Indigenous secondary school students and other Indigenous community members who attended the Print-Making Workshops, Koorie Footprints to Monash Camp, and the school visits in 2009 and 2010.

Activity	2009		2010	
	Community members	Secondary school Students	Community members	Secondary school Students
Print-Making	13	14	18	8
Camp	9	27	12	46
School visits	12	54	7	21
Total	34	95	37	75

Table 1. Participation of Indigenous Students and Other Indigenous Community Members in KFtHE Core Activities in 2009 and 2010

Print-Making Workshops

Indigenous secondary school students from Year 7 through to Year 12 and Indigenous community members in the Gippsland region participate in the Print-Making Workshops. Each workshop comprises four or five weekly sessions, and three or four workshops are run each year. During these workshops, secondary students and adult community participants explore cultural expression and develop print-making knowledge and skills through interactions with Koorie Monash University staff and mentors. The mentors include previous participants in the workshops, members of the Indigenous and artistic communities, university academic and KFtHE staff. The workshops take place at the Monash University Gippsland Centre of Art and Design. This location is intended to facilitate student familiarity with the Gippsland campus. At the end of a two year cycle of workshops, an exhibition of the artwork created by participants is held at the campus gallery. Indigenous and non-Indigenous community members and Monash university staff and students are invited to view and celebrate the work.

The objectives of the Print-Making Workshops are to:

- develop participants' skills and interest in art and design;
- demonstrate a culturally safe and supportive environment for participants;
- create collaborative space in which to share ideas and network;
- expose participants to the Gippsland campus and facilities; and,
- provide participants with information about university study opportunities and pathways in art and design.

Koorie Footprints to Monash Camp

The Koorie Footprints to Monash Camp is a residential camp for Indigenous secondary school students in Years 9 through to 12. The camp involves a one- or two-night stay on the Gippsland campus. During the camp, the students participate in activities and lessons that are relevant to a range of careers. They attend presentations from academics working in a range of disciplines represented at the regional campus, Indigenous mentors, and other Monash support services staff. The students are given the opportunity to engage in conversations with these individuals. Students are also provided with information about university programs, alternative pathways to university for students who do not have the prerequisite qualifications, scholarships and student support services. They also participate in structured activities on the campus that are culturally relevant and culturally significant.

The objectives of the Koorie Footprints to Monash Camp are to:
- inspire Indigenous secondary school students to appreciate and engage with education at school and in everyday life;
- encourage students to complete VCE and go on to university, TAFE or employment;
- expose students to Monash university life, the available university programs, and various pathways to these programs;
- inform students of available scholarships, support services, facilities and extracurricular activities (e.g., sporting and social clubs); and,
- inspire a strong sense of Indigenous pride and identity in Indigenous secondary students.

School Visits

The KFtHE program facilitates school visits where Indigenous students from schools throughout Gippsland either come to the campus or KFtHE staff visit the school. The visits take place every year for Indigenous students from Years 6 through to 12. Students who visit the campus participate in activities that assist them to become familiar and comfortable with the campus, its faculties and schools, facilities and services (e.g., challenges to locate places and facilities around the campus). Indigenous university students are also present during the campus visit as role models for the visiting students.

When KFtHE staff visit schools, the activities provided for the students include the presentation of information about university courses and pathways. The KFtHE coordinator – a university graduate herself – shares her own story about attending university. School visits are supported by different organisations and areas within the university including the GAP project, Monash University marketing (i.e., "Monash Discovery Club"), Catholic Education, and the Smith Family.

The objectives of the school visits (whether on campus or at the school) are to:
- inspire Indigenous secondary school students to appreciate and engage with education at school and in everyday life;
- encourage students to aspire to complete secondary school and possibly go on to pursue higher education;

- raise awareness of the Indigenous programs, pathways, scholarships and student support services that are available at the Gippsland campus of Monash University;
- provide students with a positive university experience (for those who visit the campus);
- assist students to develop a deeper understanding of cultural heritage and the importance of preserving that heritage; and,
- instil in students a strong sense of confidence and pride in their cultural identity.

The General Support Role of the KFtHE Coordinator

In addition to the three activities described above, the KFtHE coordinator provides general support for Indigenous school students. The KFtHE coordinator also led the Gippsland Indigenous Student Services Unit team on the Gippsland campus. This team includes the Indigenous Student Support Officer and the Indigenous Tutorial Access Scheme (ITAS) Coordinator. The KFtHE program coordinator held overarching responsibility for Indigenous access and participation at the campus. This role involved oversight of the KFtHE program, and the development and day-to-day management of the core program activities described above.

With regard to enrolment, the coordinator is generally responsible for the recruitment of Indigenous students at the Gippsland campus, whether they be secondary school students or mature-age entrants. She is the initial point of contact at the Gippsland campus for prospective Indigenous students, and provides one-to-one assistance to prospective students with the enrolment process. This assistance can take the form of course advice, the provision of general information about the university, referral of students to faculties/schools and student-support services. The coordinator also provides assistance with the Indigenous Enabling Program (IEP) and Indigenous Non-Award Pathway (INAP) and direct-entry application processes, and with scholarship applications.

The stated objective of the support role of the coordinator is to maintain ongoing support and encouragement for Indigenous students to enrol and remain enrolled at the Gippsland campus. Central to achieving this objective is building, and maintaining over time, a relationship with individual students that is based on trust. At the time our descriptive analysis was conducted, the program coordinator had been employed for three years.

These activities as described by the program staff are generally consistent with the perceived pre-university enrolment needs of Indigenous students living in regional Australia (Hossani *et al.* 2008). Hossani *et al.* examined the perceived needs, attitudes, and knowledge of Indigenous secondary school students living in Toowoomba, Queensland, when considering admission to university by way of focus groups and a survey of 80 students. At the pre-enrolment stage, Indigenous students indicated that economic information (e.g., fees, cost of books) and information about the academic programs and support services available were necessary, along with information about social activities and sporting facilities, and university liaison with their school. Students were generally unaware of the financial assistance that universities can provide.

KFtHE and the Ten Characteristics of Effective Programs

The ten characteristics and four overarching strategies of effective programs as identified by Gale, Seller *et al.* (2010: 4; Gale, Hattam *et al.* 2010: 35–37) from their research discussed above ("The Design and Evaluation Matrix for University Outreach") are summarised below. The characteristics are indicated in italics.

Assembling Resources

Effective program activities are *people-rich* in that they create opportunities for students to engage with others in extended conversations about university and develop a relationship with others who are in a position to provide them with assistance. This includes extended visits to university campuses and activities with a mentoring component (Gale, Hattam *et al.* 2010: 35). Programs are effective where *financial support or incentives* are provided to students, particularly in combination with other forms of support (Gale, Tranter *et al.* 2010: 73). Successful programs characteristically target students *early* in their schooling, provide continued support to students *over time*, and are *sustained* in terms of the funding arrangements (Gale, Tranter *et al.* 2010: 71).

Engaging Learners

Effective programs *recognise difference* and acknowledge that students from disadvantaged backgrounds bring a range of knowledge and learning capacities to formal education (Gale, Hattam *et al.* 2010: 36). Effective programs also *enhance academic curriculum* and pedagogy throughout schooling. A quality curriculum emphasises deep knowledge and intellectual engagement, and employs meaningful authentic task design and aligned systems of assessment (Gale, Tranter *et al.* 2010: 73). Whilst enhanced school curricula and pedagogy lead to improved student retention and achievement, it is rarely the focus of university programs to increase participation in higher education (Gale, Hattam *et al.* 2010: 37). *Research drives* the effective design, implementation and evaluation of successful programs, drawing on an evidence base to inform the stages in the life of a program. Programs with this characteristic use the research strengths of the university to drive design, implementation, and evaluation (Gale, Hattam *et al.* 2010: 37).

Working Together

Effective programs entail ongoing *collaboration* between stakeholders across sectors and agencies (e.g., schools, universities, non-government organisations, regional authorities, families, and communities), working together at all stages of program design, development, and delivery. Programs that are *cohort-based* (e.g., focus on classes or even larger cohorts of young people in a school or region) are more effective, enabling the program to change peer cultures as well as support individuals (Gale, Tranter *et al.* 2010: 71).

Building Confidence

Programs are effective where there is *communication* with students and *information* provided to students to assist them to learn about university life and university courses. Information and one-off communication sessions about the university may be less effective if not backed up with specific assistance for students in interpreting forms and making choices (Gale, Tranter *et al.* 2010: 72). Programs that *familiarise students with the university and provide onsite experiences* are more effective where they involve extended interactions with universities and university staff and students (Gale, Hattam *et al.* 2010: 36).

The fit between descriptors for the three KFtHE program activities and the role of the coordinator and these ten characteristics identified by Gale *et al.* (2010) is described in Table 2 through to Table 5. Each table represents a different activity. The qualitative information contained in these tables is then combined to generate what Gale, Seller *at al.* (2010) labelled the "program composition" – the first stage of applying DEMO to assess a program.

Strategy	Characteristic
Assembling resources	**People-rich:** University art students and staff are present at the weekly workshop sessions to mentor and teach the secondary students and assist them to reach their potential in terms of artistic and cultural expression. Sessions take place over an extended period of time, providing students with the opportunity to develop a relationship with the mentors and ask questions about studying art and design at the university.
	Financial support and/or incentives: The workshops are held at no expense to the students.
	Early, long-term, sustained: The workshops target Year 9–12 students, and are funded by an Australian Government grant for three years. While each workshop involves a new group of participants, previous participants are invited to use the space during the workshops to create their own prints and mentor current participating students. This provides the returning students with further opportunities to strengthen the relationships they have developed with university staff.
Engaging learners	**Recognition of difference:** The print-making workshops are designed to be culturally significant and explicitly recognise cultural knowledge. Students are encouraged to express their cultural understanding and interpretations through art. The prints which result from these workshops are "valued" by display in a public exhibition space on campus. The exhibition is attended by the local Indigenous community, Monash staff, and those in the art industry.
	Enhance academic curriculum: The workshops are skills-based: students are taught strategies to improve their skills in printmaking and artistic expression, and further develop their understanding of Aboriginal art.
	Research-driven: There has been no formal evaluation of the KFtHE program activities.
Working together	**Collaboration:** Delivery of the workshop sessions and staging of the exhibition involves collaboration between schools and teachers, Indigenous community members, the university and university staff, and local artists.
	Cohort-based: Small numbers of students from a restricted range of schools attend the workshop. The involvement of past participants as mentors further links students to their peers.
Building confidence	**Communications and information:** During the workshops, career pathways and campus information is casually discussed. The Head of Art and Design at the campus presents his own artwork to the students and formally addresses them on opportunities to pursue higher education in the area of art and design available at the University. At the end of the workshop, Monash University flyers are distributed to the participants containing course guides, enrolment, and campus information.
	Familiarisation/site experiences: The workshops and exhibition are held at the campus, thereby exposing students to the campus facilities over an extended period of time and providing opportunities for extended interaction with university staff.

Table 2. Application of the DEMO Characteristics to the Print-Making Workshops

Strategy	Characteristic
Assembling resources	**People-rich:** During the overnight camp, students interact with Indigenous community members and role models, which includes respected community members, Koorie engagement support officers, high profile entertainers, current Indigenous university students, staff, and students from the Gippsland campus. During the camp activities, Indigenous students interact with Monash general and academic staff in order to successfully solve game challenges on the campus.
	Financial support and/or incentives: The camp was held at no cost to the students.
	Early, long-term, sustained: The camp is attended by Year 9–12 Indigenous secondary school students. While the majority of participating students only attend one camp, there are some who attend consecutive years.
Engaging learners	**Recognition of difference:** Indigenous students are encouraged to discuss their culture and how it relates to learning (i.e., learning styles, support needs) during camp activities. Indigenous community members are involved in the camp and students take part in culturally relevant and significant activities.
	Enhanced academic curriculum: The activity does not relate to school or university academic curriculum.
Working together	**Collaboration:** The camps activities include presentations from Elders, organisations (job exposition), professionals, and Indigenous entertainers. Volunteer members from the Indigenous community and university students are also present as supervisors and guides.
	Cohort-based: Students from different secondary schools across Gippsland come together to attend the camp.
Building confidence	**Communication and information:** The camp involves sessions which provide students with promotional materials from Monash University, including handbooks, flyers, and show bags. The students are given the opportunity to hear the testimonials of Indigenous role models and Indigenous university students. These discussions also cover residential accommodation, university lifestyle, and pathways to university.
	Familiarisation/site experiences: Staying on-campus during the day and overnight exposes the students to the university, facilities, and services available and Monash staff and students. A variety of on-campus experiences are offered to the students, including accommodation, café visits, university classes, and sports/recreational activities.

Table 3. Application of the DEMO Characteristics to the Koorie Footprints to Monash Camp

Strategy	Characteristic
Assembling resources	**People-rich:** When students visit the campus they are able to interact with Indigenous community members and role models, Monash University staff, and students. The visits are short, taking between two and five hours.
	Financial support and/or incentives: The campus visits are offered at no cost to the students.
	Early, long-term, sustained: Indigenous students from Year 6–12 participate in the campus visits.
Engaging learners	**Recognition of difference:** There are various cultural aspects of the campus visits in the form of cultural activities and Indigenous community members' contributions.
	Enhanced academic curriculum: The campus visits include information sessions on how to recognise and utilise their own thinking strategies and learning styles. The activity is not related to school or university academic curriculum.
Working together	**Collaboration:** Participating students are given the opportunity to interact with Monash university staff and Indigenous students. Members of the Indigenous community are present during the campus visits to help guide the students through the campus.
	Cohort-based: Campus visits can combine groups of students from different schools.
Building confidence	**Communication and information:** Students are given Monash University, Gippsland campus promotional materials including handbooks, flyers, and show bags. The material includes information about courses, campus guides, residential accommodation, and pathways to university study.
	Familiarisation/site experience: Students participate in activities around the campus designed to familiarise them with the campus and services available (e.g., the library, students services, student lounge, sport/recreational activities, cultural activities).

Table 4. Application of the DEMO Characteristics to the School Visits

Strategy	Characteristic
Assembling resources	**People-rich:** A university employee is dedicated to providing one-to-one case management with prospective and currently enrolled Indigenous university students. The coordinator had held this position for three years, enabling relationships to be established with students over time, and the provision of support over time.
	Financial support and/or incentives: This activity involved the provision of information about scholarships and bursaries to prospective students.
	Early, long-term, sustained: The prospective students who actually seek information and support to enrol at university are generally mature-age students who are working. The coordinator and program in its current form have no funding to continue beyond 2012.
Engaging learners	**Recognition of difference:** The one-to-one support provided to students' allows for their individual needs, experiences, and capacities to be taken into account when providing advice and support. Students are encouraged to enter a field of study that complements their history and who they believe they are.
	Enhanced academic curriculum: This activity does not relate to school or university academic curriculum.
Working together	**Collaboration:** The coordinator is the initial contact person for this campus who is dedicated to the recruitment of Indigenous students. In other cases, the coordinator receives referrals from community workers, families, schools, and involves other people in recruitment (e.g., teachers, family, Indigenous community members, academics, and Indigenous support staff).
	Cohort-based: The support work of the coordinator is one-to-one with a particular student.
Building confidence	**Communication and information:** Information is usually provided to students on a one-to-one basis. The coordinator assists Year 12 graduates with enrolment, and more generally provides students with information about accommodation and transport, financial assistance and basic Abstudy information, scholarships and bursaries for secondary school and university students, and will introduce the student to academic staff for specific information about course/unit requirements, and other support staff as required.
	Familiarisation/site experiences: If a student shows interest in enrolling in university at Monash, the program coordinator may give the student a campus tour. This varies on an individual basis depending on the student's desire to see the campus.

Table 5. Application of the DEMO to the role of the KFtHE coordinator as a source of support

Table 6 summarises the program characteristics which have been identified and the higher level strategies to which these characteristics relate. The cells marked with an "x" are those where it is clear from our preliminary assessment that the program exhibits the characteristic.

Programs can have a maximum of ten characteristics and four strategies. The number of characteristics evident in a program determines its depth, and the number of strategies evident in a program determines its breadth. "Strongly composed programs have a depth of character within a broad strategic approach"; conversely, "weakly composed programs are shallow in character and strategically narrow" (Gale, Seller *et al.* 2010: 7). The characteristics and strategies summarised in Table 6 are used to hypothesise whether the program may or may not be operating to increase the future participation in higher education of the Indigenous secondary school students who participated in the KFtHE program activities or sought the support of the program coordinator.

Strategies		Characteristics	Print-making	K.F to Monash Camp	Campus visits	Source of support / recruitment
	Assembling resources	People-rich	X	X		X
		Financial support and/or incentives				
		Early, long-term, sustained	X			
	Engaging learners	Recognise difference	X			
		Enhanced academic curriculum				
		Research driven				
	Working together	Collaborate	X	X	X	
		Cohort-based	X	X		
	Building confidence	Communicate and inform	X	X	X	X
		Familiarise / on site experiences	X	X	X	

Table 6. Summary of the DEMO Characteristics of the KFtHE Program

Note: Empty cells mean that the activity does not clearly fit the DEMO characteristic, although the activity may reflect some aspects of the characteristic.

The information presented in Table 6 indicates that the KFtHE program, considered as a whole, appears to employ all four of the strategies: "Building Confidence", "Working Together", and to a much lesser extent, "Assembling Resources" and "Engaging Learners". With the possible exception of the Print-Making Workshops, the program does not employ the strategy of "Engaging Learners". When viewing the profile of each activity separately, the Print-Making Workshop is the activity which appears to have the greatest depth of character, exhibiting seven out of the ten DEMO characteristics and a broad strategic approach employing all four strategies, albeit to varying degrees.

Particular DEMO characteristics are evident across the three core KFtHE activities and the role of the program coordinator. These characteristics include "people rich", "collaboration", "communication and information", and "familiarisation/site experiences". The characteristics represent the strategies of "Working Together", "Building Confidence", and "Assembling Resources".

Assembling Resources

Effective program activities are people-rich in that they create opportunities for students to engage with others in extended conversations about university. The Print-Making Workshops, the role of the coordinator and, to a lesser extent, the Koorie Footprints to Monash Camp can provide this opportunity to develop relationships over time, allowing students to ask questions and explore the possibilities for further study directly with university staff. Mentors play an important role under this strategy, as they do in the KFtHE program. The program employs a range of mentors across its activities, including past participants in the activities, current Indigenous university students and graduates, academics, and Indigenous community members. Gale, Tranter *et al.* (2010) also include as a mentoring strategy a single person in a university whose position is dedicated to fostering higher education pathways and connections, such as the KFtHE coordinator. An evaluation could explore the nature and extent of this interaction between secondary students and the university staff and mentors with whom they come into contact, and examine whether these relationships do in fact enable students to seek assistance in relation to their own situation and capacities.

The program does not provide direct financial assistance to students to complete their schooling or gain access to higher education through scholarships and grants; however, the coordinator does provide students with one-to-one assistance to apply for scholarships, and emergency grants or loans through the university.

While the three core program activities predominantly target students in junior and senior secondary school, the extent to which these students are involved in activities across their schooling years is unknown. The program does not currently operate in an environment of financial sustainability. The majority of university programs surveyed by Gale, Hattam *et al.* (2010) were expected to last for more than five years. The sample included more university-based programs funded for five or more years than for periods of less than five years. The KFtHE program is funded for a three-year period and is in its final year.

Engaging Learners

In relation to the strategy "Engaging learners", none of the activities are integrated with university teaching so that the Indigenous students are able to bring into their learning environments and to the work of the university what Nakata, Nakata and Chin (2008) have describe as "assets" in the form of cultural knowledge, values, experiences and skills. With the exception of the Print-Making Workshops, which builds skills in art and design, none of the activities target enhancing school curriculum and pedagogy in ways that could lead to improved student retention and academic achievement. Nakata, Nakata and Chin (2008; see also Nakata 2011) and Pearson (2009) emphasise the importance of Indigenous student-support mechanisms at the primary, secondary, and higher education levels shifting to focus more broadly on the mastery of academic and disciplinary discourses, skills, and discipline content, while also considering Indigenous students' own knowledge and experience. Nakata *et al.* (2008) report that such adjustments to curricula and pedagogy remain minimal in the university disciplines, mainstream courses, and university-support programs run by or in conjunction with Indigenous academic staff. Pearson (2009) describes a similar pattern in the primary and secondary schooling of Indigenous children.

Working Together

Collaboration in the delivery of the three KFtHE program activities is evident. This collaboration takes place principally between schools, the university (its staff and students), and the Indigenous community. What this analysis cannot reveal is the degree to which collaboration influenced the establishment of the program activities, and continues to influence its ongoing development. The involvement of all stakeholder groups in designing and delivering interventions ensures that programs are not built around false assumptions about what assists students (Gale, Tranter *et al.* 2010: 71).

The strategy of "working together" also encompasses engaging with cohorts of school students so as to influence peer culture as well as support individual students (Gale, Seller *et al.* 2010). As Gale, Seller *et al.* (2010) identified, little is known about the qualitative aspects of groups that constitute legitimate cohorts or peers and the relational elements of the peer group that influence group attitudes towards university participation. Research by Biddle (2010) suggests that peer influences on education in the Indigenous community are complex and may cross age cohorts in unexpected ways, with Indigenous youth responding to the education level of their nearest contemporaries, rather than older adults in their community. Because of this complexity, peer group influences and cohort effects in education behaviours and aspirations are not simply reflected in activity attendance numbers.

Evaluation of the Koorie Footprints to Monash Camp, and the Print-Making Workshops in particular, provides an opportunity to explore qualitatively the nature of the peer influences associated with the different groups taking part in these activities, the relationships that participating students develop over the course of the activities, and the degree and nature of the information exchange that takes place. This group currently includes adults and elders who are planning to undertake or have undertaken a degree, contemporaries who have recently graduated from secondary school, past student participants of the activities, and Indigenous students from Years 7–12 who attend the program activities for the first time.

Building Confidence

Building Indigenous students' confidence in their ability to pursue higher education is the dominant strategy of the KFtHE program. The three core activities and the work of the program coordinator provide students with information about the university. The Print-Making Workshops provide information that is specific to art and design, while the Koorie Footprints to Monash Camp and the campus visits provide information that more broadly covers university courses and services. The coordinator provides one-to-one assistance to students and information that is relevant to the individual needs, interests, and capacities of the student.

Gale, Hattam *et al.* (2010) found that information and one-off communication sessions about universities may be less effective for school students if they are not backed up with specific assistance in interpreting forms and making choices. This entails the same students receiving broad information about courses and individual assistance specific to the student. While general information is provided to secondary school students by way of the KFtHE activities, the program coordinator reported that students who seek specific assistance from her to apply for a university place and financial assistance are predominantly mature-age students who completed their schooling at least two years prior to seeking information from the coordinator. Evaluation of the program may be able to assess the extent to which these two groups of students (secondary school students and mature-age students) overlap in the information and support they both need and receive.

It is possible that school students are not receiving the one-to-one information and assistance in the area of financial support for study that they need to allay their fears that university study is not within their financial means (and that of their family) upon leaving school. Rather, it is information that is predominantly sought by mature-age students who seek to study at the university after some time in the work force. Hossain et al. (2008) asked Indigenous university students from an Australian regional university to rate the extent of their pre-enrolment need for information (academic, social, and economic) and found that economic information, including that relating to free education pathways and assistance with other financial costs associated with university study, was identified by students as the area where they had the most substantial need for pre-enrolment information. The researchers' sample was predominantly mature-age Indigenous students from a regional campus, which reflected the characteristics of the student population on that campus. It is possible that even with this information and access to scholarships, Indigenous school-leavers and their families find it too difficult to overcome the financial barriers to participation in higher education.

All three activities and the role of the coordinator entail familiarising students with the university environment, albeit to varying degrees. Programs that familiarise students with the university and provide onsite experiences are more effective where they involve extended interactions with university staff and students (Gale, Seller *at al.* 2010: 36). Gale, Tranter *et al.* (2010) note that such opportunities can be significant in reducing fears and awakening a desire to attend university. Concrete familiarity can be particularly reassuring for students from regional and remote communities and for Indigenous students when the visits enable conversations to occur with community peers and/or Elders (Gale, Tranter *et al.* 2010: 72).

The Koorie Footprints to Monash Camp and the Print-Making Workshops, in particular, can provide opportunities for relationship-building and information exchange over time, through extensive onsite exposure to the campus and university staff. Importantly, these activities are also attended by Indigenous community peers and Elders.

Qualitative Estimate of the Strength of the KFtHE Program

Gale, Seller et al. (2010) advise against organising these overarching strategies and the characteristics that underpin them into a hierarchy of relative importance, or referencing one strategy over another. Our descriptive analysis suggests that all four program strategies are indicated by at least one program characteristic.

As discussed earlier ("Building Confidence"), program composition is assessed in terms of a balance between the total number of program characteristics (depth) and the number of program strategies from which they are drawn (breadth). Figure 1 illustrates how these two factors (characteristics and strategies) are referenced to each other for the KFtHE program. This diagram adapts the depiction by Gale, Seller et al (2010) of program composition and has been modified to locate the relative strength of the KFtHE program, as indicated by shading in grey.

Program depth (characteristics)					
	10				VS
	9				VS
	8			S	VS
	7			S	**VS**
	6		M	S	VS
	5		M	S	VS
	4		M	S	S
	3	W	M	M	
	2	W	W		
	1	W			
		1	2	3	4
	Program breadth (strategies)				
	Program strength: W = Weak M=Moderate S=Strong VS=Very strong				

Figure 1. Program Composition

Adapted from Figure 2 in Gale, Seller et al. (2010:14)

When the three core activities and the role of the coordinator are considered together, the program covers all four strategies and seven of the ten characteristics of effective programs. The program composition considered as a whole activity is classified as "Very Strong". If the Print-Making Workshops was to be considered alone, it would likewise be classified "Very Strong". This classification of the strength of the program composition means that there is a balance between the total number of program characteristics (depth) and the number of program strategies employed in their implementation (breadth).

Equity Orientation

The composition of the program, as indicated by Figure 1, provides the first stage in the process of applying the Design and Evaluation Matrix for University Outreach to the KFtHE program to obtain a qualitative assessment of the likelihood of program effectiveness. The third criterion to be taken into account is the equity orientation of the program. The overall likely effectiveness of a program in increasing the number of disadvantaged students participating in higher education depends on the strength and degree to which it is supported by an equity orientation in relation to the policy underpinning the program and in practice. Gale, Seller *et al.* (2010) consider a comprehensive equity orientation to include the following three equity perspectives.

First, the program must *unsettle deficit views* of the students it targets. This entails "a positive understanding of historically disadvantaged schools, students and their communities" (Gale, Seller *et al*, 2010: 11). In practice, this perspective involves presenting university as attainable; positioning students as intelligent and capable learners; sensitivity to alternative cosmologies and epistemologies; high intellectual challenge with high expectations and engagement of students.

Secondly, it must involve *researching "local knowledge" and negotiating local programs*: this includes "building viable relationships with specific schools and their communities, and learning about their understanding of the problems" (Gale, Seller *et al.* 2010: 11). In practice, this entails genuine reciprocal alliances and collective research into the long-term effects on a range of factors to help to build an evidence base particular to the specific context and group served by the program.

Thirdly, it includes *building capacity in communities, schools and universities.* In practice, this includes securing increased funding for programs from various sources, supporting whole school change, developing curriculum materials, professional development of university staff and teachers (Gale, Seller *et al.* 2010: 11).

The policy orientation of the KFtHE program is clearly to "Unsettle Deficit Views" to the extent that the program activities present university as attainable for Indigenous students, celebrate culture and Indigenous ways of knowing, and are based on an understanding of the challenges facing Indigenous students. The program also appears to exhibit elements of "Researching local knowledge" and "Negotiating local programs" in policy and practice. Relationships have been built between the university, schools, and the Indigenous community, and the activities have developed from an understanding amongst these groups of the barriers for Indigenous students to accessing higher education.

The program in its current form appears, however, not to be orientated towards building capacity in schools and universities through curriculum and staff development both in the schools and at the university. The high degree of community support and engagement in the activities suggests it may nevertheless be operating at the level of building capacity in the local Indigenous community, as well as facilitating cultural awareness amongst university staff. This is most obviously the case for the Print-Making Workshop.

A formal evaluation of the program would involve an examination of these three policy orientations and their articulation in the program activities and experiences of the students who participate in the KFtHE program activities.

Likelihood of Program Success

The final stage of applying DEMO references program strength with the number of equity perspectives evident in the KFtHE program. Figure 2 references the strength of the program composition against the number of equity perspectives guiding the program to derive a qualitative estimate of the likelihood of program success.

Program composition	VS	U-L	L-QL	QL-VL	VL
	S	U	L	QL	QL-VL
	M	U	L	L	L-QL
	W	U	U	U	U-L
		0	1	2	3
	Number of equity perspectives				
	Likelihood of program success: U=Unlikely L=Likely QL=Quite likely VL=Very likely				

Figure 2. Design and Evaluation Matrix for University Outreach: Likelihood of Program Success

Adapted from Figure 4 in Gale, Seller *et al.* (2010:16)

Figure 2 indicates the likely effectiveness of the KFtHE program as "Quite-Likely to Very-Likely" to assist Indigenous students to aspire to and participate in higher education. This estimate is based on the equity orientation of *Unsettling deficit* views and *Researching local knowledge and negotiating local programs*.

In deciding whether to invest time and resources in an evaluation of the KFtHE program, this qualitative assessment of the likelihood of program success should be viewed in the context of the actual pattern of Indigenous student enrolment at the Gippsland campus. The number of Indigenous students enrolled at the campus has increased since 2006, rising steeply since 2008. This pattern is in contrast to falling and now-stable non-Indigenous student enrolment numbers, yet consistent with the enrolment figures for Indigenous and non-Indigenous students across all the Victorian campuses of Monash University. The rate of increase for Indigenous student enrolments is, however, highest at the Gippsland campus (i.e., 216% increase for the Gippsland campus vs. 141% increase for all other Victorian campuses in the period 2006–2011). Figures 3a and 3b present Monash Gippsland student enrolment numbers over time (Monash University ATSI pivot tables).

These figures, at least in part, reflect broader student enrolment trends for Australian public universities. For the period 2006–2011, the percentage increase in the number of commencing Aboriginal and Torres Strait Islander students is considerably higher than the figures for all domestic students (DIISRTE 2007–2011). The highest percentage increase in commencing Indigenous students (11.8%) occurred in the period 2008–2009, at a time when Indigenous Access and Enabling Scholarships (IAS and IES) were introduced by the Australian Government in 2008. This may also have had some effect on increasing Indigenous enrolments at the Gippsland campus.

The steady increase in the enrolment of Indigenous students at the Gippsland campus may not reflect KFtHE program attendance by these students, nor do these figures provide any indication of the enrolment of Indigenous school-leavers as opposed to mature-age students. This is the ultimate question to be answered by any evaluation of the KFtHE program.

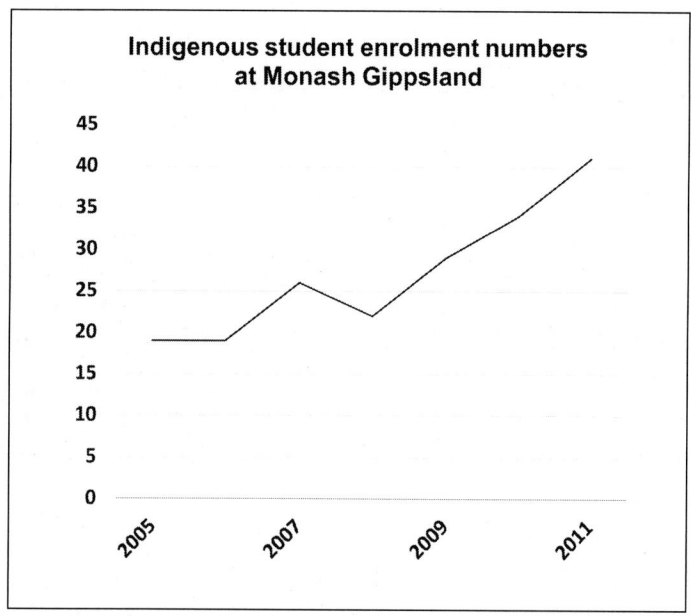

Figure 3a

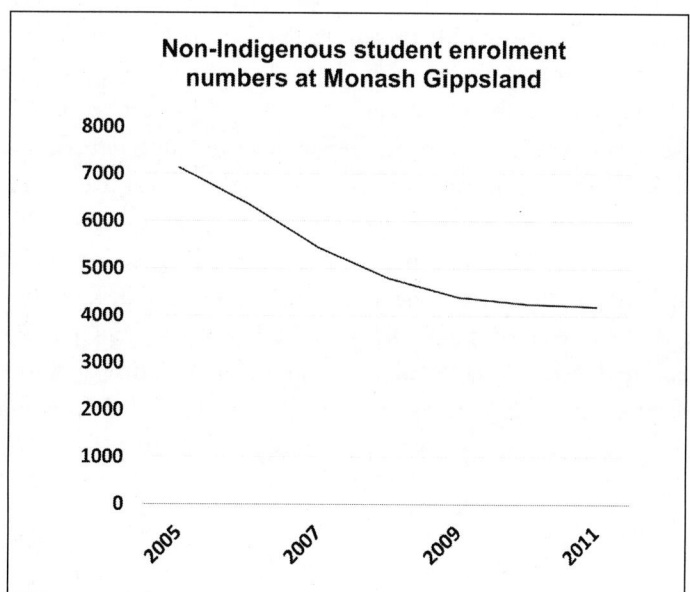

Figure 3b

Conclusion

Research and evaluation is required to demonstrate the efficacy of the KFtHE program. The conclusion that can be drawn from this proscriptive application of the DEMO to the characteristics, policy, and practice orientation of the KFtHE program is that it is both necessary and timely to quantify and qualify what appears to be a successful program. Such research would help drive the future development of the program in a context of growing Indigenous student numbers and Indigenous community engagement with the Gippsland campus. This analysis also represents a unique application of the DEMO by Gale *et al* as a proscriptive tool for designing program evaluation; one that identifies key constructs that potentially mediate and moderate program effectiveness, and offers insight into how such constructs could be measured. Indigenous evaluation research is now needed to enable Gippsland's Indigenous community to determine and develop priorities and strategies for their continued engagement with the University.

Acknowledgements

The research was conducted under the auspices of the Gippsland Access and Participation (GAP) Project. We wish to acknowledge the support of Associate Professor Jenny Mosse (GAP Project leader) and Alan Scarlett (Executive Officer and Gippsland Campus Manager), both of whom provided helpful feedback on early drafts of the paper. The GAP Project received funding from the Australian Government, Department of Education, Employment and Workplace Relations, to increase participation of rural and Indigenous students in higher education. Finally, we would like to acknowledge and pay our respects to the traditional custodians, the Brayukaloong clan of the Gunnai/Kurnai people, the Elders past and present and descendants of this Country where work on the *Koorie Footprints to Higher Education* program and associated research was conducted and presented. This paper is based on a presentation at the Education for Regional Sustainability Conference (21 November 2011, Monash University, Gippsland Campus).

References

Alloway, N., Gilbert, P., Gilbert, R., & Muspratt, S. 2004. *Factors Impacting on Student Aspirations and Expectations in Regional Australia.* Canberra: Commonwealth of Australia.

Austin, H., & Heath, J. 2010. 'Using DEMO to Evaluate and Enhance Schools Outreach Programs: An Example from the South Coast of New South Wales'. 2nd Annual Student Equity in Higher Education Conference, 11–12 October, Melbourne.

Biddle, N. 2006. 'The Age at which Indigenous Australians Undertake Qualifications: A Descriptive Analysis'. *Australian Journal of Adult Learning* 46(1): 28–50.

Biddle, N. 2010. 'A Human Capital Approach to the Educational Marginalisation of Indigenous Australians'. CAEPR Working Paper No. 67/2010. Canberra: ANU College of Arts & Social Sciences.

Craver, L., Tucker, A., Munns, G., Hinkley, J., Marsh, H., & Simpson, K. 2005. *Indigenous Students' Aspirations, Dreams, Percpetions and Realities.* Canberra: Report for the Department of Education, Science and Training.

Department of Industry, Innovation, Science, Research and Tertiary Education (DIISRTE). 2007–2011. *Selected Higher Education Statistics.* [Full Year Student Summaries.] http://www.deewr.gov.au/HigherEducation/Publications/HEStatistics/Publications/Pages/Home.aspx (accessed 8 August 2012).

Gale, T., Hattam, R., Parker, S., Comber, B., Bills, D., & Tranter, D. (2010). *Interventions Early in School as a Means to Improve Higher Education Outcomes for Disadvantaged (particularly low SES) Students. Component B: A Survey of the Nature and Extent of Outreach Activities Conducted by Australian Higher Education (Table A Providers).* Canberra: Department of Education, Employment and Workplace Relations.

Gale, T., Seller, S., Parker, S., Hattam, R., Comber, B., Tranter, D., & Bills, D. (2010). *Interventions Early in School as a Means to Improve Higher Education Outcomes for Disadvantaged (particularly low SES) Students. Compnent C: A Design and Evaluation Matrix for Unviersity Outreach in Schools.* Canberra: Department of Education, Employment and Workplace Relations.

Gale, T., Tranter, D., Bills, D., Hattam, R., & Comber, B. 2010. *Interventions Early in School as a Means to Improve Higher Education Outcomes for Disadvantaged (particularly low SES) Students. Component A: A Review of the Australian and International Literature.* Canberra: Department of Education, Employment and Workplace Relations.

Hossain, D., Gorman, D., Williams-Mozely, J., & Garvey, D. 2008. 'Bridging the Gap: Identifying Needs and Aspirations of Indigenous Students to Facilitate Their Entry into University'. *Australian Journal of Indigenous Education* 37: 9–17.

James, R. 2002. *Socioeconomic Background and Higher Education Participation: An Analysis of School Students' Aspirations and Expectations.* Canberra: Department of Education, Employment and Workplace Relations.

Lawrence, R. 2007. *Research on Strong Indigenous Communities: Brief 1.* Canberra: Indigenous Justice Clearing House, Australian Institute of Criminology.

Martin, K. 2009. 'Ways of Knowing, Being and Doing: A Theoretical Framework and Methods for Indigenous and Indigenist Re-Search'. *Journal of Australian Studies* 27(76): 203–214.

Monash University. 2005 – 2011. 'ATSI Pivot Tables'. http://www.opq.monash.edu.au/us/pivot-table/index.html (accessed 8 August 2012).

Nakata, M. 2011. 'Indigenous Slant Ciluting Diluting Core Curriculums'. *The Australian*, Higher Education Supplement. 11 August: 23.

Nakata, M., Nakata., V, & Chin, M. 2008. 'Approaches to the Academic Preparation and Support of Australian Indigenous Students for Tertiary Study'. *The Australian Journal of Indigenous Education* (37): 137–145.

Pearson, N. 2009. 'Radical Hope: Education and Equality in Australia'. *Quarterly Essay* (35): 1–105.

Porsanger, J. 2004. 'An Essay About Indigenous Methodology'. *Nordlit* 15: 105–121.

Porsanger, J. 2010. 'Self-Determination and Indigenous Research: Capacity Building on Our Own Terms'. Paper presented at the International Expert Group Meeting – Indigenous Peoples: Development with Culture and Identity Articles 3 and 32 of the United Nations Declaration on the Rights of indigenous Peoples. 12–14 January, New York.

Rigney, L. 1999. 'Internationalisation of an Indigenous Anticolonial Cultural Critique of Research Methodologies'. *Wicazo Sa Review* 14(2): 109–122.

Seller, S., Hattam, R., Bills, D., Comber, B., Tranter, D., & Gale, T. (2010). *Interventions Early in School as a Means to Improve Higher Education Outcomes for Disadvantaged (particularly low SES) Students: A Design and Evaluation Matrix for Unviersity Outreach in Schools*. Canberra: Department of Education, Employment and Workplace Relations.